European and Transatlantic Studies

Springer
Berlin
Heidelberg
New York
Barcelona
Budapest
Hong Kong
London
Milan
Paris
Tokyo

Barry Eichengreen • Jeffry Frieden
Jürgen von Hagen (Eds.)

Monetary and Fiscal Policy in an Integrated Europe

Acting Editor: Jürgen von Hagen

With 26 Figures
and 28 Tables

Springer

Professor Barry Eichengreen
University of California at Berkeley
Department of Economics
Berkeley, CA 94720
USA

Professor Jeffry Frieden
University of California at Los Angeles
Los Angeles, CA 90024-1472
USA

Professor Dr. Jürgen von Hagen
University of Mannheim
Seminargebäude A5
68131 Mannheim
Germany

Library of Congress Cataloging-in-Publication Data

Monetary and fiscal policy in an integrated Europe / Barry Eichengreen, Jeffry Frieden, Jürgen von Hagen (eds.).
p. cm. -- (European and Transatlantic studies)
Includes bibliographical references and index.
ISBN-13:978-3-642-79819-1 e-ISBN-13:978-3-642-79817-7
DOI:10.1007/978-3-642-79817-7

1. Monetary policy--European Union countries. 2. Fiscal policy--European Union countries. 3. Europe--Economic integration. I. Eichengreen, Barry J. II. Frieden, Jeffry A. III. Hagen, Jürgen von. IV. Series.
HG925.M657 1995
332.4'94--dc20 95-19315
CIP

Softcover reprint of the hardcover 1st edition 1995

43/2202-5 4 3 2 1 0 - Printed on acid-free paper

Acknowledgments

This volume is a product of the Study Group on the Political Economy of European Integration convened by the Center for German and European Studies of the University of California. The Center is supported by a Center of Excellence grant from the government of the Federal Republic of Germany. The Director of the UC Center, Professor Gerald Feldman, has provided generous support throughout. For help with this volume we thank Syd Mintzer for editorial assistance, Arthur Gordon and Philipp C. Rother for copy editing, and David Ellison for indexing. This volume is published in conjunction with: Barry Eichengreen, Jeffry Frieden, and Jürgen von Hagen, (eds.), *Politics and Institutions in an Integrated Europe.* European and Transatlantic Studies, Berlin, Heidelberg, New York: Springer, 1995.

Contents

The Political Economy of European Integration: Introduction

Barry Eichengreen, Jeffry Frieden, and Jürgen von Hagen

The process of European integration has momentous implications for the future of Europe. The Single European Act and the Maastricht treaty signaled the desire of Europe's political leaders to accelerate the pace of integration. Their initiatives represented an ambitious attempt to restructure Europe's institutions and transform its economy.

Subsequent developments have raised questions about whether these efforts will succeed. The hesitation of electorates in countries like Denmark and France to ratify the Maastricht treaty brought to the surface concern over the possibility that the European Union (EU) might run a "democratic deficit" – that institutions such as the European Commission and the European Central Bank (ECB) might acquire considerable power but not be sufficiently accountable to the voting public. The insistence of the United Kingdom and Denmark on being able to opt out of the Social Charter and the monetary union, respectively, underscored the fact that different member states have different visions of the EU's future. Speculative attacks on European currencies in 1992-1993 cast doubt over the viability of the Maastricht blueprint for completing the transition to economic and monetary union. Together with political and financial turmoil in countries like Italy and Greece, these events led German and French politicians, once enthusiastic supporters of a union of the 12, to articulate a vision of "variable geometry" or "multispeed Europe." All this occurred against the backdrop of the expansion of the EU to include Austria, Finland, and Sweden, and of the membership ambitions of Eastern Europe.

These events raise several analytical questions, each with immediate policy relevance. At one level there are questions about why the integration process took the form that it did. Why did the pace of integration accelerate in the 1980s? Why did it suffer reversals in the 1990s? At another level are equally intriguing questions about the consequences of the integration process. What form will economic and monetary union take: single or multispeed, uniform or variable geometry? Will capital, labor, and commodity market integration enhance the efficiency of the European economy? How will the institutions of social and economic governance be affected?

These are the issues that motivate the research presented here. Their analysis is far from straightforward. The difficulty of treating them results from the absence of a unified analytical framework. Political scientists, economists, and scholars from other social science disciplines do not possess a consensus model with which the relevant issues can be addressed. In this introduction, we therefore sketch some leading approaches and suggest how they might be synthesized.

The two volumes in this series are the output of a study group convened by the editors on behalf of the Center for German and European Studies of the University of California.[1] The final product is unusual in a number of respects. First, it is the output of a group of scholars concerned with European affairs who interacted in a series of meetings over a period of three years. We hope that the chapters consequently display more unity and coherence than is typical of collected works. Second, these volumes are the product of an interdisciplinary group of economists, political scientists, and sociologists sharing a common interest in European issues. European integration has economic, political, and social dimensions that cannot be adequately understood in isolation from one another. By bringing together scholars capable of analyzing these various aspects, we hope to shed light on aspects of the European integration process that to date have been inadequately appreciated.

1. Approaches to Analyzing European Integration

One might begin by distinguishing three broad sets of considerations that are central to analyzing European integration. These emphasize economic efficiency, distributional interests, and socioeconomic institutions.

1.1 The Efficiency Approach

One set of studies focuses on efficiency considerations. Some scholars, for whom these concerns arise in a largely normative context, are interested in discovering which policies or forms of economic organization are most likely to enhance economic performance. This is especially important for policymakers, and observers of policymaking, in the context of the largely unprecedented set of economic and political problems and pressures that faces the EU today. It is indeed one of the great attractions of modern social science that in many arenas of human activity, it can help to identify those socioeconomic and political arrangements that are most likely to improve aggregate well-being.

The identification of efficient policies is the starting point for scholars who seek to identify an economic logic for the integration process. They emphasize the social welfare gains that will result from the creation of a single market. They point to the reduction in transaction costs that will follow from the establishment of a single currency. They suggest that the Single European Act was motivated by the increase in incomes that Europe's citizens will reap from the successful completion of this process. Europe's politicians anticipated that they would be rewarded for the implementation of programs that promised to raise the living standards of voters. Like a 10-dollar bill lying on the sidewalk, this lure proved irresistible.

There are several problems with this approach. For one, the efficiency advantages of European integration are very much in dispute. The increase in capital and labor mobility that will result from the Single Market program threatens to erode institutional arrangements like national apprenticeship and training schemes that are widely regarded sources of European competitiveness. The reduction in transaction costs that will result from monetary union has been estimated by the European Commission as .5% of national income, hardly an impressive return on an investment whose costs involve forsaking monetary policy as an instrument of national economic stabilization. Reasonable people can argue that the efficiency gains from monetary union will turn out to be large, but equally reasonable people can disagree. It hardly seems plausible that the voting public, which is notoriously risk-averse, has found this efficiency argument compelling.

In addition, it is not obvious that the efficiency approach can explain the ebb and flow of the integration process. Granted that a single market offers efficiency advantages, why did the process suddenly gain momentum in the 1980s? Why has it encountered new difficulties recently? These questions may have plausible answers. One can argue, for example, that the rise in European unemployment in the 1980s and the intensification of Japanese and East Asian competition threatened European prosperity to the point where the efficiency gains from integration could no longer be overlooked. In rebuttal, one might respond that a free lunch (to be paid for with the 10-dollar bill referred to above) is equally attractive in times of crisis and normalcy.

One might argue that the Single Market and Maastricht initiatives were driven by technological changes that enhanced factor mobility (capital mobility in particular), increasing the cost of attempting to segment national markets and undermining the viability of the European Monetary System (EMS) of pegged but periodically adjustable exchange rates, which left no alternative to economic and monetary union. But such technological progress had been ongoing for many years; why should it have tipped the balance in the 1980s? The end of the Cold War and the collapse of communism in Central and Eastern Europe are plausible candidates to which responsibility might be assigned for the subsequent deceleration of the integration process. The attractiveness of policies designed to encourage trade with other Western European countries certainly diminished when one's logical trading partners, as in the German case, suddenly encompassed much of Eastern Europe. Structural fund transfers designed to help the economies of Southern Europe capitalize on the opportunities offered by integration became more costly when there existed new uses for these resources in the East. Perhaps such factors can explain the difficulties of the 1990s. But the answers to these questions are not obvious. Nor is it clear that the efficiency approach offers a complete explanation for the course of European integration.

1.2 The Distributional Approach

Members of a second school reject the notion that there exists an omniscient social planner seeking to maximize economic efficiency and national incomes in favor of the belief that the process of European integration is fundamentally political. Self-interested groups seek to use policy initiatives at the European level to influence the distribution of income. The insight is familiar from the literature on trade politics: liberalization initiatives have important distributional effects that lead different sectoral interests to lobby in different directions. Factors of production that are utilized intensively in the production of import-competing goods may suffer from liberalization even though the nation gains overall; conversely, factors used intensively in export-oriented sectors may gain more than proportionately. Whether liberalization takes place depends on the size of these competing constituencies. The Single Market initiative is, at its heart, a program for regional if not multilateral trade liberalization. It follows that standard pressure-group politics should come into play. Other initiatives like monetary unification stand to benefit certain groups (importers and exporters whose activities are disrupted by exchange rate fluctuations) while hurting others (currency traders, most obviously).

An attraction of this approach is that it offers a straightforward way of explaining the rise in support for European integration in the 1980s. The share of national income that European countries exported to one another rose noticeably over the two preceding decades, strengthening the export lobby. The growth of direct foreign investment and intra-European capital mobility augmented the numbers of those who suffered capital losses in the event of an exchange rate change. Overall, the growing interdependence of the European economies strengthened distributional lobbies that stood to benefit from integration and the intensity of their political activity.

Here as elsewhere, a problem with this approach is the temptation to infer causation from observed outcomes, giving rise to the *post hoc, ergo propter hoc* fallacy. It is always possible after the fact to identify a distributional interest that stood to benefit from a particular policy initiative; it is more difficult to verify that lobbying on the part of that interest group was responsible for the policy shift. Nor is it easy to know which way to cut the distributional pie; should distributional interests be disaggregated along sectoral or factoral lines (producers of traded and nontraded goods or capital versus labor), for example? Domestic electorates did not vote on the Single European Act, and only a minority of EU member states held referenda on the Maastricht treaty. How then should we suppose that the preferences of distributional interests were communicated? Can we afford to ignore the existence of principal-agent problems – that there was scope for slippage between the preferences of distributional interests and the actions of their elected and appointed representatives? Finally, the distributional approach is rarely extended to introduce a role for institutions in amplifying and dissipating political pressures.

1.3 The Institutional Approach

The institutional approach aims precisely to incorporate the impact of institutions on sociopolitical outcomes. Members of the institutional school argue that the process of European integration is shaped by national and international institutions that give it direction and momentum. For example, support for monetary unification is buttressed by its linkage to the Common Agricultural Policy, since floating exchange rates between separate national currencies (some would argue separate national currencies themselves) greatly complicate efforts to peg the domestic-currency prices of agricultural products in a European market free of internal barriers to trade. The domestic political systems of member states amplify the influence of the farmers who benefit from this program. The very existence of the Common Agricultural Policy as an EU institution – indeed, as the single most important EU institution judged on the basis of budgetary spending – renders agricultural policy difficult to modify and monetary unification difficult to resist. To cite another example, the division of responsibility among the European Commission, the European Parliament, and other agencies of the EU bestows considerable autonomy on members of the European Commission and increases its president's room to maneuver. This allows one to argue that the integration process was accelerated by the personal and political influence of Commission President Jacques Delors, who believed in its economic and political efficacy, not least for his own career, and who had the capacity to make a difference by virtue of the particular institutional structure in which he operated. Similarly, the unanimity rules under which the European Commission has operated has given smaller member states disproportionate bargaining power and allowed them to influence EU policymaking in ways that cannot be understood without taking institutional considerations into account.

Observing these facts is easier than analyzing them. Like the weather, everybody talks about institutions but no one does anything about them. Modeling the role of institutions strains the limits of existing social science. Predicting when and how institutions matter is therefore problematic. We know that institutions are most likely to make a difference when information is costly, so that their agenda-setting function can be important. We know that they will matter when the cost of market transactions is relatively high, so that their existence makes possible outcomes that will not be feasible in their absence. When there exist coordination problems that give rise to multiple equilibria, institutions can serve as the selection mechanism or focal point that causes individuals to agree on a particular solution. Institutions can serve as commitment technologies to solve the time-inconsistency problems that otherwise bedevil the conduct of economic policy and to lend credibility to otherwise unsustainable plans.

Beyond these generalizations, the way forward is not entirely clear. Modeling the role of institutions confronts the investigator with the social scientist's dilemma of how to trade off rigor for realism. Minimal rigor often requires alarming sacrifices of realism, and vice versa. Hence, institutional analysis remains underdeveloped.

1.4 Synthesis

It will come as no surprise that we believe that understanding European integration requires drawing on each of these approaches. The efficiency considerations that are the economist's bread and butter, the self-interested political behavior whose analysis comes naturally to the political scientist, and the institutional approach that has gained increasing favor under the banner of "the new institutionalism" need to be blended to provide a balanced picture of the integration process. Progress along these lines will hinge on the completion of serious empirical work on specific aspects of the process of European integration – case studies, if one will. Pitched at a high level of abstraction, the insights of the efficiency, distributional, and institutional schools are both obvious and intractable. They are at the same time self-evident and difficult to operationalize. They need to be tailored to specific questions and evaluated empirically in order for their explanatory power to be assessed and their specification to be refined. Social-scientific studies of European integration need to proceed as normal science, in which relevant questions are formulated, hypotheses specified, and propositions subjected to detailed empirical examination. We like to think that the studies collected here illustrate how this might be done.

2. The Contents of the Book

The contributions to this volume focus on the political economy of macro-economic policy in the EU. (The companion volume is concerned with the politics and institutions of European integration.) Its chapters reflect a combination of the efficiency, distributional, and institutional approaches described above.

The first four chapters focus on the political economy of European monetary relations. Carl Walsh begins with an assessment of some leading issues in monetary policy. One of the more controversial aspects of contemporary EU politics is the degree of independence appropriate for an ECB. In this context, Walsh analyzes the implications of central bank independence for the inflation-unemployment trade-off.

Walsh starts with the observation that independent central banks tend to be associated with lower levels of inflation. The standard case for central bank independence is indeed based on the inability of politically dependent central banks to credibly commit to low inflation policies. As independence strengthens the credibility of the institution's monetary commitment, however, it creates expectations among the public that may make wages and prices more rigid. When inflation is low and stable, agents will reduce the frequency of nominal wage and price changes in order to minimize menu costs. In such an environment, a reduction in inflation may cause a significant rise in unemployment.

Central bank independence can therefore give rise to economic expectations that *increase* the real impact of whatever discretionary monetary policy the authorities in fact pursue. On the one hand, inflation will be regarded as so unlikely that the authorities can more easily "surprise" the public. On the other hand, attempts to reduce inflation further face the barrier of fixed expectations. This raises the "sacrifice ratio," the amount of unemployment associated with a percentage-point decrease in inflation. Walsh finds that this effect is strongly present in the European data. On this basis he warns that the creation of an independent ECB may actually exacerbate problems of short-term macroeconomic adjustment.

How wages respond to disinflationary shocks depends not just on expectations of central bank policy but also on the distributional interests and institutions represented in the labor market. These interests and institutions are the focus of the chapter by Geoffrey Garrett and Christopher Way. Garrett and Way show that the structure of national trade unions can have profound implications for labor's response to macroeconomic shocks. They argue that unions representing workers in sectors of the economy not exposed to international competition – the "sheltered" sectors – are far less concerned about aggregate inflation levels than those in the exposed sectors, for which inflation can threaten loss of competitiveness and unemployment.

For this reason, Garrett and Way expect that such countries as Denmark and Sweden, in which the annual bargaining round is led by unions in the sheltered sector (especially public-sector unions), are more likely to experience political pressure for undesirable macroeconomic policies. In contrast, in countries like Austria and Germany where the union movement is led by unions in the exposed sector, pressures are greater for policies to avoid higher levels of inflation. This set of distributional and institutional considerations implies that the Nordic countries, where public-sector unions are large and influential, may have difficulty achieving the lower inflation rates associated with a commitment to European monetary integration.

The next two chapters, by Maurice Obstfeld and by Andrew Rose and Lars Svensson, analyze the 1992-1993 crises in the EMS. They assert that neither institutional nor distributional factors were responsible for the difficulties in the EMS. In their view, characteristics of the foreign exchange markets themselves, especially the self-reinforcing actions of currency traders, inflicted severe welfare costs on the national and regional economies.

The official explanation for the 1992-1993 crises is that countries whose currencies were attacked – Italy, Britain, Spain, and others – had excessively expansionary monetary and fiscal policies and failed to adjust to the shock of German reunification. Obstfeld casts doubt on this presumption. He shows that a second class of explanations, based on theoretical models of self-fulfilling speculative attacks, provides a more plausible explanation of this experience. The key to Obstfeld's analysis is the government's response to the markets.

Governments whose currencies were attacked and that were forced to raise interest rates in response found themselves in an unsustainable position. High interest rates exacerbated unemployment, undermined the stability of banking systems, raised the burden of the public debt, and, where mortgage interest rates are indexed, increased the cost of homeownership. Thus, a policy of exchange-rate pegging that would have remained viable indefinitely in the absence of an attack had to be abandoned for political reasons once pressure was applied to the currency. Self-fulfilling attacks on Exchange Rate Mechanism currencies could thereby prove rational and succeed.

Rose and Svensson use empirical methods from the recent literature on exchange rate target zones to shed light on this and related propositions. They present a range of findings on the behavior of financial markets in the period leading up to the 1992-1993 Exchange Rate Mechanism crises. Their most remarkable result is the absence of evidence that the markets attached a significant probability to realignment until immediately before the crises occurred. If political economy fundamentals like budget deficits, inflation, and unemployment explain why currencies were attacked and currency pegs had to be abandoned, then one would expect realignment expectations to have risen gradually, along with these fundamentals. In fact, there is little evidence of this. These findings seem easiest to reconcile with Obstfeld-style models of self-fulfilling attacks.

As monetary integration continues, it raises a host of issues related to national fiscal policies in the EU. The next two chapters, by Giancarlo Corsetti and Nouriel Roubini and by Michael Hutchison and Kenneth Kletzer, analyze fiscal policy in the transition to monetary union. Corsetti and Roubini consider the potential inefficiencies that institutional characteristics of democratic political systems can introduce into fiscal policymaking. They evaluate a government that, owing to divergences between its preferences and those of the public, runs deficits that are excessive from a social welfare standpoint. However, such a government is still likely to engage in socially efficient tax smoothing, running larger deficits in recessionary periods. One implication of their analysis is that a binding fiscal ceiling adopted to reduce the socially undesirable excessive-deficits bias will also discourage socially desirable tax smoothing. There is thus no unambiguous welfare argument in favor of the debt and deficit limits included in the convergence criteria that member states must meet in order to qualify for participation in European Monetary Union.

A political bias toward excessive deficits is likely to be exacerbated by increased openness and especially by growing international capital mobility. If capital is mobile, excessive deficits will not be discouraged by upward pressure on domestic interest rates. This might appear to strengthen the argument for fiscal restrictions in a monetary union. But Corsetti and Roubini show that if the private sector is able to borrow abroad on the same terms as the government, the latter will finance its deficits by borrowing from domestic residents who will refinance their bond purchases abroad. To be effective, then, a fiscal restriction would have to apply to all public-sector borrowing, both domestic and foreign.

Hutchison and Kletzer evaluate problems related to those discussed by Corsetti and Roubini, starting with a review of the debate over the Maastricht treaty's debt and deficit limits. They point to fallacies in several standard efficiency cases for fiscal ceilings. It is incorrect to argue, for example, that excessive deficit spending immiserizes neighboring countries by raising regional or world interest rates; in the absence of preexisting distortions, this pecuniary externality merely redistributes income from debtors to creditors without affecting national welfare. Preexisting distortions can change this picture, particularly political distortions that cause some governments to systematically run excessive deficits as in the model of Roubini and Corsetti. Of course, the first-best solution to this problem is for countries to eliminate the domestic political distortions that are the source of the problem rather than adopting the second-best solution of binding themselves with an international treaty.

Hutchison and Kletzer go on to suggest that the real danger of excessive deficits in Europe may result from the expectation that policymakers at the EU level will be forced to "bail out" national fiscal authorities. Once monetary autonomy is eliminated, there will be increased need to use fiscal policy for stabilization. But national fiscal autonomy will be limited by the mobility of the tax base in an integrated Europe. In response to this constraint, the EU itself will inevitably assume greater responsibility for stabilization policy; new initiatives are likely to take the form of a system of fiscal federalism, which transfers resources to states suffering temporary recessions. The governments of member states will realize, of course, that the cost of debt service will eventually be assumed by an EU-wide authority and that the transfers the nation receives from the fiscal authority will depend in part on the debt burden it inherits. Hence, national governments will have an incentive to run excessive deficits over the transition, providing a rationale for the fiscal limits set down by the Maastricht treaty.

Hutchison and Kletzer demonstrate that European fiscal policies will be affected by the level of intra-European labor mobility. This last point, which also affects other political and economic developments in the EU, is the focus of Christopher Erickson's chapter. Erickson seeks to draw lessons by analogy, comparing wage differentials within manufacturing industries in the 50 U.S. states and the 12 EU countries. Surprisingly, he finds that wage differentials are not dramatically larger in the EU than in the United States when they are computed using purchasing power parity exchange rates. Differences across EU countries in the cost of living go a considerable way toward equalizing real earnings, despite the persistence of wage differentials. This suggests that the completion of the Single Market will not necessarily lead to massive labor-market dislocations or to a flight of labor from high- to low-tax jurisdictions. If the mobility of national tax bases is a problem, Erickson concludes, it is most likely to operate through the behavior of internationally mobile capital, not labor.

Another aspect of European labor relations that has received a great deal of attention is the high and persistent level of unemployment in much of the region. In their chapter, Karl Ove Moene and Michael Wallerstein present one explanation of this phenomenon. They start with two observations. First, substantial unemployment differentials have persisted even among such relatively similar economies as those in Scandinavia, despite the fact that there are no legal barriers to labor migration within the region. Second, unemployment has jumped from extremely low to extremely high in some Scandinavian countries in recent years – from under 3% to about 13% in Sweden between 1989 and 1993, for example.

Moene and Wallerstein present a model in which firms pursue two sorts of employment (especially layoff) policies, depending on the general labor market setting. Where labor markets are tight, firms hoard labor even in times of slack demand so that they do not face difficulty restaffing once the macroeconomy recovers. Where unemployment is relatively high, firms lay off workers with impunity in difficult times, with the expectation that they will be able to rehire new workers as necessary. This behavior is self-reinforcing: the more firms hoard workers, the greater the incentive for each individual firm to hoard workers, and vice versa.

The possibility of such polar outcomes is important for members and prospective members of the EU for many reasons. Perhaps the most important is that European integration can subject countries to shocks that drive them from one equilibrium to another – specifically, from the low-unemployment to the high-unemployment state. This is especially the case to the extent that monetary integration reduces the ability of individual countries to respond independently to macroeconomic disturbances.

The final chapter in this volume, by Jeffrey Frankel and Shang-Jin Wei, evaluates the degree of European economic integration. Frankel and Wei consider the development of intra-European financial and commercial links, especially with an eye to their potential impact on the efficient allocation of resources regionally and globally. Specifically, they ask whether European integration has created a covert Fortress Europe by biasing trade toward European partners. Frankel and Wei also explore the possibility that the stabilization of exchange rates within Europe has encouraged the differential growth of intra-European trade, possibly at the expense of trade with other parts of the world. While intra-European exchange-rate stabilization has been dramatic, Frankel and Wei find only a small effect on the growth of intra-European trade. Nor do they find much evidence that the EU has been a source of trade diversion; the growth of intra-European trade has not occurred at the expense of trade with the rest of the world. Frankel and Wei describe a number of mechanisms whereby regional integration can strengthen support for multilateral liberalization as appears to have been the case in the European Community.

Endnotes

1. The center is funded by a grant from the German government. For support in the course of this project we thank the center's past and present directors, Richard Buxbaum and Gerald Feldman, respectively. This book is published in conjunction with: Barry Eichengreen, Jeffry Frieden, and Jürgen von Hagen, (eds.), *Politics and Institutions in an Integrated Europe.* European and Transatlantic Studies, Berlin, Heidelberg, New York: Springer, 1995.

Central Bank Independence and the Short-Run Output-Inflation Trade-off in the European Community

Carl E. Walsh[1]

1. Introduction

The member countries of the European Community (EC) have established a process for moving toward a common monetary policy conducted by a single European Central Bank (ECB). The structure of this new policy institution, modeled after the German Bundesbank, has been specifically designed to guarantee it a high degree of independence from political influences. Empirical evidence linking independent central banks with low average inflation played an important role in giving impetus to the creation of a common central bank with substantial political independence.[2]

The benefits of central bank independence are usually attributed to the ability of independent central banks to commit credibly to a low inflation policy. An independent ECB, it has been argued, would gain the same credibility for a low inflation policy as currently enjoyed by the Bundesbank; the transfer of this credibility would enable the European Monetary Union to sustain a low average rate of inflation. To reinforce the commitment to low inflation during the transition to a monetary union, the Maastricht Treaty requires EC countries to reform their own national central banks to grant them greater political independence.

While the arguments in favor of independent central banks have emphasized the lower average inflation such independence seems to produce, it is also important to examine the possible real economic effects of independence. Alesina and Summers (1993) have shown that several measures of real economic performance, such as average real growth rates, average unemployment rates, and their variances, seem unrelated to a measure of central bank independence. They conclude by suggesting, "The monetary discipline associated with central bank independence reduces the level and variability of inflation but does not have either large benefits or costs in terms of real macroeconomic performance" (p. 159). Similar findings for a much larger sample of developed and developing countries and an alternative measure of central bank independence are reported in Walsh (1994).

These findings have important implications for a monetary union under the ECB. Extrapolating experience under the Bundesbank would suggest the ECB will deliver relatively low inflation with no detrimental effects on the real growth and unemployment of the monetary union members. However, there are other aspects of an economy's real performance that might be affected by the degree of central bank independence. Among the most important is the slope of the short-run trade-off between inflation and unemployment. For example, if inflation should rise due to exogenous disturbances, the costs of subsequent policies to reduce inflation will depend on both the speed with which inflationary expectations adjust and the slope of the short-run Phillips Curve. And the inflationary consequences of monetary expansions will also vary with the slope of the short-run Phillips Curve.

If greater credibility does accrue to independent central banks, this should reduce the costs of policies designed to lower inflation. This is the argument of Sargent (1982); a credible disinflationary policy can reduce the rate of inflation with little output or unemployment cost. Hence, greater central bank independence might be expected to reduce the costs of disinflation by ensuring that the public's expectations of inflation decline rapidly, shifting the short-run Phillips Curve in toward the origin.

Ball, Mankiw, and Romer (1988), however, have shown that the short-run trade-off between output and inflation varies with the mean rate of inflation; lower average inflation is associated with greater output effects of changes in nominal income growth. While they attribute the effect of mean inflation on the trade-off to the relationship between mean inflation and the frequency of price changes, their results indicate that attempts to lower inflation will be more costly in countries that have generally achieved low average inflation. To the extent the ECB is able to mimic the Bundesbank's success in fighting inflation, the inflation-output trade-off in a monetary union may differ from that currently faced by the individual members of the EC.

If independence results in lower and less variable average inflation, the work of Lucas (1973), Gray (1978), and Canzoneri (1980) suggests additional reasons the slope of the Phillips Curve may be affected. In the model of Lucas (1973), the slope of the Phillips Curve reflects the outcome of a signal extraction problem that individual agents in the economy face. A reduction in the variance of nominal aggregate shocks implies that movements in prices are more likely to be the result of relative price movements that require real adjustments in output and employment. Thus, given the expected rate of inflation, a disinflationary shock leads to a larger output response than would be the case if inflation had been more variable. That is, the Phillips Curve would be flatter under an independent central bank that generates low inflation variability.

Gray (1978) and Canzoneri (1980) construct models in which nominal shocks have real effects because of the existence of nominal wage contracts. They show that a reduction in the variance of nominal shocks will tend to increase the optimal contract length and reduce the optimal degree of indexation. Both of these effects, by increasing nominal wage rigidity, work to increase the real effects of a nominal shock.

Increased central bank independence, therefore, should affect both the position of the Phillips Curve and its slope, shifting the short-run trade-off between inflation and unemployment in toward the origin and flattening its slope. The effect on the slope of the short-run trade-off between unemployment and inflation will increase the real economic costs of a policy to reduce average inflation and, conversely, lower the inflationary costs of economic expansion. These changes will affect the incentives monetary authorities face to engage in activist stabilization policies. If changes in the degree of central bank independence affect the short-run trade-off between output and inflation, then the policies of central bank reform currently under way in the EC may have a greater impact on the future macroeconomic performance of member countries than would be suggested by discussions that have emphasized only the likely effects on credibility and average inflation.

This article examines the relationship between central bank independence and the short-run trade-off between output and inflation among the EC countries. In the next section, a simple model of the joint determination of nominal rigidity and optimal discretionary monetary policy is developed. Private agents optimally choose the degree of nominal wage indexation, and this choice is shown to depend on the weight the central bank places on its inflation objectives. Changes in this weight lead to private sector responses that affect the slope of the short-run Phillips Curve. The following section examines existing measures of the costs of disinflation among the EC countries and shows that they appear to be positively correlated with measures of central bank independence. That is, those EC countries with greater central bank independence also appear to face higher costs of disinflation. This suggests that any credibility effect associated with greater central bank independence has been offset by systematic differences in the Phillips Curves different central banks face. The next section explores this empirical finding further by using time series data on EC member countries to estimate the relationship between central bank independence and the short-run trade-off between output and inflation. The empirical evidence seems to suggest that increased central bank independence, as is occurring among national central banks under the Maastricht Treaty and will occur if a monetary union is eventually formed, is associated with changes in the short-run trade-off between inflation and output that result in a flatter short-run Phillips Curve. A flat Phillips Curve may then reflect the benefit of low and stable inflation that allows private agents to reduce contracting and menu costs by limiting the frequency of nominal price and wage changes. Such a development simultaneously increases the temptation to inflate while raising the costs of inflation reduction.

2. Indexation, Central Bank Independence, and the Trade-off Parameter

The channel through which the institutional structure of the central bank might affect the slope of the short-run trade-off between output and inflation is suggested by the work of Gray (1978) and Canzoneri (1980). They examine the manner in which the degree of wage indexation and the length of nominal wage contracts will depend on the nature of real and nominal economic disturbances. Their models imply that the variability of output and the flexibility of wages and prices are jointly endogenous (see also Gray and Kandil, 1991). If independent central banks tend to generate an economic environment that produces longer nominal wage contracts or less indexation, the degree of nominal rigidity in the economy will rise. This flattens the aggregate supply curve (in inflation-output space) and raises the short-run output effects associated with changes in the rate of inflation. That is, the nature of contracts is endogenous and may be affected by the conduct of monetary policy.

Central banks affect the relative importance of real and nominal disturbances by their stabilization policies. And the extent to which a central bank engages in activist stabilization policies will depend on the weight it places on its inflation goals (Rogoff, 1985). A central bank that places greater weight on inflation stabilization will offset less of the output effects of a supply shock. If this increases the impact of real shocks on output, the optimal degree of wage indexation will fall (Gray, 1978). However, variations in the degree of indexation will also affect the optimal central bank response to aggregate supply shocks. Thus, to examine the role of central bank independence on the slope of the aggregate supply function, it is necessary to determine jointly the optimal degree of wage indexation and the optimal monetary policy.

To illustrate the relationship between central bank policy and nominal wage rigidities, I use a framework that is similar to that employed by Devereux (1987), Ball (1988), and Waller and VanHoose (1992). In contrast to these articles, however, I allow for monetary policy to conduct stabilization policy in response to aggregate supply disturbances. Wage setters in segmented labor markets choose the degree of local wage indexation; the central bank chooses average money growth and its response to aggregate supply shocks. The central bank's stabilization decision -- its decision about how to respond to the realization of the aggregate supply shock -- will depend on the aggregate degree of nominal wage indexation in the economy, while private agents' decisions about wage indexation will depend on the extent to which the central bank engages in stabilization policies. Thus, modeling the joint determination of indexation and central bank policy requires some assumptions about the strategic interactions between private agents and the central bank. There are several ways this interaction could be modeled. Since the point of the model is illustrative, I portray this interaction in the simplest terms possible.

Consider an economy that produces a homogenous output that is sold in an economywide competitive market but is produced by a continuum of firms, each of which faces a perfectly inelastic supply of workers as in Ball (1988) or Waller and VanHoose (1992). Assuming all firms have identical Cobb-Douglas production functions and suppressing unnecessary constant terms, it can be shown (see, e.g., Waller and VanHoose, 1992) that output of firm i is given by

$$y_i = c\,(1-\gamma_i)(p - p^e) + (1 + c)u \qquad [1]$$

where y_i is (log) output, $0 \leq \gamma_i \leq 1$ is the degree of indexation (0 corresponds to no indexation, 1 to full indexation), $c = \alpha/(1 - \alpha)$ where α is labor's share of income, p is the (log) aggregate price level, p^e is the level of p private agents expect, and u is a common aggregate supply disturbance, assumed to be mean zero and serially uncorrelated with variance σ_u^2. Assuming a constant supply of labor, full information output is normalized to equal $y_i^0 = u \equiv y^0$.

Letting m denote the (log) nominal money supply, the demand side of the economy is represented by a simple quantity equation:

$$p = m - y + v \qquad [2]$$

where v is a mean zero, serially uncorrelated velocity disturbance with variance σ_v^2. For convenience, u and v are assumed to be uncorrelated. The equilibrium price level, given p^e, can be found by integrating Equation 1 over all firms--to obtain $y = c(1 - \gamma)(p - p^e) + (1 + c)u$, where γ is the aggregate degree of wage indexation--and substituting this expression for y into Equation 2. Taking expectations of the resulting expression, under the assumption that wage contracts are set prior to observing either u or v, yields an expression for p^e. Finally, eliminating p^e from the equation for p allows one to show that

$$p = m^e + \frac{1}{1 + c(1 - \gamma)}[m - m^e + v - (1 + c) \qquad [3]$$

so that $p^e = m^e$. Equation 3 then implies that output from firm i will be equal to

$$y_i = \frac{c(1 - \gamma_i)}{1 + c(1 - \gamma)}(m - m^e + v) + \frac{(1 + c)[1 + c(\gamma_i - \gamma)]}{1 + c(1 - \gamma)}u. \qquad [4]$$

Employers and employees in each sector are assumed to set the degree of nominal wage indexation so as to minimize the variance of sector output around its full information level. With many sectors, each of which is small, it is appropriate to assume that each sector takes the aggregate average degree of wage indexation as given. In order to set γ_i optimally, however, private agents must form expectations about the behavior of the money supply. So it is necessary to examine the decision problem the central bank faces.

Suppose the central bank attempts to minimize an expected loss function that depends on price fluctuations and output deviations around a level of output that exceeds the full information level by $k > 0$:

$$L = \frac{1}{2}E[(y - y^0 - k)^2 + \beta p^2]. \qquad [5]$$

Policy under discretion is taken to mean that the central bank treats the private sector's expectations and the degree of wage indexation as given in setting the nominal money supply to minimize L. In this case, the time-consistent optimal money rule under rational expectations is given by

$$m = \frac{c(1 - \gamma)k}{\beta} + bu \qquad [6]$$

where

$$b \equiv \left[1 + \frac{c\,[\beta - c\,(1-\gamma)]}{[c\,(1-\gamma)]^2 + \beta}\right]. \qquad [7]$$

The coefficient b determines the policy response to aggregate supply shocks and is a function of the aggregate indexation parameter γ. Equation 7 defines the locus BB in Figure 1, which shows the central bank's optimal stabilization response to supply shocks to be a function of the aggregate degree of wage indexation when the central bank takes the degree of wage indexation as given.[3] Greater nominal wage indexation increases the effect of supply shocks in generating deviations of output from its full information level and reduces the output effect of monetary surprises. With a reduced ability to affect output, monetary policy acts to offset more of the price effects of a supply shock; this is accomplished by increasing b.

Since $m - m^e = bu$ from Equation 6, Equation 4 implies that the variance of firm i's output around u will be equal to

$$\sigma_i^2 = c^2\left[1 - \frac{(1-\gamma_i)(1+c-b)}{1+c\,(1-\gamma)}\right]^2 \sigma_u^2 + \left[\frac{c\,(1-\gamma_i)}{1+c\,(1-\gamma)}\right]^2 \sigma_v^2. \qquad [8]$$

In choosing γ_i to minimize Equation 8, individual wage setters take the aggregate indexation parameter γ as given. Since the central bank's response to supply shocks, b, is a function of γ, individual agents also take b as given in setting γ_i. The value of γ_i that minimizes σ_i^2 is

$$\gamma_i = 1 - \frac{[1 + c\,(1-\gamma)]\,(1+c-b)\,\sigma_u^2}{\sigma_v^2 + (1+c-b)^2 \sigma_u^2}. \qquad [9]$$

In a symmetric Nash equilibrium, $\gamma_i = \gamma$ for all i, which, from Equation 9, implies that

$$\gamma = 1 - \frac{(1+c-b)\,\sigma_u^2}{\sigma_v^2 + (1-b)(1+c-b)\,\sigma_u^2}. \qquad [10]$$

As is well-known, an increase in the variance of nominal shocks (v) relative to real shocks (u) increases the optimal degree of indexation. Equation 10 also illustrates that the optimal degree of indexation will depend on the extent to which the central bank responds to supply shocks (b). The locus WW in Figure 1 shows the optimal degree of indexation as a function of b. As b increases, the impact of an aggregate supply shock on the deviation of output from its full information value also increases.[4] This raises the importance of real shocks relative to nominal shocks and lowers the optimal degree of indexation.

In a Nash equilibrium, γ and b are given by the joint solutions to Equations 7 and 10.[5] At point A in Figure 1, the degree of indexation is optimal, given the central bank's stabilization policy; and the central bank's stabilization policy is optimal, given the degree of wage indexation.

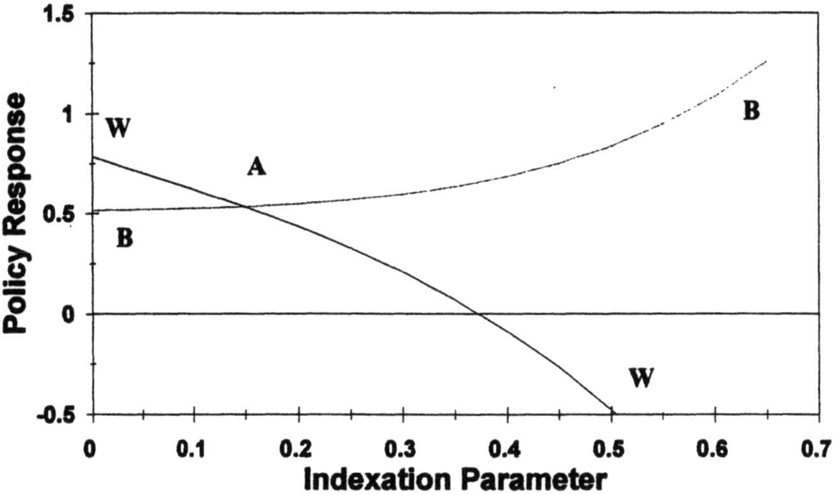

Figure 1: Equilibrium Indexation and Policy Response to Supply Shocks

The WW locus is independent of β, the weight on inflation in the central bank's loss function. The BB locus, however, does depend on β. An increase in β shifts BB upward, increasing b at each γ as the central bank acts to insulate prices more fully from aggregate supply shocks at the cost of greater output fluctuations. In the new equilibrium, b increases while γ decreases.[6]

While the notion of central bank independence is multidimensional, it is often associated with a greater emphasis on inflation objectives -- a higher β in terms of the model (see, e.g., Cukierman, 1992, or Debelle and Fischer, 1994). Hetzel (1990) and Debelle and Fischer (1994) have emphasized the distinction between goal independence -- the ability to specify the goals toward which policy will be directed -- and instrument independence -- the ability to set policy tools freely to achieve specified goals. Goodhart (forthcoming) has suggested the term *autonomy* -- as opposed to independence -- as a more appropriate characterization of the objective of recent central banking reform proposals. These proposals, while pursued under the banner of greater central bank independence, have actually involved reducing goal independence by explicitly assigning low inflation objectives to the central bank. This is certainly the case with the proposed ECB as set out in the Maastricht Treaty. Consequently, central banking changes in the EC are likely to be associated with an increase in the parameter β in the central bank's loss function. Adopting this interpretation, a rise in central bank independence results in a fall in the degree of nominal wage indexation. As a result, nominal wage rigidity increases; this is reflected in an increase in the real output effect of a nominal shock. Figure 2 plots the (inverse) slope of the short-run aggregate

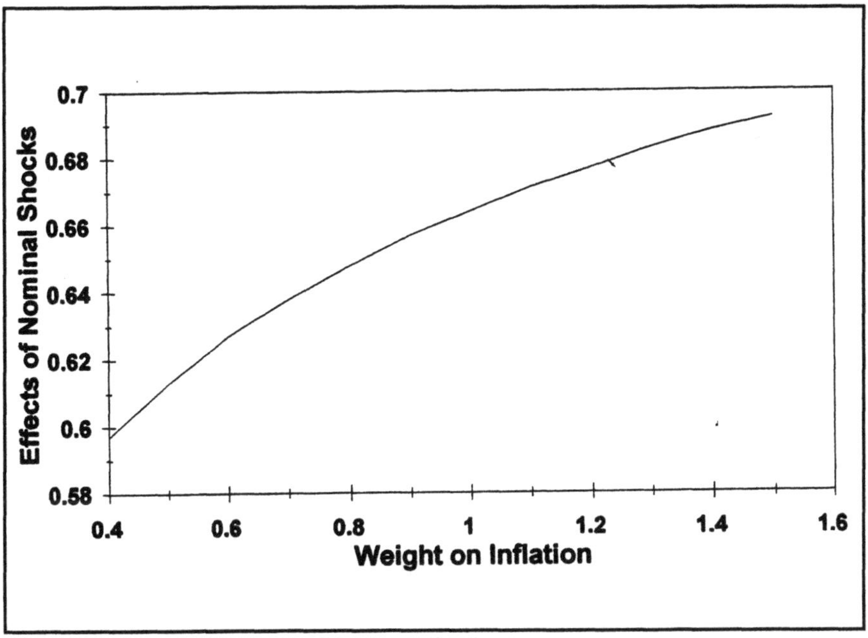

Figure 2: Output Effect of a Nominal Shock

supply function -- the coefficient of money surprises in the solution for aggregate output -- against the degree of central bank independence, proxied by β.

While the model presented here has focused on the wage indexation parameter, similar implications hold for the optimal contract length. As Gray (1978), for example, has shown, an increase in the relative importance of real shocks will tend to increase the optimal contract length. This has the effect of increasing nominal rigidities. An increase in the weight the central bank places on its inflation objective is predicted to raise the degree of nominal rigidity in the economy both by lowering wage indexation and by increasing contract length.

This section has illustrated one channel through which greater central bank independence, to the extent it implies an increased focus on price stabilization, can affect the degree of nominal wage rigidity in the economy. If inflation should rise as the result of exogenous disturbances, the real costs of subsequent policies to reduce inflation will be affected by the credibility of the central bank and the degree of nominal rigidity. If central bank independence raises both credibility and nominal rigidities, the net outcome is an empirical question. In the absence of a credibility bonus -- of which there seems to be little evidence, at least for moderate inflations (see Egebo and Englander, 1992, Judd and Beebe, 1993, and Debelle, 1994, although evidence consistent with some credibility effects in the United States is presented in Croushore and Kroot, 1994) -- the wage indexation model predicts that greater central bank independence would raise the output cost of disinflation and increase the output effects of monetary expansions.

3. Central Bank Independence and the Sacrifice Ratio

This section provides a preliminary analysis of the empirical relationship between central bank independence and the costs of disinflation among the EC countries using existing estimates of short-run inflation-output trade-offs and disinflation costs. The section begins, however, with a description of the measures of central bank independence employed in the empirical analysis.

As is well-known, measures of central bank independence are negatively correlated with average inflation; greater independence is associated with lower inflation (Alesina, 1988; Alesina and Summers, 1993; Bade and Parkin, 1982; Banaian, Laney, and Willett, 1983; Cukierman, 1992; Cukierman, Webb, and Neyapti, 1992; Cukierman, Kalaitzidakis, Summers, and Webb, 1993; Grilli, Masciandaro, and Tabellini, 1991). While various indices of independence have been used in these studies, the findings are generally consistent.[7]

Measures of central bank independence are designed to reflect the institutional framework within which central banks operate, and they depend on various legal aspects of the central banking structure in each country. In this article, I use three indices. The first, denoted CWN, is the measure of legal independence constructed by Cukierman, Webb, and Neyapti (1992). This measure is also used by Cukierman (1992, see in particular Chapter 19) and Cukierman, Kalaitzidakis, Summers, and Webb (1993). Cukierman, Webb, and Neyapti (1992) have assembled an extensive database of legal characteristics of central banks for a large sample of developed and developing countries. The data categories range from information on who appoints the central bank's chief executive officer and the provisions for that officer's dismissal to information on the terms of government borrowing from the central bank. Cukierman, Webb, and Neyapti use these data to construct their measure of legal independence, and the index is available for 11 of the EC countries (Belgium, Denmark, France, Germany, Greece, Ireland, Italy, Luxembourg, Netherlands, Spain, and the United Kingdom).

The second index is that used by Grilli, Masciandaro, and Tabellini (1991) and is denoted GMT. These authors make a distinction between "political" and "economic" independence. Political independence involves the ability of the central bank to define its policy objectives free from government influence, while economic independence refers to the ability of the central bank to freely determine the manner in which it implements policy to achieve its (possibly politically determined) objectives. The GMT index is the sum of separate measures of political and economic independence. This index is available for 11 EC countries (Belgium, Denmark, France, Germany, Greece, Ireland, Italy, Netherlands, Portugal, Spain, and the United Kingdom).

Results are also reported using a measure from Fratianni and Huang (1992) and denoted FH. This index is an average of nine measures of central bank independence and is available for nine of the EC countries (Belgium, Denmark, France, Germany, Ireland, Italy, Netherlands, Spain, and the United Kingdom). Since both GMT and CWN are among the nine indices Fratianni and Huang used, FH does not provide an independent measure of central bank independence.

However, it does incorporate information from several other indices; with each individual index subject to measurement error, there is some argument for using an average index such as FH. The FH measure gives the Bundesbank a value of 1. The value of the index for each of the other central banks is based on the average and the standard deviation of the nine individual index measures. A central bank is included only if measures from at least four of the nine indices are available.

Table 1 reports the correlations among the three measures of central bank independence. Simple correlations are shown above the diagonal, rank correlations below. The simple correlations among all three indices are quite high. Since GMT and CWN are component measures used in FH, the high correlation between these two and FH is not surprising. CWN, however, is based on a much more detailed set of legal characteristics than is GMT.[8] The rank correlation between CWN and GMT is, in contrast, only .311. To see why, Table 2 presents the rankings implied by each index. For all three, Germany is ranked as having the most independent central bank. The most marked differences are between the CWN and GMT rankings for Belgium and Greece. CWN places Belgium at the bottom of its ranking, while GMT ranks it as fourth (tied with France) out of 11. GMT ranks Greece as tenth out of 11, while CWN places Greece as the most independent central bank after Germany among the EC countries. Eliminating Greece from the comparisons, the rank correlation between CWN and GMT jumps from .311 to .732. For a more complete discussion of measures of central bank independence, see Pollard (1993).

Table 1: Measures of Central Bank Independence Correlations (Rank Correlations Below Diagonal)

Variable	CWN	GMT	FH
CWN	1.000	.620	.939
GMT	0.311	1.000	.850
FH	0.949	0.677	1.000

While new estimates of the short-run output-inflation trade-off for the EC countries are provided in the next section, it is useful to examine first the relationship between measures of central bank independence and existing estimates of the costs of disinflation. Such estimates for the EC countries are provided by Ball, Mankiw and Romer (1988), Schelde-Andersen (1992), and Ball (forthcoming). Ball, Mankiw and Romer report a trade-off parameter (denoted here as BMR) that measures the extent to which a nominal shock affects real output. This parameter is the estimated coefficient on the growth rate of nominal income in an equation for the level of real output (gross domestic product, GDP, or gross national product, GNP). The lagged level of output and a time trend are also

Table 2: Rankings of Central Bank Independence

Country	CWN	GMT	FH
Belgium	11	4	7
Denmark	3	3	2
France	8	4	5
Germany	1	1	1
Greece	2	10	-
Ireland	5	4	3
Italy	9	8	7
Luxembourg	6	-	-
Netherlands	4	2	4
Portugal	-	11	-
Spain	10	8	6
U.K.	7	7	4

included in the regression, and results are reported for 43 countries. In order to focus on the flexible exchange rate period, the most relevant estimates from BMR are those for the EC nations using annual data for the period 1973 to 1986 (Ball, Mankiw, and Romer, 1988: 36). A high value of the estimated parameter implies that nominal shocks have large real output effects and, consequently, that the sacrifice ratio -- the output or unemployment costs per percentage point reduction in inflation -- will tend to be large.

A second measure of the sacrifice ratio is obtained from Schelde-Andersen's study of disinflation among the Organization for Economic Cooperation and Development countries. Schelde-Andersen presents four estimates of the sacrifice ratio, all based on the disinflation experiences of the early 1980s. These differ in two ways: the time period over which the change in inflation is measured and the measure of the real costs (unemployment or output). The index I use is a simple average of the four estimates Schelde-Andersen (1992: 124) reported.

While the BMR estimates are regression-based, Ball (forthcoming), like Schelde-Andersen, adopts a case study approach to estimating the sacrifice ratios associated with specific disinflationary periods for the developed countries. I employ Ball's measure obtained from annual data and reported in his Table III. Table 3 presents the correlations between the three estimates of the trade-off between inflation and real economic activity and the three alternative measures of central bank independence. For all combinations, the correlations are positive, suggesting that a greater degree of central bank independence is associated with increased

Table 3: Central Bank Independence and Sacrifice Ratios: Correlations

Index of Central Bank Independence	Ball, Mankiw, and Romer (1972-1988)	Schelde-Andersen	Ball
CWN	0.650	0.506	0.428
GMT	0.571	0.785	0.453
FH	0.658	0.561	0.619

costliness of policies to reduce inflation. Debelle and Fischer (1994), using the GMT index and Ball's measure of the sacrifice ratio, have also noted this positive correlation. Most arguments for policy independence, however, cite the increased credibility of a low inflation policy when monetary policy is conducted by an independent central bank. Increased credibility should reduce the output cost of disinflations, an implication that does not appear to hold empirically. Thus, while countries with highly independent central banks experience lower average inflation, they also seem to bear a higher than average output cost in order to reduce inflation.

A common argument is that the costs of disinflation are smaller at high inflation rates. Since central bank independence is usually associated with lower average inflation, the positive correlation between central bank independence and sacrifice ratios may simply reflect the impact of low average inflation on the sacrifice ratio.[9] Alesina and Summers (1993) report average inflation rates and the variance of inflation during the 1973 to 1988 period for most EC countries (they exclude Greece, Ireland, Luxembourg, and Portugal). Table 4 reports correlations between these measures, central bank independence, and the trade-off estimates. All three measures of central bank independence are strongly negatively correlated with average inflation and with its variance. In turn, the mean and variance of inflation are negatively correlated with the estimates of the costs of disinflation. Thus, the positive correlations reported in Table 3 could arise because inflation is more

Table 4: Average Inflation, Sacrifice Ratios, and Central Bank Independence: Correlations

Var.	CWN	GMT	FH	BMR	Schelde Ander-sen	Ball Ann.
Infl 73-88	-0.643	-0.829	-0.582	-0.180	-0.890	-0.156
Var 73-88	-0.700	-0.857	-0.660	-0.551	-0.603	-0.139

costly to reduce at low levels and because countries with independent central banks tend to experience lower levels of inflation. If this is the case, a higher sacrifice ratio may simply reflect the success of low- inflation policies. By using a measure of the output-inflation trade-off, it is possible to investigate whether the positive correlation between central bank independence and the inflation-output trade-off simply reflects the negative correlation between independence and both average inflation and its variance.

Table 5: Dependent Variable: BMR73-86 (Sample Size: 8)

Var.	Eq. 1	Eq. 2	Eq. 3	Eq. 4	Eq. 5	Eq. 6
Const.	-0.89 (0.46)	-2.29*** (0.58)	-0.12 (0.39)	-.00 (0.92)	-0.01 (1.93)	0.53 (0.74)
INFL 73-88	0.06 (0.03)	0.13*** (0.04)	0.04 (0.04)			
SD 73-88				-0.02 (0.16)	-0.03 (0.03)	-0.06 (0.16)
CWN	2.65*** (0.70)			1.71 (1.07)		
GMT		0.23*** (0.04)			0.08 (0.12)	
FH			1.13** (0.41)			0.73 (0.56)
R^2	.75	.85	.61	.59	.43	.54

*** Significant at the 1% level. ** Significant at the 5% level.

Table 5 reports the results obtained when the BMR trade-off parameter for a cross- section of EC countries is regressed on average inflation and on the standard deviation of inflation as reported by Alesina and Summers and the measures of central bank independence.[10] For each equation reported in Table 5, the dependent variable is the BMR estimated trade-off parameter; a high value of the dependent variable corresponds to a greater output effect of nominal income changes -- that is, a flatter Phillips Curve. Equations 1 to 3 in Table 5 include average inflation and a measure of central bank independence. Only when GMT is used is average inflation statistically significant, while the measure of central bank independence is estimated to have a statistically significant positive effect on the trade-off parameter no matter which index is used. This suggests that central bank independence is not simply serving as a proxy for the effect of average inflation on the short-run output-inflation trade-off.

Table 5 also reports the results of regressing the BMR trade-off parameter on the standard deviation of inflation. If the slope of the short-run Phillips Curve depends on the variance of nominal disturbances as in Lucas (1973), then less volatile inflation should be associated with a flatter Phillips Curve and a higher value of the BMR trade-off parameter. Since inflation volatility is negatively correlated with central bank independence, this channel could account for the positive association between the trade-off parameter and the measures of central bank independence. When the trade-off parameters are regressed on the standard deviation of inflation and measures of central bank independence, however, neither variable is statistically significant. Since the regressions in Table 5 are based on only eight observations (Belgium, Denmark, France, Germany, Italy, Netherlands, Spain, and the United Kingdom) -- the EC countries in Ball, Mankiw, and Romer's sample for which Alesina and Summers report average inflation -- the results should be viewed as suggestive only.

This section has employed existing measures of the short-run trade-off between inflation and output to provide a preliminary look at the relationship between disinflation cost measures and central bank independence. Countries with highly independent central banks seem to face the largest real costs of inflation reduction. Since central bank independence is negatively correlated with average inflation rates, the positive correlation between disinflation costs and the independence indices may reflect increasing marginal costs of disinflation. The BMR trade-off parameter, however, was significantly and positively related to central bank independence even after controlling for average inflation in a cross-section of EC countries.

4. The Output-Inflation Trade-off in the EC

To investigate further the relationship between central bank independence and the costs of disinflation, new estimates of the trade-off between output and inflation were obtained for the 12 EC countries for which at least one of the three measures of central bank independence was available. These are Belgium, Denmark, France, Germany, Greece, Ireland, Italy, Luxembourg, Netherlands, Portugal, Spain, and the United Kingdom. Following Ball, Mankiw, and Romer (1988), I estimate regressions of the following form for each country:

$$y_{i,t} = a_i + b_i(\Delta y_{i,t} + \Delta p_{i,t}) + c_i y_{i,t-1} + Trend_i + e_{i,t} \qquad [11]$$

where $y_{i,t}$ is the log of GDP (GNP) for country i in period t, $p_{i,t}$ is the log of the GDP deflator, and Trend is a simple linear time trend. The relevant parameter governing the short-run trade-off between output and inflation for country i is b_i. As Ball, Mankiw, and Romer note, this type of equation has been estimated by Lucas (1973) and Schultze (1984) among others. A higher value of b_i implies that more of any change in nominal income appears as a change in real output in the first year. A large b_i corresponds, therefore, to high output costs of a disinflation.

Data on real and nominal GDP were obtained from the International Financial Statistics (IFS); GNP is used for Belgium and Germany. The log price deflator was defined as log nominal GDP (GNP) minus log real GDP (GNP). The estimation period is 1973 to 1992 (to 1991 for Belgium, Greece, and Portugal).

Table 6 reports the estimates of b_i for each country. Since the residuals from each equation are likely to be correlated across countries, results obtained by the joint estimation of all 12 equations using Seemingly Unrelated Regression (SUR) for the period 1973 to 1991 are also presented in Table 6. These estimates should

Table 6: Estimated Trade-off Parameters1973-1992

Country	OLS	SUR
Belgium	0.446** (0.18)	0.471*** (0.08)
Denmark	1.221*** (0.26)	1.286*** (0.19)
France	0.430* (0.20)	0.539*** (0.06)
Germany	0.860*** (0.09)	0.806*** (0.05)
Greece	0.371* (0.20)	0.272** (0.11)
Ireland	0.076 (0.15)	0.195*** (0.07)
Italy	0.527*** (0.10)	0.432*** (0.06)
Luxembourg	0.955*** (0.20)	0.486*** (0.07)
Netherlands	0.597*** (0.12)	0.527*** (0.06)
Portugal	0.225 (0.16)	0.285*** (0.07)
Spain	0.309 (0.22)	0.169 (0.11)
U.K.	0.063 (0.22)	0.052 (0.12)

Note: Sample ends in 1991 for Belgium and Greece.
***, **, *; Significant at the 1%, 5%, 10% level

be quite similar to those obtained by Ball, Mankiw, and Romer since they estimate the same equation using the same data source (IFS). Their most comparable sample is from 1972 to 1986 and the correlation between their estimates and my ordinary least squares (OLS) estimates is .917. The correlation with my SUR estimates is .875. Table 7 reports the simple correlations between the estimated b_i's and the various measures of central bank independence. In all cases, central bank independence is positively correlated with the trade-off parameter. The correlation is smallest for the measure constructed by Cukierman, Webb, and Neyapti (1992) and largest for the index of Grilli, Masciandaro, and Tabellini (1991). These positive correlations confirm the results reported above using previous estimates of either sacrifice ratios or the slope of the short-run aggregate supply relationship.

Table 7: Estimated b's and Central Bank Independence Correlations

Variable	OLS	SUR
CWN	.434	.449
GMT	.559	.553
FH	.459	.465

Note: The number of countries covered by each index differs (11 countries for CWN and GMT and nine for FH).

In order to more formally investigate the possible dependence of b_i on the degree of central bank independence, the effect of central bank independence on the trade-off parameter can be jointly estimated for all the countries. The constant term and the coefficients on lagged GDP and the trend are still allowed to differ across countries, but b_i is assumed to be equal to $\alpha + \beta CBI_i$ where CBI_i is the index of central bank independence for country i. That is, the following equation was estimated:

$$y_{i,t} = a_i + (\alpha + \beta\, CB_i)(\Delta y_{i,t} + \Delta p_{i,t}) + c_i y_{i,t-1} + Trend_i + e_{i,t} \qquad [12]$$

The estimates of α and β when the GMT index of central bank independence is employed are given in column 1 of Table 8. The results reflect the positive correlations reported in Table 7; the effect of independence on the trade-off parameter is positive and statistically significant. Columns 2 and 3 replace the GMT index with the CWN index and the FH index, respectively. In all cases, increased central bank independence is associated with an increase in the trade-off parameter, indicating that the short-run aggregate supply relationship is flatter for EC countries with more independent central banks.

The positive estimated coefficients are consistent with the model in which greater central bank independence was associated with a decline in nominal wage indexation and, as a result, increased nominal rigidity. However, a variety of other explanations for the positive association between the independence indices and the

Table 8: Determinants of the Trade-off Parameter: Central Bank Independence

Explanatory Variable	Equation 1	Equation 2	Equation 3
Constant	.060	.128**	.262***
Measures of central bank independence:			
GMT	.047***		
CWN		.714***	
FH			.366***
Number of countries	11	11	9

Notes: Each column shows the estimated effects of the explanatory variables on the *coefficient* of nominal income growth in a SUR system estimated using annual data from 1973 to 1991.
***, **: Significant at the 1%, 5% level.

impact of nominal income changes on real output are possible.

If sacrifice ratios are lower at high rates of inflation, the positive effect of central bank independence could, as noted earlier, simply be serving as a proxy for the lower average inflation rates experienced by countries with more independent central banks. However, as Ball, Mankiw, and Romer (1988) have noted, this argument is not necessarily correct. Greater central bank independence, if it is associated with lower average inflation, shifts the Phillips Curve downward; but the slope of the Phillips Curve evaluated at the sample mean unemployment rate would be unaffected if the sample mean provides an estimate of the natural rate of unemployment. The estimated trade-off parameter would, in this case, be independent of both central bank independence and average inflation.

Ball, Mankiw, and Romer (1988) propose a New Keynesian model in which the slope of the Phillips Curve does depend on the mean rate of inflation. Higher average inflation is associated with more frequent changes in individual prices; this implies that the degree of nominal rigidity will be decreasing in the mean rate of inflation. With the short-run output-inflation trade-off dependent on the extent of nominal rigidities, the trade-off parameter should be a decreasing function of the mean rate of inflation. Because of the negative correlation between central bank independence and average inflation, the Ball, Mankiw, and Romer argument would be consistent with the apparent positive correlation between the independence indices and the trade-off parameter.

Equations 1 and 5 of Table 9 report the results of allowing the trade-off parameter to depend on average inflation; in Equation 1, the average rate of inflation is calculated for the sample period (1973-1991), while in Equation 8, the average for a preestimation sample period is used (1966-1972). If the slope of the short-run Phillips Curve reflects nominal contracting behavior that would tend to change slowly over time, the average inflation rate from the earlier period may be the most relevant determinant. In fact, both Equations 1 and 5 show that the trade-off parameter is negatively and statistically significantly related to average inflation, as Ball, Mankiw, and Romer argued.

In Equations 2-4 and 6-8, each of the indices of central bank independence is added. If the positive effect of independence on the trade-off arises simply because independence is proxying for average inflation, independence should not have a significant effect when average inflation is also included in the regression equation. As is clear from Table 9, however, the coefficients on the independence indices continue to be highly significant. When average inflation for the within-sample period (1973-1991) is used, the coefficient on the inflation variable is actually *positive* and significantly different from zero with a marginal significance level of under 3% when GMT is used. It appears that independence is not simply serving as a proxy for the average level of inflation.

According to the earlier model, central bank independence matters for the trade-off parameter because independence is related to the relative variance of real and nominal output disturbances. Table 10 reports the results of adding the standard deviation of the growth rate of nominal income as a determinant of the trade-off parameter.

Table 9: Determinants of the Trade-off Parameter: Central Bank Independence and Average Inflation

	Equation							
Explanatory Variable	1	2	3	4	5	6	7	8
Constant	.631***	.430***	.452***	1.04***	.602***	-.461**	.392***	.61***
Measures of central bank independence:								
GMT		.062***				.087***		
CWN			.561***				.597***	
FH				.307***				.148**
Average inflation 1973-1991	-2.32***	2.52**	-2.66***	-3.55***				
Average inflation 1966-1972					-4.90***	-8.34***	-4.90***	-12.39***
Number of countries	12	11	11	9	12	11	11	9

Notes: Each column shows the estimated effects of the explanatory variables on the *coefficient* of nominal income growth in a SUR system estimated using annual data from 1973 to 1991.
***, **: Significant at the 1%, 5% level.

Both the Lucas signaling and the nominal wage indexation/contract length arguments imply that an increase in nominal volatility should reduce the trade-off parameter. This prediction holds when the standard deviation is measured over 1973-1991 (Equation 1, Table 10), but it fails to hold when the standard deviation is measured over the presample period 1966-1972 (Equation 5). When the indices of central bank independence are added, only GMT continues to be significant (Equation 2) when nominal volatility is measured over the sample period. However, the central bank independence measures remain positive and highly significant if nominal volatility is measured over the presample period (Equations 6-8). The measure of nominal volatility remains correctly signed and statistically significant only if it is measured over the 1973-1991 sample period.

Table 10: Determinants of the Trade-off Parameter: Central Bank Independence and Nominal Variability

	Equation							
Explanatory Variable	1	2	3	4	5	6	7	8
Constant	.953***	.674***	.843**	1.04***	.227***	.074***	.038***	.222***
Measures of central bank independence:								
GMT		.033***				.048***		
CWN			.188				.695***	
FH				.064				.347***
Standard deviation of nominal income growth, 1973-1991	-13.9***	-12.6***	-12.5***	-16.0***				
Standard deviation of nominal income growth, 1966-1972					4.342***	-.769	2.695*	1.532
Number of countries	12	11	11	9	12	11	11	9

Notes: Each column shows the estimated effects of the explanatory variables on the *coefficient* of nominal income growth in a SUR system estimated using annual data from 1973 to 1991.
***, **, *: Significant at the 1%, 5%, 10% level.

Equations 1-8 of Table 11 allow the trade-off parameter to be a function of central bank independence, average inflation, and the standard deviation of nominal income growth. Here, the results again depend importantly on whether inflation and nominal volatility are measured over the sample period (Equations 1-4) or the presample period (Equations 5-8). Focusing on the sample- period measures, Equation 1 shows that both mean inflation and nominal volatility have the

Table 11: Determinants of the Trade-off Parameter:
Central Bank Independence, Average Inflation, and Nominal Variability

	Equation							
Explanatory Variable	1	2	3	4	5	6	7	8
Constant	1.10***	.64***	.96***	1.01***	.51***	.41***	.39***	.97***
Measures of central bank independence:								
GMT		.036**				.061***		
CWN			.176				.573***	
FH				.116				.284***
Ave. inflation 1973-1991	-1.90***	.112	-2.14***	1.97				
Ave. inflation 1966-1972					-4.76***	-8.38***	-4.77***	-12.13***
Standard deviation of nominal income growth, 1973-1991	13.08***	-12.68***	-10.84***	-19.33***				
Standard deviation of nominal income growth, 1966-1972					3.412**	1.070	1.226	2.208
Number of countries	12	11	11	9	12	11	11	9

Notes: Each column shows the estimated effects of the explanatory variables on the *coefficient* of nominal income growth in a SUR system estimated using annual data from 1973 to 1991.
***, **, *: Significant at the 1%, 5%, 10% level.

predicted effects on the trade-off parameter, with both being statistically significant. However, when the GMT measure is added (Equation 2), mean inflation has the wrong sign (positive) and is not statistically significant, while central bank independence is significant at the 5% level. With the other two indices (CWN and FH), mean inflation remains significant (and negative) when CWN is used but has a nonsignificant (but large) positive coefficient when FH is used. Neither CWN nor FH is statistically significant.

When the presample period is used to measure mean inflation and the standard deviations of nominal income growth, the results are quite different. In Equations 5-8, mean inflation always has a negative and statistically significant estimated coefficient. The standard deviation of the growth rate of nominal income, however, always has a positive estimated coefficient; it is significant only when no measure of central bank independence is included. Ball, Mankiw, and Romer (1988: 42) also report finding a positive coefficient on aggregate demand variability for their pre-1972 sample. Central bank independence remains correctly signed and statistically significant at the 1% level regardless of which index is used.

The empirical evidence reported in this section casts some doubt on the argument that central bank independence delivers lower inflation with no real effects. Central bank independence appears to be related to the short-run inflation-output trade-off. This suggests an increased cost of inflation reduction and larger output effects of monetary surprises in countries with more independent central banks and is consistent with the model in which an increase in the weight the central bank places on its inflation objective increases the degree of nominal rigidity in the economy. However, the empirical association between independence and the trade-off parameter is clearly consistent with other interpretations. The reported results have indicated the existence of a relationship that, given the recent trends toward increasing the political independence of central banks around the world, warrants further study. For the EC nations, the empirical results suggest that the changing monetary environment associated with greatly increased autonomy on the part of national central banks and the ECB under a monetary union will affect the economic structure in ways beyond simply lowering average inflation. If the short-run output-inflation trade-off shifts, the macroeconomic adjustments to aggregate shocks among the EC will be altered by the institutional reforms designed to achieve price stability

5. Conclusions

The evidence presented here, together with the findings in Debelle (1994) and Debelle and Fischer (1994), indicates that there exists a positive association between a country's cost of reducing inflation and the degree of independence the country's central bank enjoys. This runs directly counter to the general presumption in the literature that increased central bank independence brings with it a credibility bonus that should lessen the costs of any disinflationary policy. At least for the EC countries, the moves toward increasing the political independence of central banks may have greater real effects than previous discussions have suggested. The indexation model illustrates one channel through which changes in central bank independence might affect the short-run output-inflation trade-off by altering the structure of nominal wage contracts in the economy.

As with the evidence of the negative correlations between central bank independence and average rates of inflation, the empirical results reported here cast little direct light on the important issue of causality. Does the establishment of central bank independence lead to labor market structures that make reducing inflation more costly? Or are countries with flat aggregate supply curves more likely to establish independent central banks? Flat short-run supply curves raise the temptation to engage in expansionary policies and boost the inflationary bias of discretionary policy. Both these factors might increase the value of an independent central bank that maintains a low rate of inflation.

Just as correlations do not imply causality, they do not yield any particular welfare conclusions. Even if it is the institution of an independent central bank that is responsible for the changing trade-off, increasing central bank independence may still be welfare-improving.[11] In the analysis of Rogoff (1985), increasing the weight the central bank places on its inflation objectives lowers average inflation at the cost of increasing the output variance due to aggregate supply disturbances. Rogoff shows that it is optimal for the central bank to give more weight to inflation goals than does society as a whole. Changing the central bank's objective function affects the degree of wage indexation the public finds optimal. Greater central bank independence leads to less wage indexation. While this tends to increase the real effects of nominal disturbances, it also acts to reduce the deviations from full information output of supply disturbances. Thus, the increase in output variance associated with a greater weight on inflation may be partially offset by the induced changes in labor contracts caused by less-activist stabilization policies.

If inflationary episodes originate from nonpolicy disturbances, the cost of policies to lower inflation will depend on the output effects of slowing nominal income growth. The incentives to engage in stabilization policies and the inflationary bias of discretionary monetary policy also will depend on the short-run trade-off between inflation and output. The analysis presented here suggests the increased central bank independence that will characterize the EC countries in the future may affect the degree of nominal rigidity. Even if a monetary union is still several years off, the Maastricht Treaty means that individual countries will have more independent national central banks than previously. It is important to recognize that these changes will do more that just lower average inflation; there will be real effects as well. The empirical evidence suggests that both the incentive to inflate and the costs of reducing inflation may increase with greater central bank independence.

Endnotes

1. This research was partially supported by grants from the Study Group on the Political Economy of European Integration of the Center for German and European Studies at the University of California, Berkeley, and the National Science Foundation. I would like to thank Jeff Frieden, Jürgen von Hagen, Pierre Siklos, Chris Waller, Judy Walsh, and participants at the National Bureau of Economic Research Summer Institute, Monetary Economics Program, for helpful comments, though responsibility for errors remains with the author alone. Any opinions expressed are not necessarily those of the Federal Reserve Bank of San Francisco or the Federal Reserve System.

2. This evidence is surveyed in Cukierman (1992, Chapter 19).

3. In Figure 1, the share of labor income is set at .7 so that the parameter c in Equation 7 is equal to 7/3, and β, the weight on the price term in the central bank's objective function, is set equal to 1.

4. The coefficient on u in the expression for the deviation of y from its full information value is given by $c[\gamma + b(1 - \gamma)]/[1 + c(1 - \gamma)]$, which is increasing in b.

5. For European economies characterized by centralized wage bargaining, a more relevant equilibrium concept might be that of Stackelberg. With centralized bargaining, wage setters would no longer take the central bank's action as independent of their choice of indexation parameter. In this case, γ would be set taking into account the impact that varying γ would have on the central bank's behavior. That is, the dependence of b on γ given in Equation 7 would be explicitly taken into account in setting γ. In this environment, Equation 7 continues to hold (under the assumption that the central bank sets policy after private agents have chosen the degree of wage indexation), but in place of Equation 10, γ solves $\{[c^2(1-\gamma)^2+\beta]\}/\{[1+c(1-\gamma)]\}^3 = 2(c\beta)^2\sigma_u^2/\sigma_v^2$. The degree of wage indexation no longer depends on b since private agents take into account the dependence of b on γ in choosing γ. It will still depend on β, however.

6. Devereux (1987) and Waller and VanHoose (1992) have noted that the inflationary bias of discretionary monetary policy will depend on the indexation parameter; a fall in the degree of indexation raises the average inflation rate under discretion. An increase in β, the weight placed on inflation, lowers the optimal degree of wage indexation. However, this effect is small, and the net effect of a rise in β is to reduce the average inflation rate. For $\alpha = .7$, equal variances of v and u, and $k = 0.05$, a rise in β from 1 to 2, which cuts the average inflation rate by 50% when γ is treated as constant, reduces average inflation by 38.5% when γ is endogenous.

7. More skeptical interpretations of the data can be found in Capie and Wood (1991), Posen (1993), and Cargill (1994).

8. Interestingly, Cukierman, Webb, and Neyapti (1992) also report an index based on survey responses to questions about a central bank's actual independence in the conduct of monetary policy, and the correlation between this survey measure and the index based on legal characteristics is essentially zero. See also Walsh (1993). Johnson and Pierre (1993) examine the role of political variables in empirical reaction functions for a number of central banks and conclude that the presence of such political effects is not closely related to standard rankings of central banks in terms of their political independence.

9. Ball, Mankiw, and Romer (1988) have suggested that this argument may not be correct.

10. Since the Schelde-Andersen and Ball measures of the sacrifice ratio are based on specific time periods (Schelde-Andersen from the 1980s, Ball from the 1960s to the 1980s), BMR's trade-off parameter estimated using data from 1973 to 1986 is the most appropriate one to relate to Alesina and Summers's average inflation data.

11. For example, for some parameter values, the loss function in Equation 5 is decreasing in β.

References

Alesina, A. "Macroeconomics and politics." In Fischer, S. (ed.), *NBER Macroeconomics Annual*. Cambridge, MA: MIT Press, 1988.

Alesina, A., and Summers, L.H. "Central bank independence and macroeconomic performance: some comparative evidence." *Journal of Money, Credit and Banking* 1993, 25: 157-162.

Bade, R., and Parkin, M. "Central bank laws and inflation - a comparative analysis." University of Western Ontario, 1982.

Ball, Laurence. "Is equilibrium indexation efficient?" *Quarterly Journal of Economics* 1988, 103: 299-311.

Ball, Laurence. "What determines the sacrifice ratio?" Unpublished manuscript, Princeton University, March 1993.

Ball, Laurence, Mankiw, N. Gregory, and Romer, David. "The new Keynesian economics and the output-inflation trade-off." *Brookings Papers on Economic Activity* 1988 (1), 1-65.

Banaian, K., Laney, L.O., and Willett, T.D. "Central bank independence: an international comparison." *Federal Reserve Bank of Dallas Economic Review* 1983, 1-13.

Canzoneri, Matthew. "Labor Contracts and Monetary Policy." *Journal of Monetary Economics* 1980, 6: 241-255.

Capie, F.H., and Wood, G.E. "Central banks and inflation: an historical perspective - Part I." *Central Banking* 1991, 2: 27-46. Capie, F.H. and Wood, G.E. "Central banks and inflation: an historical perspective - Part II." *Central Banking* 1991, 2: 38-57.

Cargill, Thomas. "The statistical association between central bank independence and inflation." Unpublished manuscript, University of Nevada, Reno, 1994.

Croushore, Dean C., and Kroot, Ronald S. "A measure of Federal Reserve credibility." *Journal of Policy Modelling* 1994, 16: 215-231.

Cukierman, Alex. *Central Bank Strategy, Credibility and Independence*. Cambridge, MA: MIT Press, 1992.

Cukierman, A., Kalaitzidakis, P., Summers, L., and Webb, S. "Central bank independence, growth, investment and real rates." *Carnegie-Rochester Conference Series on Public Policy* 1993, 39: 95-140.

Cukierman, A., Webb, S.B., and Neyapti, B. "Measuring the independence of central banks and its effects on policy outcomes." *World Bank Economic Review* 1992, 6: 353-398.

Debelle, Guy, "The ends of three small inflations: Australia, New Zealand and Canada," MIT, March 1994.

Debelle, Guy, and Fischer, Stanley. "How independent should a central bank be?" Paper presented at the Center for Economic Policy Research and Federal Reserve Bank of San Francisco Conference on Monetary Policy in a Low Inflation Regime, March 1994.

Devereux, Michael. "The effect of monetary variability on welfare in a simple macroeconomic model." *Journal of Monetary Economics* 1987, 19: 427-435.

Egebo, Thomas, and Englander, A. Steven. "Institutional commitments and policy credibility: a critical survey and empirical evidence from the ERM." *OECD Economic Studies* 1992, 18: 45-84.

Fratianni, Michele, and Huang, Haizhou. "Reputation, central bank independence and the EBC." Indiana University Working Paper No. 92-031, December 1992.

Goodhart, Charles. "Central bank independence." *Journal of International and Comparative Economics* (forthcoming).

Gray, Jo Anne. "On indexation and contract length." *Journal of Political Economy* 1978, 86: 1-18.

Gray, Jo Anne, and Kandil, Magda. "Is price flexibility stabilizing? a broader perspective." *Journal of Money, Credit and Banking* 1991, 23: 1-12.

Grilli, Vittorio, Masciandaro, Donato, and Tabellini, Guido. "Political and monetary institutions and public financial policies in the industrial countries." *Economic Policy* 1991, 13: 342-392.

Hetzel, Robert L. "Central banks' independence in historical perspective." *Journal of Monetary Economics* 1990, 25: 165-176.

Johnson, David R., and Siklos, Pierre L. "Political effects on central bank behavior: some international evidence." Wilfrid Laurier University, March 1993.

Judd, John P., and Beebe, Jack H. "The output-inflation trade-off in the United States: has it changed since the late 1970s?" *Federal Reserve Bank of San Francisco Economic Review* 1993, 3: 25-34.

Lucas, Robert E., Jr. "Some international evidence on output-inflation tradeoffs." *American Economic Review* 1973, 63: 326-344.

Pollard, Patricia S. "Central bank independence and economic performance." *Federal Reserve Bank of St. Louis Review* 1993, 75: 21-36.

Posen, Adam S. "Why central bank independence does not cause low inflation: there is no institutional fix for politics." O'Brien, R. (ed.), *Finance and the International Economy: 7* (The 1993 Amex Bank Review Prize Essays). Oxford, England: Oxford University Press, 1993.

Rogoff, Kenneth. "The optimal degree of commitment to an intermediate monetary target." *Quarterly Journal of Economics* 1985, 100: 1169-1189.

Sargent, Thomas. "The ends of four big inflations." In Hall, R. (ed.), *Inflation: Causes and Effects*. Chicago: University of Chicago Press, 1982, pp. 41-98.

Schelde-Andersen, Palle. "OECD country experiences with disinflation." In Blundell-Wignall, A. (ed.), *Inflation, Disinflation and Monetary Policy*. Sydney, Australia: Reserve Bank of Australia, 1992, pp. 104-173.

Schultze, Charles L. "Cross-country and cross-temporal differences in inflation responsiveness." *American Economic Review* 1984, 74: 160-165.

Waller, Christopher J., and David, VanHoose. "Discretionary monetary policy and socially efficient wage indexation." *Quarterly Journal of Economics* 1992, 107: 1,451-1,460.

Walsh, Carl E. "Central bank strategies, credibility and independence: a review essay." *Journal of Monetary Economics* 1993, 32: 287-302.

Walsh, Carl E. "Is there a cost to central bank independence?" *Federal Reserve Bank of San Francisco Weekly Letter*, 94-05, February 4, 1994.

The Sectoral Composition of Trade Unions, Corporatism, and Economic Performance

Geoffrey Garrett and Christopher Way[1]

There has been considerable debate as to whether powerful trade unions in European Union (EU) member states are compatible either with the internal market or with monetary union. As macroeconomic performance has deteriorated in many corporatist countries since the 1980s - Sweden providing the paradigmatic case - doubts about the compatibility of strong labor movements and EU membership have grown. Is corporatism a relic of a different age, a luxury of the long postwar boom? Are strong unions detrimental to and destabilizing for the internal market and monetary union in the EU? This article answers these questions in the negative. We contend, however, that existing arguments about the macroeconomic consequences of corporatism should be significantly modified to take into account the impact of the growth of public sector unions on the relationship between institutional structure of labor movements and economic outcomes. The deteriorating performance commonly attributed to corporatism in the 1980s was limited to countries where public sector unions increasingly dominated national labor movements. Encompassing trade union movements can still generate wage restraint, but only where the union movement is dominated by unions in the exposed sector that are subject to the constraints posed by international market competition. Hence, countries, such as Austria and Finland, with strong labor movements led by exposed sector unions are likely to enjoy the benefits of EU membership without suffering great costs, whereas the costs will be greater for countries with strong public sector unions such as Sweden and Norway.

1. Introduction

There has been considerable discussion as to whether powerful trade unions in European Union (EU) member states are compatible either with the internal market or with monetary union. Since the governments of Austria and the Nordic countries have agreed to join the EU, this issue is likely to become more contentious because these states have long had the most powerful organized labor movements in Europe. Will the competitive position of EU members with powerful unions be eroded vis-à-vis those member states with weaker unions and with countries outside the EU as the remaining barriers to trade are removed? If so, will this generate pressures for upward harmonization on the social dimension in Europe or for increasing nontariff barriers with the rest of the world? Would the costs of participating in the European Monetary Union (EMU) be higher in countries with strong unions? If so, could this potentially destabilize monetary union?

Two basic answers to these questions can be delineated. On the one hand, some neoclassical economists (and public proponents of this position such as the British Conservative government) argue that trade union power inevitably worsens economic performance by pushing wages above levels that the market would otherwise bear. From this perspective, the EU should aggressively pursue deregulation of labor markets and resist at every turn increases in the social dimension within Europe. Moreover, one might argue that EMU should be imposed on members with strong unions to provide external discipline on wage militancy as an international equivalent to independent central bank reforms within countries.

On the other hand, many suggest that while this critique of trade unions may apply under some circumstances - most notably, where individual trade unions bargain autonomously for their members' wages - strong unions can allow countries to compete successfully in free markets if the behavior of discrete unions is coordinated by powerful labor confederations or if wage setting is centralized at the national level (as historically has been common in postwar northern Europe). The basic logic underpinning this position is that such "corporatist" institutions internalize the potential negative externalities of wage militancy - resulting in wage levels that do not retard growth, increase inflation, or decrease employment. From this perspective, there is no reason to deregulate European labor markets. Instead, one could argue that unions should be strengthened to spread the benefits of corporatism throughout the EU.

For much of the 1970s and 1980s, the balance of scholarly opinion supported the proposition that strong unions and centralized wage setting generated macroeconomic outcomes that were at least as good as those in countries with much less organized labor markets (such as Canada or the United States).[2] However, recent events have cast doubt on this claim. The paradigmatic case is Sweden. Long considered the exemplar of a successful corporatist political economy - with powerful unions, centralized wage setting, and full employment without high inflation - stagnant growth and rising prices plagued Sweden in the 1980s. Even its vaunted employment record deteriorated in the early 1990s. This decline in macroeconomic performance was accompanied by the breakdown of centralized wage setting, leading many commentators to proclaim the demise of corporatism, not only in Sweden but elsewhere as well (Martin, 1991; Moene and Wallerstein, 1992; Pontusson and Swenson, 1992).

Is corporatism a relic of a different age, a luxury of the long postwar boom? Is the existence of strong unions detrimental to and destabilizing for the internal market and monetary union in the EU? This article answers these questions in the negative. It contends, however, that existing arguments about the macroeconomic consequences of trade unions should be significantly modified to take into account the impact of the growth of public sector unions on the relationship between the institutional structure of labor movements and macroeconomic outcomes.[3] The deteriorating performance commonly attributed to corporatism in the 1980s was limited to cases where public sector unions increasingly dominated national labor movements (such as Denmark, Norway, and Sweden). In contrast, macroeconomic outcomes continued to be good (in terms of international comparisons) in countries with cohesive labor movements led by unions in the exposed sector (notably, Austria and Germany).

In turn, this suggests that given membership in the EU cuts trade protection and that EMU would reduce the macroeconomic policy autonomy of member governments, accession will be significantly more costly for Norway and Sweden than for Austria and Finland. Moreover, this even split among the new members suggests that the latest round of accession will not alter the balance of power in the EU over economic issues.

The article is divided into four sections. The first section elaborates the theoretical argument. The second section presents data on the organization of trade unions and the size of public sector unions for 16 industrial countries over the period 1975-1990.[4] The third section tests the theoretical argument against inflation and unemployment. The implications of these findings for the dynamics of European integration are discussed in the last section by way of conclusion.

2. Corporatism and the Sectoral Composition of Trade Unions

Debates about the macroeconomic effects of labor market institutions can be arrayed on two dimensions - whether the relationship between union organization and economic performance is linear and which institutional features best explain this relationship. The underlying logic of arguments about the consequences for economic performance of variations in labor movement structure is straightforward. Workers face a pervasive collective action problem. Maximizing wages is the objective of every worker. If all workers pursue this strategy, however, the collective outcome will be suboptimal. Nominal wage increases will be eroded by higher economy-wide inflation, and unemployment will increase. Early work suggested that increasing the power of trade unions would always improve macroeconomic outcomes. This argument for a linear relationship between union organization and performance was based on the assumption that as more workers became unionized, the incentives for their leaders to engage in wage restraint would increase. From this perspective, stronger unions would always have greater incentives to internalize the externalities associated with wage militancy (Cameron, 1984; Crouch, 1985; Korpi and Shalev, 1979). There were two basic flaws in this simple argument. First, it neglected the basic insight of neoclassical economics that the free play of market forces is likely to result in very good performance. By definition, trade unions give their members the capacity to bid up their wages above what the market would otherwise bear. Second, the linear hypothesis failed to distinguish the case of highly centralized union movements with the incentives and capacity to generate economy-wide wage restraint (and national-level wage setting) from the case of individually powerful but collectively decentralized unions (with industry-level wage bargains) - leading to upward pressures on wages throughout the economy.

Calmfors and Driffill (1988) combined these insights by arguing that the relationship between labor market institutions and economic performance is U-shaped. Where unions are very weak and wage setting is dominated by collective bargaining at the firm level, it is possible simultaneously to have low inflation and high levels of employment - in accordance with basic neoclassical theory. Where individual unions are strong but collectively decentralized, however, they will push up wages regardless of the deleterious consequences for the economy as a whole or for the employment prospects of nonunionized workers. Finally, wage militancy will be mitigated by the existence of powerful central labor confederations and national-level bargaining arrangements.

The second dimension of debate concerns whether the level of wage setting or the internal organization of trade unions is the more important facet of labor market institutions. It is common in economics to concentrate on the location of wage setting - that is, whether wage bargains are struck at the firm, industry, or national level (Bruno and Sachs, 1985; Newell and Symons, 1987; Rowthorn, 1992). Other scholars emphasize the degree of "encompassment" (Olson, 1982) in the organizational structure of national labor movements - the extent to which leaders of peak labor confederations can effectively deliver the support of their membership to any decisions they make about wages, working conditions, and the like (Cameron, 1984; Schmitter, 1981).

The level of wage setting and the internal structure of trade unions tend to be conflated because they are quite highly correlated. In a recent analysis, however, Golden argues persuasively that the internal structure of labor movements is the more important variable for explaining economic performance (Golden, 1993). Consider, for example, Britain and Italy in the latter 1970s (Gourevitch et al., 1984; Lange, Ross, and Vanicelli 1982). In both countries, national wage agreements were struck in efforts to reduce the inflationary consequences of the first Organization of Petroleum Exporting Countries (OPEC) oil shock. But the efficacy of these agreements was quickly undermined by the inability of the central labor confederations in both countries to enforce these deals on their members. These cases and others[5] suggest that wage drift will render less effective national-level wage setting unless central labor confederations have power over rank-and-file unionists.

Two institutional features of labor movements are particularly important in mitigating the collective action problem unions face (Lange, Wallerstein, and Golden, 1993). First, the fewer the number of unions, the smaller the temptation to free ride, and hence the greater their ability to act collectively. Second, the greater the portion of organized labor in a single peak confederation, the greater the concern of its leaders to internalize the negative externalities associated with wage militancy and the greater their ability to deliver their members for any decisions they make.

In sum, the state of the art on labor market institutions concentrates on their internal organizational characteristics and asserts that their relationship to macroeconomic performance is not linear, but U-shaped. In recent years, however, the empirical veracity of the U-shaped relationship has been questioned. The basic criticism is that while the deleterious consequences of strong but decentralized unions continue to be felt, the ability of powerful centralized labor confederations to generate beneficial wage restraint has declined. As a result, it is now frequently assumed that the relationship between labor market institutions and economic performance is linear and negative. Increasing union power is always bad for the economy.[6]

In this article, we take issue with these arguments about labor market institutions and question the current pessimism pertaining to the macroeconomic consequences of union strength. Existing cross-national analyses implicitly assume that the interests of all workers are the same. Yet case studies on the northern European countries indicate that if this assumption was ever valid, it certainly has not been in recent years (Iverson, 1994; Pontusson, 1992; Swenson, 1992). Among other things, these studies point to the destabilizing effects of increasing conflicts between unions in the sector of the economy exposed to international competition and those sheltered from it.[7] In practice, the best available proxy for the sheltered part of the economy is the public sector.[8]

The strategic calculus of workers in the public sector is very different from that of workers in the exposed sector. Wage growth has great and immediate consequences for the welfare of workers in the exposed sector. International market conditions determine the price of goods and services. Thus, changes in output and employment are directly affected by changes in labor costs (relative to productivity).[9] However, this relationship is much weaker in the public sector. There is nothing akin to a "world market price" for public sector products. The proximate determinant of employment is government preference rather than the global competitiveness of public goods and services. Moreover, there are strong incentives for governments not to cut public sector jobs (or to expand them) to prop up employment in hard times because in so doing they can gain the short-term benefits from maintaining overall employment levels while putting off paying the costs (through borrowing).[10]

This political economy of government employment creates powerful incentives for public sector workers to push up wages, in the expectation that this will not adversely affect their employment prospects. Instead, they fully expect that the costs of their wage militancy will be borne throughout society through larger public sector deficits and higher inflation. The more extensively the public sector is unionized, the more powerful should be upward wage pressures, and the greater should be negative externalities of public sector militancy. Exposed-sector workers, in particular, will be adversely affected because higher deficits and inflation will put upward pressures on interest rates and the exchange rate, decreasing the competitiveness of national products in international markets. Moreover, increases in the prices of nontradable inputs put upward cost pressure on producers of tradable goods. One should expect the net consequence of this dynamic to be either higher unemployment in the economy at large (if governments cannot endlessly create public sector jobs to replace those lost in the exposed sector) or similar levels of unemployment at ever high rates of inflation (if governments can continue to fund public sector expansion through borrowing).

It is at this point that one can integrate the power of public sector unions into conventional arguments about corporatism. As a first cut, we simply split evenly our sample of 16 countries according both to the strength of public sector unions and to more conventional measures of labor organization.[11] Figure 1 illustrates our theoretical expectations. The institutional structure of trade union movements is divided into "strong" and "weak" types. Those characterized by high union density, small numbers of unions, and encompassing peak confederations are labeled strong. Conversely, those with low density, many affiliates, and nonencompassing confederations are deemed weak. The second dimension divides labor movements in terms of the sectoral composition of trade unions ("public sector dominant" and "exposed-sector dominant"). Our expectations about inflation and unemployment in the four types of labor movements are indicated by the - and + signs. The number of signs reflects the hypothesized magnitude of these effects.

	Union Strength	
Sectoral Composition of Union Movement	weak	strong
Exposed Sector Dominant	Market-Exposed **inflation --** **unemployment -**	Coporatist-Sheltered **inflation -** **unemployment --**
Public Sector Dominant	Market-Sheltered **inflation +** **unemployment ++**	Corporatist-Sheltered **inflation ++** **unemployment +**

Figure 1: A Typology of Labor Movements

Economic performance in the Weak Unions/Exposed-Sector Dominant cell is likely to be good. Organized labor as a whole is not strong enough to alter significantly market-determined allocations of wages, and the weakness of public sector unions minimizes the negative externalities generated by sectoral divisions in the economy. One should thus expect very low inflation in these cases. Business cycles in this type of system will likely create some short-term job losses, but unemployment should be better than where public sector unions dominate the organized labor movement.

Performance should also be good in the Strong Unions/Exposed-Sector Dominant case. Powerful labor movements are strong enough to affect market outcomes, but the dominance of exposed-sector unions means that this power will be directed to maximizing employment in tradables by constraining wage growth in the whole economy (including the public sector) to global market conditions. Consequently, unemployment is likely to be very low in these systems. Given the fact that incentives for politicians to smooth business cycles are likely to be stronger where unions are very strong (as a result of stronger left parties, for example), one should expect inflation to be somewhat higher than in the Market-Led/Exposed-Sector Dominant case. This is the paradigmatic case of successful corporatism in the contemporary period.

Both inflation and unemployment are hypothesized to be higher in the Weak Unions/Public Sector Dominant cell than in either case where the labor movement is dominated by exposed-sector unions. Public sector unions will push up wages, despite the negative externalities of this behavior. The weakness of organized labor overall, however, will likely mute wage-push inflation, but unemployment should be very high. Finally, performance is also likely to be poor in the Strong Unions/Public Sector Dominant category. Given the overall power of trade unions (and the political pressures they are likely to exert on governments), however, one should expect employment to be propped up somewhat at the cost of higher inflation. Nonetheless, employment performance in this cell is hypothesized to be considerably worse than in the Strong Unions/Exposed-Sector Dominant case.

3. Measuring the Sectoral Composition and Organizational Structure of Labor Movements

Most studies of the effects of labor market institutions have relied on snapshots at a single period of time (usually the mid-1970s) comprising the portion of the workforce in trade unions and crude qualitative codings for the internal organization of labor movements. In the past few years, however, two research projects have generated data that facilitate the formulation of more fine-grained and time-variant indicators of theoretically important attributes of labor market institutions. First, Visser (1991) has compiled for the Organization for Economic Cooperation and Development (OECD) annual cross-national data on the size of trade union membership up to 1990 and for selected years the composition of unions as well, including separate measures for public sector unions. Second, a team of American political scientists has collected data on the structural attributes of labor movements - including the level of wage bargaining and the centralization of authority in trade unions - at five-year intervals from 1970 to 1990 (Golden, Lange, and Wallerstein, 1993; Lange, Wallerstein, and Golden, 1993).

We have used these data sets to construct measures of two facets of labor movement institutions that reflect the power of public sector unions and the internal organizational capacity of labor movements for collective action. The first indicator comprises the portion of total union members in public sector unions and the proportion of total employment in the public sector.[12] Higher combined scores are indicative of greater public sector strength in the labor movement. The internal structure measure incorporates the percentage of the working age population in trade unions, the portion of all union members in the largest confederation of labor, and the number of affiliate unions in this confederation. The higher the union density, the greater the portion of union members in the largest union

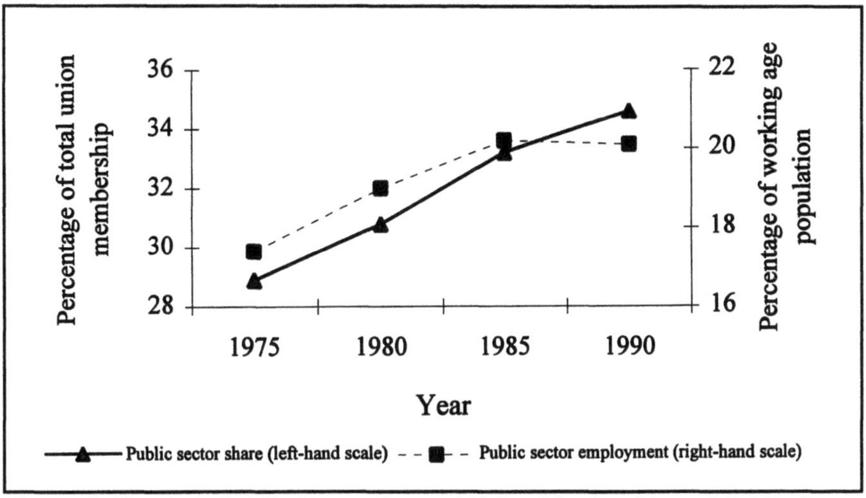

Figure 2: Trends in Public Sector Share of Union Membership and Public Sector Employment, 1975-1990

confederation; the smaller the number of unions affiliated with this confederation, the greater the capacity for the labor movement to act collectively.

Figures 2 and 3 depict the evolution of the strength and sectoral composition of labor over the past two decades, averaged over the 16 countries in this study. Visser's (1991) data make it clear that there has been no secular decline in trade union density since the 1970s. Average union density increased from the 1960s to the mid-1980s and since then has stabilized (Garrett, forthcoming). To be sure, individual countries experienced dramatic changes -- from the weakening of unions in the United Kingdom and France to the burgeoning growth of membership in the Scandinavian countries -- but on balance union density has not changed appreciably. But clearly the composition of trade unions has changed considerably. Figure 2 plots the public sector share of union membership (left-hand scale) and the public sector share of total employment (right-hand scale). The sectoral balance of power within trade unions tilted strongly in favor of public sector unions throughout the period under investigation. Moreover, this proportion increased in every country in the sample except for France. Until the mid-1980s, much of this was explicable in terms of the expansion of public sector employment, but the public sector share of union membership grew still higher by 1990 even though public employment declined somewhat. This suggests that the propensity for workers to join unions in recent times has been higher in the public than the private sector, perhaps reflecting the rapid growth in part-time work in the private sector.

Figure 3 plots changes in the average major confederation monopoly (left-hand scale) and the average number of unions affiliated with the major confederations (right-hand scale).[13] The major confederation share of union membership, while slightly lower in 1990 than in the mid-1970s, exhibits no drastic changes.[14]

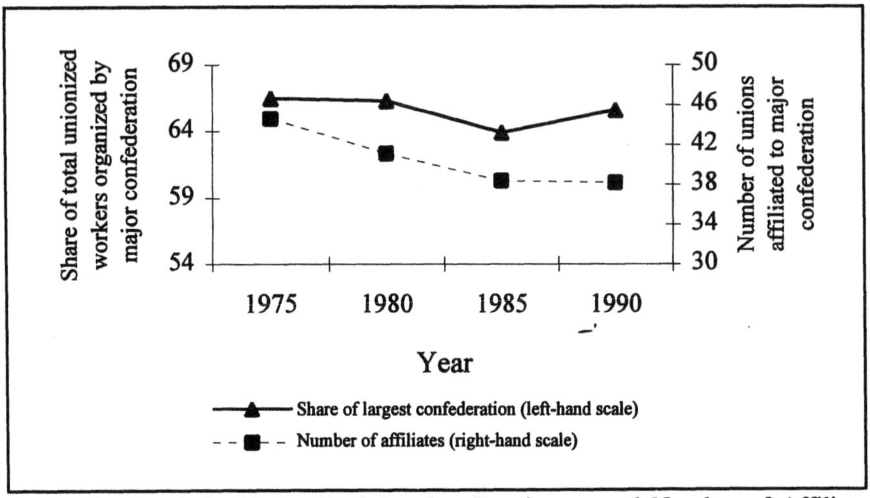

Figure 3: Trends in Major Confederation Dominance and Number of Affiliate Unions in 16 OECD Countries, 1975-1990

Nonetheless, the data clearly refute the notion that large shifts in confederal monopoly have undermined labor's ability for collective action. Moreover, the data in Figure 3 reveal a clear downward trend in the average number of unions affiliated with the major confederations, which should have enhanced the ability of labor movements to generate wage restraint by reducing the difficulty of acting collectively.

In general, these data suggest that there were no great changes in the structural attributes of national trade union movements in the 1980s. Indeed, if anything, the organizational structure of unions is more conducive to corporatism now than it was 20 years ago. However, it is also clear that the sectoral composition of labor movements has changed greatly in the past two decades, with the power of the public sector increasing in almost all countries.

For the purposes of our typological analysis, we divided the countries in our study on both dimensions of labor market institutions. For public sector power, we ranked countries at five-year intervals according to the portion of total union members in public sector unions and the portion of total employment in the public sector. We then summed these two ranks and divided the countries into two categories: exposed-sector dominant and public sector dominant. Similarly, we divided labor movements into strong and weak categories after combining their rankings on union density, major confederation share, and the number of affiliate unions. Figure 4 reports each country's classification for 1975, 1980, 1985, and 1990.

This scheme produces important similarities with and differences from existing efforts to classify the internal organization of labor movements (Cameron, 1984; Schmitter, 1981). The most general observation to be made is that, consistent with most assumptions that labor market institutions are very stable and slow to change,

Figure 4: Classification of Labor Movements in 16 Countries, 1975-1990

Year	Strong Labor / Exposed-Sector Dominant	Strong Labor / Sheltered-Sector Dominant	Weak Labor / Exposed-Sector Dominant	Weak Labor / Sheltered-Sector Dominant
1975	Austria Finland Germany	Australia Denmark Norway Sweden United Kingdom	Italy Japan Switzerland United States	Canada France Netherlands New Zealand
1980	Austria Finland Germany	Australia Denmark Norway New Zealand Sweden	Italy Japan Switzerland United States	Canada France Netherlands United Kingdom
1985	Austria Finland Germany Switzerland	Australia Denmark Norway Sweden United Kingdom	Canada Italy Japan United States	France Netherlands New Zealand
1990	Austria Finland Germany	Australia Denmark Norway Sweden United Kingdom	Italy Japan Switzerland United States	Canada France Netherlands New Zealand

there was very little movement in the classification of cases (even though the ranking of countries, not surprisingly, was less stable).

Let us begin with the strong/exposed cases. Austria, Finland, and Germany are in this category over the whole period of the study. Few would quibble with the classification of Austria, and Germany's position is consistent with Golden's arguments about the importance of union monopoly (Golden, 1993). The placement of Finland is slightly more contentious because most studies rank this country as only a borderline corporatist system.

Of more interest, however, are the cases that were classified as strong overall labor movements but with powerful public sector unions. We expect economic performance to have been poorer in this category, and this is consistent with most views about the consequences of labor market institutions in Australia and Britain.[15] But this category also contains three countries identified at different times as exemplars of corporatism - Denmark, Norway, and Sweden. In each of these countries, however, public sector unions have always been relatively strong, and, moreover, public sector employment has increased more rapidly than in other OECD countries since the 1970s. If our theoretical arguments are correct this should have had deleterious consequences for the macroeconomy and especially for inflation.

Turning to the cases with weak unions, three countries are consistently classified in the weak unions/exposed-sector dominant cell - Italy, Japan, and the United States. Switzerland was usually in this cell, but its labor organization structure continually bordered on moving into the strong union category. The American case is unproblematic. Japan's classification can be criticized for ignoring informal coordination in the economy organized by business association (Soskice, 1990), but this is true for any argument built on the organization of labor movements or the level of wage setting. The placement of Italy is more troubling because of its chronically poor economic performance and scholarly views about the disorganization of Italian unions (Lange, Ross, and Vanicelli, 1982). However, public sector unions have always been relatively weak in Italy, hence the classification in this article. Perhaps other factors, such as the chaotic nature of Italian party politics, have more to do with its poor economic performance (Roubini and Sachs, 1989).

Finally, Canada, France, the Netherlands, and New Zealand tended to be located in the market-sheltered grouping. The only case worth mentioning here is the Netherlands, which in the 1960s was often considered a clear instance of corporatism because of its national wage-setting arrangements. According to our data, however, unions were never sufficiently strong to be able to act collectively to generate wage restraint, and the presence of powerful public sector unions exacerbated this problem.

4. Labor Organization and Economic Performance, 1972-1991

Having described national labor movements in terms of the strength of public sector unions and the organizational structure of trade unions as a whole, let us

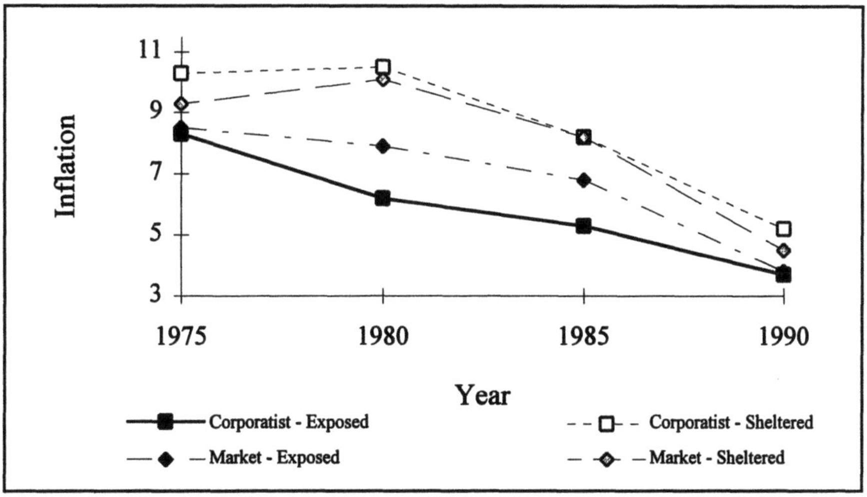

Figure 5: Average Inflation by Type of Labor Organization, 1975-1990

now explore the consequences of these two variables for economic performance. As a first cut, inflation and unemployment (and a "misery index" combining them[16]) in each of the four types of labor movement setting were compared over four time periods: 1972-1976, 1977-1981, 1982-1986, and 1987-1991.[17] After calculating the average performance of the 16 countries for each time period, group averages for each of the four types of labor movements were tabulated.

Figure 5 plots the average inflation for each category from 1972 to 1991. These data reveal three important trends. First, for both the strong and weak union categories, the exposed-sector dominant cases tended to enjoy lower inflation than the sheltered-sector dominant countries (although these differences declined over time as the consequences of the OPEC oil shocks dissipated). Second, contra our expectations, inflation was always lower in the strong/exposed category than in the weak/exposed case, suggesting that wage restraint organized by strong unions was more effective in limiting wage push than were market mechanisms in the weak-union case. This may reflect the fact that even in countries such as the United States, unions have been strong enough to exert some power in labor markets (Alvarez, Garrett, and Lange, 1991). Finally, inflation was always highest in the strong/sheltered category, implying that where public sector unions are very strong, they were able to use the collective action capacity of centralized labor movements to further their own interests, at the expense of workers in sectors that are exposed to international competition.

An examination of outliers reveals important exceptions to these general trends. The inflation performance of the weak/exposed systems is more impressive when it is recalled that Italy - which persistently endures the highest inflation among our 16 countries - was always in this category. Despite Italy's dismal performance, this group still boasted lower average inflation than the weak labor countries with strong public sectors. On the other hand, the Netherlands, despite its strong public

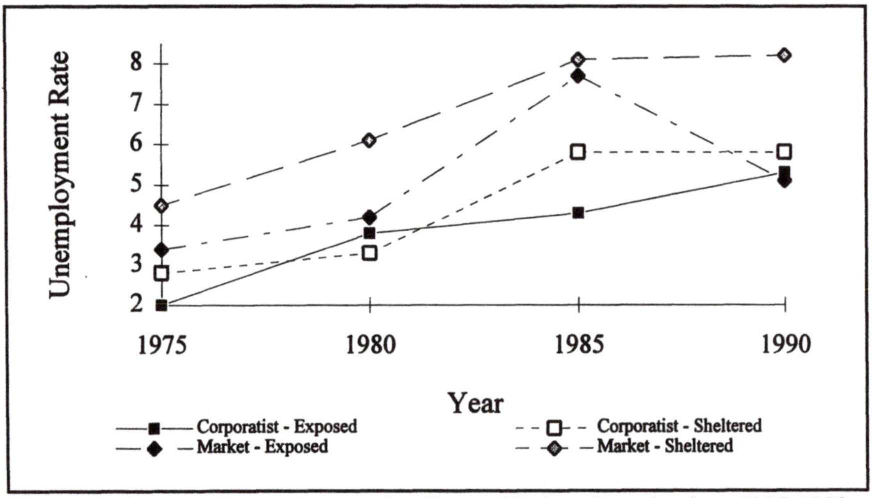

Figure 6: Average Unemployment by Type of Labor Organization, 1975-1990

sector unions, displayed surprisingly low inflation, perhaps as a result of the policy of pegging the guilder to the deutsche mark. Without the Netherlands, average inflation in the weak/sheltered category would have been considerably higher.

The unemployment results are similar to those for inflation (see Figure 6). Unemployment was lower in the exposed-sector dominant categories than in the sheltered-sector dominant cases (with the exception of the strong/exposed case in 1980). Moreover, both types of strong union countries suffered less unemployment than did the weak labor systems. These differences were relatively small in the mid-1970s, but the divergences widened in the recessionary climate of the 1980s (although it should be noted that unemployment was very low in the weak/exposed category in the last period). As with inflation, examining individual cases helps flesh out this analysis. Once again, Italy's poor performance stood out in the weak union/exposed dominant category. On the other hand, Norway's good performance improved the results for the strong union/sheltered-sector dominant countries, but Norway's robust performance was largely a consequence of its North Sea oil bounty (Garrett and Lange, 1986).

Finally, we used the misery index to provide a single indicator of overall economic performance. Figure 7 reveals that the strong union/weak public sector cases consistently had the lowest average misery indices of the four categories (although this was matched by the weak/exposed category in the last period). Moreover with the exception of 1985, overall performance was better in the exposed-sector dominant cases than in the sheltered-sector dominant countries, irrespective of the strength of organized labor overall. As with inflation and unemployment, Italy and Norway were the two most notable outliers. Italy's misery index was always at least twice that of any other case in its category, while Norway persistently had the lowest score in the strong sheltered group. Even though these two outliers both work against our hypothesis, the expected pattern

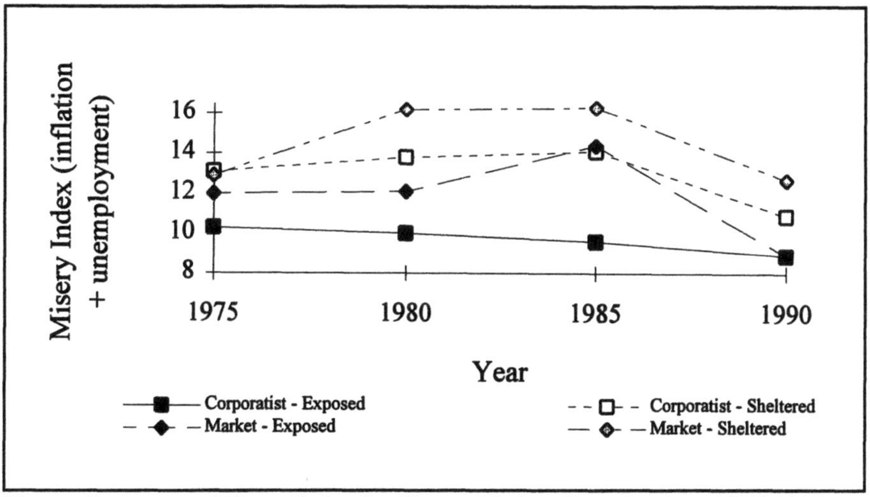

Figure 7: Average Misery Index by Type of Labor Organization, 1975-1990

between exposed- and sheltered-sector dominant countries still holds.

Taken together, the descriptive data presented in figures 5-7 seem strongly to support our theoretical arguments. However, there are significant limitations to this analysis. First, the typology does not take into account the Calmfors-Driffill hypothesis that the relationship between union structure and macroeconomic performance is U-shaped, not linear. Second, the analysis discriminates between countries at a given point of time in terms of the composition and internal structure of labor movements, but it does not identify the effects of changes over time within countries. Third, the comparison of performance according to labor market institutions neglects any other factors that may have influenced inflation and unemployment. Finally, the descriptive data do not tell us how statistically significant were the differences in performance between various configurations of labor market institutions.

To remedy these deficiencies, we regressed inflation and changes in unemployment on four types of variables.[18] First, we included the vulnerability of national economies to changes in OECD demand conditions and their dependence on imported oil to control for the effects of changes in the international economy on a given country. Second, period dummy variables were included to take into account any secular changes across all countries in inflation and unemployment (reflecting, for example, changes in government priorities).[19] Third, we explicitly modeled the Calmfors-Driffill argument by including a squared term for union strength. Finally, we isolated the effects of the sectoral composition of unions with a public sector strength variable. Both of the union measures vary over time and between countries and are arrayed on standardized scales.

Table 1 records the regression estimates. The control variables were very effective in the inflation equation. Inflation declined with higher growth in the OECD and increased with dependence on imported sources of oil. Furthermore, the

Table 1: Union Structure, Union Composition, and Economic Performance

Independent Variables	Inflation	Unemployment
1972-1976	1.33 (2.62)	-0.78 (1.43)
1977-1981	-4.06* (2.67)	-0.47 (1.43)
1982-1986	-5.92*** (2.63)	0.39 (1.41)
1987-1991	-5.35** (2.70)	-2.31* (1.48)
Lagged Dependent Variable	0.55*** (0.10)	-0.07 (0.07)
OECD demand conditions[a]	-0.0013** (0.00078)	0.0027 (0.006)
Oil Dependence[b]	12.99* (8.42)	9.55 (7.65)
Union Strength[c]	27.00*** (10.79)	6.14 (5.50)
Union Strength Squared	-26.08*** (9.89)	-7.49* (4.96)
Public Sector Strength[d]	3.91** (2.21)	2.06*** (0.93)
Observations	64	64
Adjusted R^2	0.67	0.37

Notes: All entries are least square estimates using White's (1980) correction for heteroscedastic residuals, with standard errors in parentheses.

* $p < 0.10$,** $p < 0.05$, *** $p < 0.01$, one-tailed test, each.

a) Annual average OECD gross domestic product growth rates weighted by trade openness (exports/GDP) for each of the 16 countries.

b) The price of oil (in constant 1980 $US) multiplied by a country's net oil imports (as a % of total energy requirements).

c) This index combines union density, major confederation monopoly, and number of affiliate unions by converting each to a [0,1] scale, with the highest value on each measure set equal to one. The three indicators are then weighted equally in creating an index of union strength on a [0,1] scale.

d) This index combines public sector union membership as a percentage of total union membership and public sector employment as a percentage of total employment. Each measure is converted to a [0,1] scale by setting the highest value equal to one, and then the two indicators are weighted equally in creating an [0,1] index of public sector strength.

period dummies suggest that after the first oil shock, inflation declined significantly in Western countries - even controlling for these factors. Of more interest for present purposes, however, are the parameter estimates for the labor market institution terms. The union strength and union-squared coefficients were both highly significant and consistent with the Calmfors-Driffill hypothesis. Inflation was lower where labor movements were either very weak or very strong than in intermediate cases. Controlling for all these factors, however, public sector strength was significantly associated with higher inflation. This is strongly supportive of our basic argument about the damaging macroeconomic effects of strong public sector unions.

The unemployment results are less clear-cut. Oil dependence, OECD demand conditions, and the period dummies had little impact on changes in unemployment. The two variables testing the U-shaped argument about union structure and economic performance were in the expected directions, but the parameter estimates were not strong enough to meet standard criteria of statistical significance. Notwithstanding these limitations, however, the regression equation again strongly suggests that increased public sector union strength has deleterious consequences for overall levels of unemployment.

5. Conclusion

This article has demonstrated that the sectoral composition of trade unions affects inflation and unemployment. In the period 1972-1991, inflation and unemployment were consistently lower in countries where the labor movement was dominated by unions in the exposed sector than where public sector labor was more powerful. This suggests an important amendment to the literature on corporatism and helps reconcile traditional arguments about the beneficial consequences of powerful trade unions with the poor performance of some northern European economies, most notably Sweden since the mid-1980s. Encompassing trade union movements can still generate wage restraint, but only where the union movement is dominated by unions in the exposed sector that are subject to the constraints posed by international market competition.

We believe that this finding has significant consequences for the dynamics of European integration, and specifically for the political economy of accession for the governments that have agreed to join the EU: Austria, Finland, Norway, and Sweden. All of these countries have powerful labor movements. However, public sector unions are much stronger in Norway and Sweden than they are in Austria and Finland. In order to analyze what will likely follow from this divergence in labor market institutions, let us break down the discussion into two dimensions. First, we will distinguish between the effects on the new members of joining the EU from the likely behavior of these countries in the EU. Second, we will separate the political economy of joining the EU's internal market from that of potential membership in EMU.

Our analysis suggests that both Austria and Finland are well-positioned to join both the internal market and monetary union. These economies are likely to enjoy the benefits of membership without suffering great costs. They can be expected to respond well to the competitiveness pressures of the internal market and to the macroeconomic disciplines of EMU - because the bulk of the unionized workforce is in the exposed sector, and hence directly subject to the constraints that operate in international goods and services and capital markets. In turn, this suggests that these countries will merge easily into the coalition between Germany and the Benelux countries supporting free trade and strict adherence to the conditions for the transition to EMU set out in the Maastricht treaty.

The situation is very different with respect to Norway and Sweden. At first blush, one might expect that joining the internal market would be costly for these countries because wage militancy by powerful public sector unions either would put upward pressure on exchange rates (if interest rates rise) or would lead to large-scale capital flight (if they do not). In turn, this might suggest that these countries would be more likely to join the (admittedly less clear-cut and consistent) protectionist coalition in the EU, comprising some combination of France, Italy, and the southern European countries. Moreover, one might think that membership in EMU would be very damaging for these countries (because wage militancy would result in higher real exchange rates).

However, the events of 1991 and 1992 suggest that the Norwegian and Swedish governments viewed membership in the EU (and particularly participation in the European Monetary System and potentially EMU) as the best method for constraining domestic wage militancy. The logic behind this position requires reconsideration of the basic theoretical argument we have made in this article about public sector unions. We have suggested that public sector unions are not subject to competitiveness constraints because they believe governments will respond to recessions by increasing public employment - and the history of Sweden in the 1980s, in particular, supports this proposition. But this argument can be turned on its head.

A government might join a fixed exchange-rate regime precisely to tie its hands to prevent itself from expanding the public economy. This is what was attractive to the Swedish government about linking the kroner to the deutsche mark. This policy proved disastrous because the financial markets doubted the government's resolve. It is reasonable to assume that the government hoped to remove this credibility problem by membership in the EU, and particularly by signing the Maastricht treaty. The evidence from the European Monetary System for countries with fiscal imbalances, however, is not encouraging, and it is not clear that the EMU treaty will rein in these problems (Alesina and Grilli, 1991; Eichengreen, 1992; Garrett, 1993). It seems more prudent to believe that the relationship of Norway and Sweden to EMU will be closer to that of Italy than that of Germany.

In sum, if, as this article argues, the strength of public sector unions is a powerful determinant of political economic dynamics in OECD countries, one should expect that the effects of accession on would-be EU members and their likely behavior within the union will be very different. Austria and Finland can gain the fruits of membership without suffering serious costs. Conversely, the costs of accession are likely to be great for Norway and Sweden. This will put these countries on opposite sides over debates about how to govern the internal market and about the path to monetary union. Hence unlike most commentators, we do not think that accession will tip the political balance even more in the favor of Germany and its near neighbors, but rather preserve the existing balance of power.

Endnotes

1. This article was prepared for the Study Group on the Political Economy of European Integration at the Center for German and European Studies, University of California, Berkeley. We would like to thank Barry Eichengreen, Robert Franzese, Jeffry Frieden, Miriam Golden, Torben Iverson, and David Soskice for helpful discussions on the themes in this article. Special thanks to Thomas Cusack for providing us with much of the data. Garrett also acknowledges the financial support of the Hoover Institution, Stanford, and the Research School of Social Sciences, Australian National University, Canberra.

2. For a recent review of the economic literature, see Calmfors (1993). For the political science literature, see Golden (1993).

3. For a recent study that also places considerable emphasis on the problems associated with public sector union strength, see Crouch (1993).

4. The countries in the study are Australia, Austria, Canada, Denmark, Finland, France, Germany, Italy, Japan, the Netherlands, New Zealand, Norway, Sweden, Switzerland, the United Kingdom, and the United States. Public sector union data were not available for Belgium. We have not included the other Organization for Economic Cooperation and Development members either because of data problems or because they cannot be considered as stable advanced industrial economies over the period under analysis.

5. Golden (1993:441-442) makes a similar point in a comparison between Germany and Sweden in the 1980s.

6. For an excellent discussion of the northern European cases, see Scharpf (1991).

7. Pontusson and Swenson (1992) argue that conflict between high- and low-value-added producers in the exposed sector puts additional pressure on corporatism in the 1980s.

8. The relationship between the public sector and the portion of the economy insulated from international competition is not isomorphic. It is very difficult, however, to make judgments about precisely what is and what is not exposed to trade outside the public sector. Moreover, available data on the composition of trade unions are based on the distinctiveness of the public sector. As a result, we assume that public sector unions are a good approximation for organized labor in the sheltered sector.

9. In this article, we assume that other factors are constant, such as the exchange rate and supply and demand conditions in the international economy.

10. Governments are unlikely to finance public sector expansion with higher taxes because doing so would prove politically unpopular. Moreover, a tax increase, by reducing private consumption, would counteract the increase in public consumption resulting from expansion of the public sector, thus defeating the purpose of the fiscal stimulus.

11. For the purposes of this exercise, we have not incorporated the U-shaped hypothesis about the macroeconomic effects of labor movement structures because this would entail a three-way division of our 16 cases on this dimension. Combined with a dichotomous split of the cases on public sector strength, we would be left with an average of fewer than three cases in each cell. It would be difficult to make any strong conclusions on the basis of such small samples. It should be noted, however, that our arguments about the deleterious effects of public sector union strength are supported both by the typological exercise and by the regression analysis that controls for the Calmfors-Driffill argument.

12. Data for total public sector employment are from the OECD. Public sector share of all union members was calculated from data in Visser (1991) and from the OECD.

13. Data on confederation monopoly and number of affiliated unions are from Golden, Lange, and Wallerstein [1993] and Lange, Wallerstein, and Golden (1993).

14. This masks large changes in a handful of countries, usually due to the merger or dissolution of confederations. In Japan, for example, the major confederation's monopoly grew from 36% to 62% after several large confederations merged to form Rengo in the late 1980s.

15. The exception to this is the "Accord" process of centralized wage setting in Australia in the 1980s, which scholars suggest was successful in overcoming the structural weaknesses of the labor movement - the inability of the peak labor confederation, the ACTU, to organize its members and the size of public sector unions - to generate effective wage restraint (Chapman, Dowrick, and Junankar, 1991).

16. Following Okun, the "misery index" is simply the sum of unemployment and inflation.

17. Although data limitations dictated our choice of time periods, restricting the analysis to the 1972-1991 period does have the advantage of focusing on the post-Bretton Woods era of increasing economic interdependence and floating exchange rates. Since the theoretical argument assumes an open economy, this time span is the most appropriate.

18. It was necessary to use the first difference in unemployment rather than levels of unemployment because the lag structure for unemployment suggests a unit root. The estimates are ordinary least squares using White's (1980) correction for heteroscedasticity.

19. The intercept terms were suppressed so that the period dummies represent estimates of what performance would have been, controlling for the variables in the equations.

References

Alesina, Alberto, and Grilli, Vittorio. "The European Central Bank: Reshaping Monetary Policy Politics in Europe." National Bureau of Economic Research, Working Paper No. 3860, Cambridge, MA, 1991.

Alvarez, Michael, Garrett, Geoffrey, and Lange, Peter. "Government Partisanship, Labor Organization, and Macroeconomic Performance." *American Political Science Review* 1991, 85: 539-556.

Bruno, Michael, and Sachs, Jeffrey. *The Economics of Worldwide Stagflation.* Cambridge, MA: Harvard University Press, 1985.

Calmfors, Lars. "Centralization of Wage Bargaining and Macroeconomic Performance - A Survey." Institute for International Economic Studies, Seminar Paper No. 536, Stockholm University, 1993.

Calmfors, Lars, and Driffill, John. "Bargaining Structure, Corporatism and Macroeconomic Performance." *Economic Policy* 1988, 3: 13-61.

Cameron, David. "Social Democracy, Corporatism, Labour Quiescence, and the Representation of Economic Interest in Advanced Capitalist Society." In Goldthorpe, John H. (ed.), *Order and Conflict in Contemporary Capitalism.* Oxford, England: Oxford University Press, 1984.

Chapman, Bruce, Dowrick, Steve, and Junankar, P.N. "Perspectives on Australian Unemployment: The Impact of Wage Setting Institutions." In Gruen, Fred (ed.), *Australian Economic Policy: Conference Proceedings.* Canberra: Australian National University, Center for Economic Policy Research, 1991, 21-57.

Crouch, Colin. *Industrial Relations and European State Traditions.* Oxford, England: Clarendon Press, 1993.

Crouch, Colin. "Conditions for Trade Union Wage Restraint." In Lindberg, Leon N., and Maier, Charles S. (eds.), *The Politics of Inflation and Economic Stagnation.* Washington, DC: Brookings Institution, 1985.

Eichengreen, Barry J. *Should the Maastricht Treaty Be Saved?* Princeton, NJ: International Finance Section, Department of Economics, Princeton University, 1992.

Garrett, Geoffrey. "Trade, Capital Mobility and the Politics of Economic Policy." *International Organization* (forthcoming).

Garrett, Geoffrey. "The Politics of Maastricht." *Economics and Politics* 1993, 5: 105-123.

Garrett, Geoffrey, and Lange, Peter. "Performance in a Hostile World." *World Politics* 1986, 38: 517-545.

Golden, Miriam. "The Dynamics of Trade Unionism and National Economic Performance." *American Political Science Review* 1993, 87: 439-454.

Golden, Miriam, Lange, Peter, and Wallerstein, Michael. "Trends in Collective Bargaining and Industrial Relations in Non-Corporatist Countries: A Preliminary Report." Paper presented at the Annual Meetings of the American Political Science Association, Washington, DC, September 2-5, 1993.

Gourevitch, Peter, Martin, Andrew, Ross, George, Allen, Christopher, Bornstein, Stephen, and Markovits, Andrei. *Unions and Economic Crisis*. New York: Allen and Unwin, 1984.

Iverson, Torben. "Power, Flexibility and the Breakdown of Centralized Wage Bargaining." Harvard University, manuscript, 1994.

Korpi, Walter, and Shalev, Michael. "Strikes, Industrial Relations, and Class Conflict in Capitalist Societies." *British Journal of Sociology* 1979, 30: 164-187.

Lange, Peter, Ross, George, and Vanicelli, Maurizio. *Unions, Change and Crisis*. New York: Allen and Unwin, 1982.

Lange, Peter, Wallerstein, Michael, and Golden, Miriam. "The End of Corporatism? Wage Setting in the Nordic and Germanic Countries." In Jacoby, Sanford (ed.), *Global Capital, Local Labor*. Oxford, England: Oxford University Press, 1993.

Martin, Andrew. "Wage Bargaining and Swedish Politics." Center for European Studies, Working Paper Series No. 36, Harvard University, 1991.

Moene, Karl-Ove, and Wallerstein, Michael. "The Decline of Social Democracy." Paper presented at the Annual Meetings of the American Political Science Association, Chicago, September 2-5, 1992.

Newell, A.T., and Symons, J. "Corporatism, Laizzez-Faire, and the Rise in Unemployment." *European Economic Review* 1987, 31: 567-614.

Olson, Mancur. *The Logic of Collective Action*. Cambridge, MA: Harvard University Press, 1965.

Olson, Mancur. *The Rise and Decline of Nations*. New Haven, CT: Yale University Press, 1982.

Pontusson, Jonas. "The Political Economy of Class Compromise: Labor and Capital in Sweden." *Politics and Society* 1992, 20: 305-332.

Pontusson, Jonas and Swenson, Peter. "Markets, Production, Institutions and Politics." Paper presented at the 8th International Conference of Europeanists, Chicago, March 27-29, 1992.

Roubini, Nouriel and Sachs, Jeffrey. "Fiscal Policy." *Economic Policy* 1989, 9: 99-132.

Rowthorn, R.E. "Centralization, Unemployment, and Wage Dispersion." *Economic Journal* 1992, 102: 506-524.

Scharpf, Fritz. *Crisis and Choice in European Social Democracy*. Ithaca, NY: Cornell University Press, 1991.

Schmitter, Philippe C. "Interest Intermediation and Regime Governability in Contemporary Western Europe and North America." In Berger, Suzanne D. (ed.), *Organizing Interests in Western Europe*. New York: Cambridge University Press, 1981.

Soskice, David. "Wage Determination: The Changing Role of Institutions in Advanced Industrialized Countries." *Oxford Review of Economic Policy* 1990, 6: 36-61.

Swenson, Peter. "Union Politics, the Welfare State, and Intra-Class Conflict in Germany and Sweden." In Golden, Miriam, and Pontusson, Jonas (eds.),

Bargaining for Change: Union Politics in North America and Europe. Ithaca, NY: Cornell University Press, 1992.
Visser, Jelle. "Trends in Trade Union Membership." In *OECD Employment Outlook*. Paris: Organization for Economic Cooperation and Development, 1991.
White, H. "A Heteroskedasticity-Consistent Covariance Matrix Estimator and a Direct Test for Heteroskedasticity." *Econometrica* 1980, 48: 149-170.

The Logic of Currency Crises

Maurice Obstfeld[1]

Once one recognizes that governments borrow international reserves and exercise other policy options to defend fixed exchange rates during currency crises, the question arises: What factors determine a government's decision to abandon a currency peg or hang on? In a setting of purposeful action by the authorities, the possibility of self-fulfilling crises becomes important. Speculative anticipations depend on conjectured government responses, which depend, in turn, on how price changes that are themselves fueled by expectations affect the government's economic and political positions. This circular dynamic implies a potential for crises that need not have occurred, but that do because market participants expect them to. In contrast to this picture, most literature on balance-of-payments crises ignores the response of government behavior to markets. That literature, I argue, throws little light on events such as the European Exchange Rate Mechanism collapse of 1992-1993. This article presents two different models in which crisis and realignment result from the interaction of rational private economic actors and a government that pursues well-defined policy goals. In both, arbitrary expectational shifts can turn a fairly credible exchange-rate peg into a fragile one.

1. Introduction

The dramatic currency crisis that culminated in the August 1993 widening of exchange-rate bands within the European Monetary System (EMS) challenges economists to rethink their models of how markets may force governments to alter supposedly fixed exchange rates. Some European governments, notably Italy's, clearly lacked the full confidence of the markets as a result of fiscal trends incompatible with a fixed exchange rate in the long run. But the scale and scope of the turmoil that began in the summer of 1992 were so great that ultimately even apparently sustainable currency pegs were shaken. The disparate circumstances of the many currencies successfully attacked by speculators have led observers such as Eichengreen and Wyplosz (1993) and Portes (1993) to argue that, at least in the European context, recent speculative crises have been driven in part by self-fulfilling forces.

Economists have rightly tended to be wary of such accounts: finance ministers past and present have preferred to blame crises on gnomes of Zurich or *agioteurs* rather than face the reality of fundamental factors, including policy errors.

Krugman's (1979) seminal article provided a convincing theoretical rationale for the economists' view. Krugman set out a simple model in which a currency peg must be abandoned once the pegging nation's foreign-exchange reserves run out. He went on to analyze how the peg collapses in situations where the eventual exhaustion of reserves is inevitable. His remarkable finding was that speculators with foresight *inevitably* attack the currency before reserves are fully depleted and purchase all remaining reserves at that moment--a moment that can be defined precisely. This prediction follows from the simplest principles of currency arbitrage.[2]

In this article I argue that one cannot adequately understand recent European currency experience in terms of Krugman's model. For industrial European countries with access to world capital markets, reserve adequacy per se is far less of a concern than it was in the early 1970s; this factor no longer deserves the primacy assigned it in Krugman's analysis.[3] Clearly a number of other factors, notably the effects of high interest rates and growing unemployment, came into play in determining how different governments responded to the 1992-1993 crisis.

Once one acknowledges that governments may borrow reserves and exercise other policy options in the face of a crisis, the question arises: What factors determine a government's decision to abandon a currency peg or hang on? In a setting of purposeful action by the authorities, however, the possibility of self-fulfilling crises cannot be easily dismissed. Speculative anticipations depend on conjectured government responses, which depend, in turn, on how price changes that are themselves fueled by expectations affect the government's economic and political positions. This circular dynamic implies a potential for crises that need not have occurred, but that do occur because market participants expect them to.

The next section reviews Sweden's 1992 currency crisis, illustrating some restrictive features of the standard model and suggesting factors that should play roles in more-general models of currency crisis. The following section presents two different models in which crisis and realignment result from the interaction of rational private economic actors and a government that pursues well-defined policy goals.[4] In the first of these models, high nominal interest rates associated with devaluation expectations can force a government to devalue a currency whose peg would have been viable under another set of private expectations. This model is based on the effects of high interest rates on the government's fiscal position, but one could devise similar models in which high interest rates induce the government to realign through their impact on the banking system, firms' balance sheets, mortgage interest rates, and so on. A second model shows how realignments may reflect authorities' desire to offset shocks to competitiveness and employment. This model, too, is subject to multiple equilibriums. In it, arbitrary expectational shifts can turn a fairly credible exchange-rate peg into a fragile one.[5]

Both models in the market forces section portray government decisionmaking as the minimization of a social loss function that is increasing in alternative indicators of economic misery: tax rates, inflation, and unemployment are the ones chosen below. Nothing in the analysis precludes, however, a political motivation on the government's part or an influence of political rivalry on the particular economic variables of greatest current concern. I suspect that an explicit modeling of political processes, avoided here only for the sake of simplicity, would reveal an even greater scope for self-fulfilling crises.[6]

The results of this article have clear implications for the feasibility of gradualist approaches to economic and monetary unification, such as the transitional fixed exchange-rate arrangements underlying the Maastricht blueprint and the earlier Delors plan. If speculative attacks on fixed rates can be avoided indefinitely through government commitment to policies consistent with those rates, then the gradualist approach can work. Moreover, it can work without recourse to capital controls, which are at the same time costly to enforce and inimical to both economic integration and official credibility. If, instead, policies respond to the immediate political and economic imperatives created by sharp movements in interest rates, unemployment, and other sensitive variables, then the outlook is much bleaker. The unfolding and *dénouement* of the Swedish crisis, which I take up first, illustrate the pessimistic scenario.

2. Sweden's Crisis and the Standard Model

In the most basic model of currency crisis, authorities pursue unsustainable macroeconomic policies that must eventually force a fixed exchange rate to be abandoned. Krugman (1979) showed that in a world of perfect foresight, the moment of transition between the fixed-rate regime and its successor generally involves a speculative attack in which private participants in the foreign-exchange market acquire in an instant all the foreign-currency reserves central banks commit to the existing parity's defense.

Models in the spirit of Krugman (1979) provide elegant parables of how rational financial markets respond to unsustainable macroeconomic policies. The models ignore, however, the policy options available to authorities and the ways in which the marginal costs of exercising these options are balanced. Since the actions of rational speculators must be conditioned on the conjectured response of the authorities, the class of models reviewed gives relatively little general guidance on the factors generating crises and determining their outcomes.

Some interesting recent models have offered explicit political underpinnings for models such as Krugman's. Guidotti and Végh (1992) develop a model in which a war of attrition over balancing the national budget leads to continuing finance through reserve drains; if agreement is not reached in time, a crisis can occur. Velasco (1993) considers a scenario with divided government in which reserve drains occur because individual ministries fail to internalize the overall public-sector constraint. Stein and Streb (1993) propose an asymmetric-information model in which governments may rationally deplete foreign reserves so as to push inflation into the future, thus risking a crisis later. These articles yield important insights into the genesis of crises in countries where fiscal profligacy is the sole underlying cause of currency instability, but they do not cover the entire range of factors at work, particularly in the European context.

Consider, for example, the travails of the Swedish krona during 1992.[7] Sweden announced a unilateral peg to the European Currency Unit (ecu) in May 1991. The Danish rejection of the Maastricht treaty on June 2, 1992, was the occasion for a small immediate rise in krona interest rates; these rates rose sharply as uncertainties intensified over the summer (Figure 1). The culmination of these developments was an attack on non-European Community (EC) Nordic currencies in late August and early September, during which Swedish interest rates rose to unprecedented levels. While the krona peg survived this battle, it lost the war soon after, succumbing to a new attack on November 19 and entering a float.

Figure 2, which shows 1992 data on the Sveriges Riksbank's foreign-exchange reserves and net forward position in foreign currencies, reflects a story quite different from that in Krugman's (1979) account.[8] Sweden's foreign-exchange reserves were trendless (or slightly increasing) through early June, dropping only slightly by early August. There was virtually no net central bank forward intervention in this period. Starting July 24, the Riksbank began to raise the marginal interest rate it charged the domestic banks.

At the height of the August-September attack, the Riksbank intervened heavily in the krona's defense, borrowing reserves for this purpose in the second week of September. The resulting reserve shifts are apparent in Figure 2. Most intervention took the form of spot foreign-currency sales, although the Riksbank also intervened in the forward market. After the initial storm had passed, however, total central bank assets rose, interest rates fell, and reserves rose--until, quite suddenly, the ecu peg collapsed in mid-November.

A model to illuminate these events must encompass many more variables than

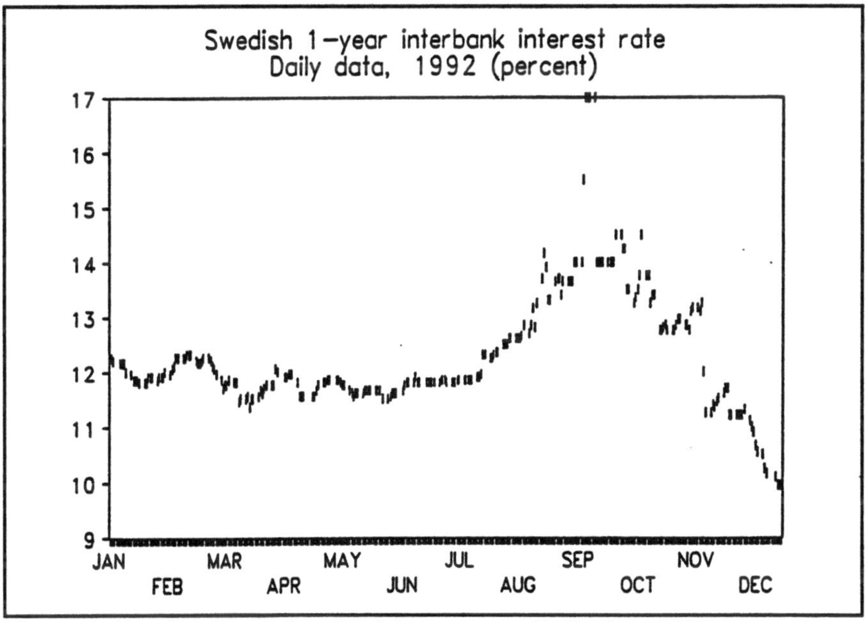

Figure 1: Swedish 1-year interbank interest rate. Daily data, 1992 (percent)

(a)

Riksbank foreign exchange reserves
Weekly data, 1992 (billion kronor)
190
180
170
160
150
140
130
120
110
100
90
JAN
FEB
MAR
APR
MAY
JUN
JUL
AUG
SEP
OCT
NOV
DEC

(b)

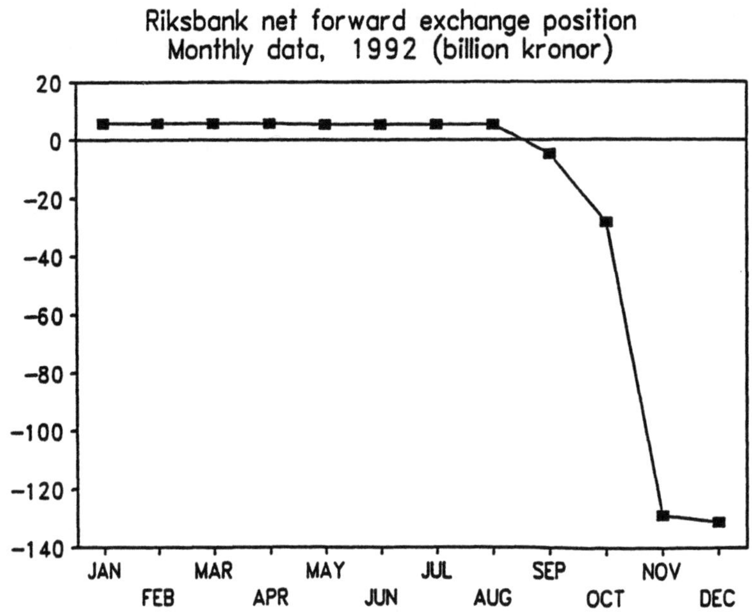
Riksbank net forward exchange position
Monthly data, 1992 (billion kronor)
20
0
-20
-40
-60
-80
-100
-120
-140
JAN
FEB
MAR
APR
MAY
JUN
JUL
AUG
SEP
OCT
NOV
DEC

Figure 2

simply the level of Sweden's foreign-exchange reserves. Sweden was in recession in the summer of 1992; its unemployment rate jumped sharply from a 1982-1991 average of 2.4% to 5.3% over all of the following year. In addition, the government's budget deficit had recently surged from an average surplus of 2.5% of gross domestic product over 1987-1991 to a deficit of 7.1% of gross domestic product in 1992. Nonetheless, the legislature seemed far from agreement on a deficit-reduction package. A troubled domestic banking system unable to tolerate high interest rates was straining the public finances. Finally, the krona had appreciated sharply in real terms since the end of 1990, and Sweden's switch from a trade-weighted basket peg to an ecu peg in the spring of 1991 made it more vulnerable to the dollar's depreciation over 1992.

In these circumstances, Sweden's maintenance of the krona's ecu peg was possible only at the cost of considerable short-term pain; and the conservative government naturally found its popularity falling. The perceived benefits from holding on were twofold. First, even though inflationary pressures were, for the moment, at bay, the government believed its long-term credibility would be damaged by a retreat from its announced nominal-anchor rule. Second, Sweden wished to demonstrate its readiness for EC membership by successfully pegging to the ecu--a strategy also followed by Finland and Norway.

This second motivation was crucial, for it implied that any event that made devaluation more "excusable" in the eyes of EC members, or that lessened the expected benefits of EC membership, would shake the government's resolve to tolerate further pain. The rejection of the Danish referendum on the Maastricht treaty, which made European unification look less likely for the near term, was the first shock: it signaled that the costs of abandoning an ecu peg, not only for Sweden but also for de jure Exchange Rate Mechanism members, might turn out to be lower than previously reckoned. To counter these impressions and restore stabilizing expectations, on June 3 France announced a September 20 referendum on the Maastricht treaty. But this tactic soon backfired as French public opinion shifted against Maastricht.

Finland, which had most recently devalued at the end of 1991, was the first country to come under pressure. Once the markka was floated on September 8, Sweden's resolve was put to the test and its fierce, temporarily successful defense of the krona began in earnest; by September 16 the Riksbank had been forced to increase its overnight lending rate to 500% per annum, an act that placed strain on private-sector balance sheets as well as on the government's. After a subsequent political agreement to cut public expenditures, the foreign-exchange market stabilized, and the Riksbank began to lower interest rates and regain foreign reserves. The central bank simultaneously increased its exposure in the forward market, perhaps to signal its resolve.

Surprisingly, in light of their painful struggle with the markets only two months earlier, the Swedish authorities floated the krona on November 19 without an aggressive interest-rate defense like the one in September. Instead, the response to renewed speculation was a strategy of limited interest-rate increases and mostly sterilized intervention, a strategy that led to massive reserve losses (see Figure 2).[9]

But these losses were a symptom and not the cause of the krona peg's political and economic unsustainability.[10]

What explains the Swedish government's surrender? Economic pain has a cumulative effect; the government had taken all it could during the August--September crisis and had little stomach for more. Furthermore, the indefinite exit of England and Italy from the Exchange Rate Mechanism on Black Wednesday, September 16, coupled with the Spanish devaluation, left Sweden with little more to prove concerning its convergence to EC policies. These events and the French *petit oui* on Maastricht left the future of the EMS itself in doubt.

What lessons does the Swedish example teach? In general, governments have several options that can be exercised in defense of an exchange parity, including borrowing foreign reserves, raising interest rates, reducing government borrowing requirements, and, as was the case for some Exchange Rate Mechanism members, tightening or imposing exchange controls. These strategies, if followed to the limit, have some chance of success. But they are painful, especially when unemployment is high and the public and private sectors are acutely vulnerable to high ex post real rates of interest. Governments therefore will balance the costs of such defenses against the benefit of resisting realignment pressures; and often they will conclude that the pain is not worth the gain. Any economic event that raises the market's estimation of the government's susceptibility to pain, or that lowers the perceived gains from a successful parity defense, can trigger a speculative attack. There need be no long prologue to such an attack: market sentiment can shift almost overnight.

If governments determine the extent of their resistance through a cost-benefit analysis, however, self-fulfilling crises become likely in situations where economic distress already places the government under pressure. The reason is that the cost of resisting an attack depends in part on *endogenous* variables. If markets expect devaluation, for example, domestic interest rates will rise, thus creating an incentive to devalue. Similarly, expectations of devaluation may be incorporated in wage demands, raising authorities' incentive to accommodate. These processes are circular, thus their timing is basically arbitrary and can be brought into play by seemingly minor events.

3. Market Forces and Government Incentives in Crises

This section explores two economic models of self-fulfilling crisis that highlight the government's endogenous response to market expectations. In the first, devaluation expectations feed into interest rates and thus can sap the government's resolve to resist a validating realignment. In the second, expectations feed into wages and competitiveness, creating similar incentives by raising unemployment.

While the first model shows how strategic exchange intervention may alter the likelihood and severity of a crisis, both models assume that foreign reserves can be freely borrowed in the world capital market, subject only to the government's consolidated intertemporal budget constraint. The two models neither assume additional reserve constraints nor assign to reserve levels per se a special role in generating balance-of-payments crises.

3.1 The Role of Nominal Interest Rates

A factor often cited in explaining why a government accedes to devaluation pressures is the increased cost of servicing the public debt. Ultimately, accounts of crises based on limited foreign reserves must also be based on overall fiscal weakness: were the public fiscal position robust, it would be credible and feasible to borrow sufficient reserves to repurchase a large portion of the high-powered money supply and thereby fend off any attack. The model of this section extends the insightful contribution of Giavazzi and Pagano (1990) by modeling the intertemporal decisions of an explicitly purposeful government.[11] Two factors that turn out to play a key role in affecting the likelihood of crises are the maturity structure of the government's domestic obligations (as in the Giavazzi-Pagano analysis) and the currency composition of the overall public debt.[12]

Let us divide the world into two periods, labeled 1 and 2. I will consider the position of a government that issues a domestic currency unit (called the "lira") but also participates in the market for a foreign currency (the "mark"). The government enters period 1 with obligations to pay to claimants the nonnegative amounts ${}_0D_1$ lire in period 1 and ${}_0D_2$ lire in period 2. In parallel notation, the government enters period 1 entitled to receive payments of ${}_0f_1$ marks in period 1 and ${}_0f_2$ marks in period 2. The levels of real government consumption in the two periods, g_1 and g_2, are given exogenously. Finally, the government can levy taxes on output at rate τ to balance its budget, but only in period 2.

The pair $\{{}_0D_1, {}_0D_2\}$ defines the maturity structure of the government's lira debt--its intertemporal endowment of domestic-currency liabilities. When ${}_0D_1 = 0$ any government debt is long term, but when ${}_0D_2 = 0$ any government debt is short term and must be rolled over in period 1. This, as shown below, is a potential source of difficulties for a government that lacks credibility.

The model assumes E=P, where E is the lira/mark exchange rate and P the lira price level. In period 1 the lira/mark exchange rate is fixed at E_1, but in period 2 the rate may be changed to E_2. The letter i denotes the nominal interest rate on loans made in period 1 and repaid in period 2.

Public-sector "cash-flow" constraints[13] reveal how the government's maturity and currency exposure change its vulnerability to market developments. I denote by ${}_1D_2$ new lira obligations due in period 2 that are incurred by the government in period 1. The period 1 constraint (where i^* is the mark interest rate) is

$$ {}_1D_2 = (1+i)\left[{}_0D_1 + E_1 g_1 - E_1({}_0f_1) + \frac{E_1({}_1f_2)}{1+i^*} \right]. \qquad [1] $$

In Equation 1, ${}_1f_2$ signifies the new mark-denominated claims due in period 2 that the government acquires in period 1 (including new central bank foreign-exchange reserves). In words, Equation 1 implies that in period 2 the government will subtract from its original lira cash flow the principal and interest on its period 1 lira borrowing. The latter, in turn, equals lira debt service, government consumption expenditure, and the acquisition of new mark assets, less mark receipts that accrue in period 1. The government's only choice in period 1 (given the assumed setup) is the currency composition of borrowing.

What is the government's position in period 2? It must meet all period 2 obligations, whether incurred in period 1 or before, and spend E_2g_2 lire besides. The revenue to finance these obligations comes from mark assets, taxes on domestic output y, and any increase in the amount of (high-powered) money residents wish to hold in period 2, M_2, over the amount held in period 1, M_1.[14] The implied period 2 constraint is:[15]

$$ {}_1D_2 + {}_0D_2 - E_2({}_1f_2 + {}_0f_2) + E_2g_2 = E_2\tau y + M_2 - M_1. \qquad [2] $$

Under the assumptions of capital mobility and uncovered interest-rate parity, perfect-foresight equilibrium entails the ex post equality of lira- and mark-asset returns, measured in lire,

$$ 1 + i = (E_2/E_1)(1 + i^*). \qquad [3] $$

Given Equation 3, Equations 1 and 2 may be combined to yield the familiar intertemporal government budget constraint (expressed in lira terms),

$$ E_1({}_0f_1) - {}_0D_1 + \frac{E_2({}_0f_2) - {}_0D_2}{1 + i} = E_1g_1 + \frac{E_2g_2 - \tau y - (M_2 - M_1)}{1 + i}. \qquad [4] $$

Private money demand obeys the simple quantity equation:

$$ M_t = kE_ty \quad (t = 1,2), \qquad [5] $$

where real output is assumed to be constant. Incorporating a nonzero nominal interest elasticity of money demand would add nothing to this model, despite its centrality in models of the Krugman (1979) variety, so Equation 5 is adopted to simplify the algebraic analysis.[16] Note the unrealistic assumption that the public holds money in period 2 even though that period is the economy's last and agents could raise consumption by spending it all. This situation arises in certain models of money demand (e.g., Brock, 1975), but different assumptions about the disposition of period 2 real balances could be made without altering the model's main thrust.

Consider next the government's position. The government cares only about the distorting effects of (ex post) inflation and the tax rate. Since both of these variables are, by assumption, zero in period 1, the objective function the government minimizes can be written as

$$ \mathcal{L} = \frac{1}{2}\tau^2 + \frac{\theta}{2}\varepsilon^2, \qquad [6] $$

where ε is the lira's depreciation rate against the mark (the inflation rate of lira prices) between periods 2 and 1,

$$\varepsilon = (E_2 - E_1) / E_2, \quad [7]$$

and $\theta > 0$ measures the weight placed on depreciation relative to other taxes. The simple quadratic specification in Equation 6 is chosen for simplicity only. There is nothing in Equation 6 to capture the notion that a realignment per se, even if small, can cause the government permanently to lose credibility or face. Such an additional fixed cost of realignment alters the analysis substantially, as is shown later, but it is easier to see why once the implications of the simpler loss function (in Equation 6) have been laid out.

In analyzing the government's behavior, it is convenient to translate Equations 1 and 2 into forms that clarify the fiscal role of the depreciation rate ε. Let the symbol ${}_td_s$ denote the real value *at the period 1 price level* of the lira government debt payment promised on date t for date s > t. Then Equations 2 and 1 translate into

$$\varepsilon({}_1d_2 + {}_0d_2 + ky) + \tau y = {}_1d_2 + {}_0d_2 + g_2 - {}_1f_2 - {}_0f_2, \quad [8]$$

where

$${}_1d_2 = (1 + i)\left({}_0d_1 + g_1 - {}_0f_1 + \frac{{}_1f_2}{1 + i^*} \right). \quad [9]$$

Equation 8 states that on date 2 the proceeds of the inflation levy plus conventional taxes must suffice to repay the government's net debt and pay for current spending. (Of course, ${}_1d_2 + {}_0d_2 + ky$ is the total inflation-tax base.)

In period 2 the government chooses ε and τ to minimize Equation 6 subject to Equation 8. Importantly, all variables in Equation 8 other than ε and τ are predetermined when the government makes its choices in period 2. In particular, the interest rate i that prevailed in period 1 as well as the government's mark purchases then (${}_1f_2$) are history. If the government could precommit its period 2 actions in period 1, the government's choice problem would look quite different and the possibility of multiple equilibriums would not arise: under precommitment the government would minimize Equation 6 subject to Equation 3 through Equation 5, in effect choosing the interest rate between dates 1 and 2. The assumption here, instead, is that when period 2 begins the government does whatever minimizes Equation 6 given the inherited budgetary situation. The private sector has rational expectations about the government's objectives, and the forecast of lira depreciation incorporated in the nominal interest rate i is based on the assumption that the government will behave in this way.

Minimization of Equation 6 subject to Equation 8 requires the critical necessary condition:

$$\frac{\theta' \varepsilon}{({}_1d_2 + {}_0d_2 + ky)} = \frac{\tau}{y}. \qquad [10]$$

Equation 10 states that at an optimum, the marginal cost of extra depreciation per lira raised equals the marginal cost per lira of higher conventional taxes. Using Equation 10 to eliminate τ from Equation 8 gives ε as

$$\varepsilon = \frac{({}_1d_2 + {}_0d_2 + ky)({}_1d_2 + {}_0d_2 + g_2 - {}_1f_2 - {}_0f_2)}{({}_1d_2 + {}_0d_2 + ky)^2 + \theta y^2}. \qquad [11]$$

Use of Equation 9 to substitute for ${}_1d_2$ above shows how the government's preferred depreciation rate is affected by the market interest rate prevailing in period 1 and by the currency composition the government chooses for its debt then.

Figure 3 shows two schedules that together determine the set of equilibrium period 1 nominal interest rates. The first is the depreciation reaction function of the government, which shows the depreciation rate ε it chooses in period 2 when confronted with a lira interest rate of i. As noted above, this rate can be found by using Equation 9 to eliminate ${}_1d_2$ from Equation 11. I have assumed that the reaction function is positively sloped, although this depends on the government's fiscal position. Intuitively, the positive slope of the reaction function reflects the possibility that a higher period 1 nominal interest rate, by raising the inflation tax base in period 2, makes greater currency depreciation optimal then. For the moment, the quantity ${}_1f_2$, equal to period 1 official acquisition of mark assets, is taken as given. Its role, which clarifies the factors that lend a positive slope to the reaction function, is explored later.

The second upward-sloping schedule in Figure 3, the interest parity curve, shows the expected rate of depreciation ε consistent with the lira interest rate i prevailing in period 1. Equations 3 and 7 show the equation for this schedule is:

$$\varepsilon = (i - i^*)/(1 + i),$$

which can be viewed as the reaction function of the lira bond market, that is, the interest rate it sets based on its expectation of ε.

In a perfect-foresight equilibrium, the depreciation rate the market expects must equal the depreciation rate the government finds optimal, given market expectations. Thus, intersections of the government reaction function and the interest parity curve determine possible equilibriums of nominal interest rates and currency depreciation. Figure 3 shows a case in which this equilibrium is not unique. Notice that the inflation and interest rates illustrated in the figure seem implausibly high, but remember that this is a two-period model in which the government must repay its entire debt on date 2.

In Figure 3 there are two equilibriums.[17] Obviously the government's loss is

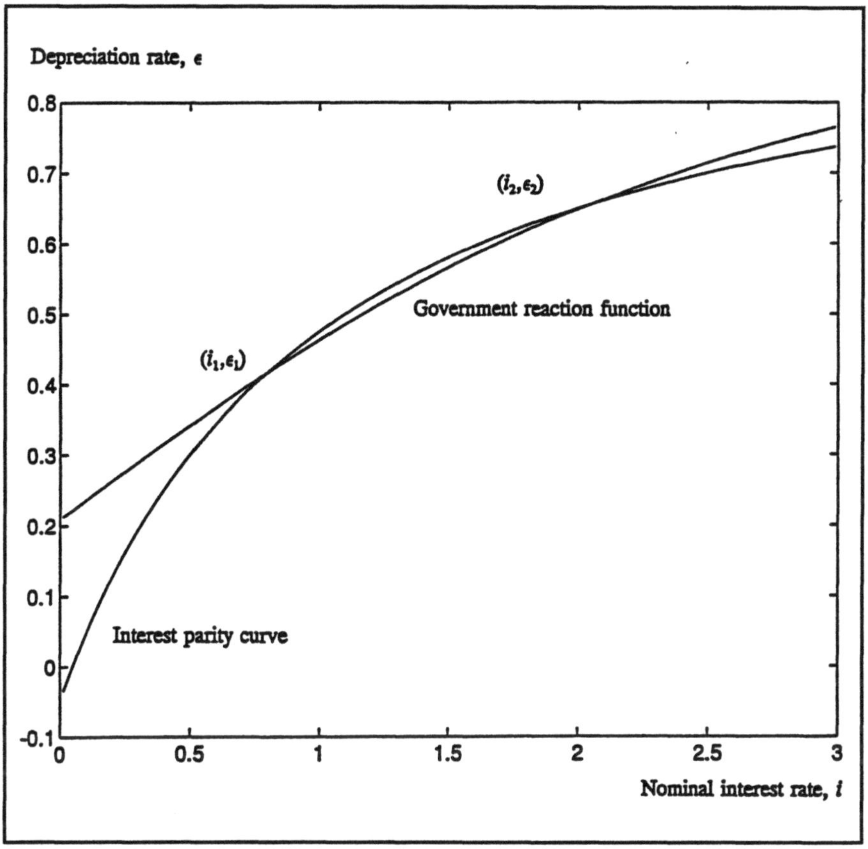

Figure 3: The set of equilibrium period 1 nominal interest rates

lower in the low-depreciation equilibrium, but there is no way to ensure that the bond market coordinates on the relatively low lira interest rate. The government faces a dynamic inconsistency problem: much as it would like to, it cannot credibly promise not to validate expectations if the bond market settles on the high-inflation equilibrium's interest rate.

Next consider the implications of this analysis for a regime of fixed exchange rates. International exchange rates are never irrevocably fixed. A sovereign government can always abandon a currency peg if economic conditions warrant a realignment. Assume, however, that the government faces a fixed cost c of realigning--a cost that could reflect political embarrassment and lost credibility, among other factors.[18] In this case the loss function is:

$$\mathcal{L} = \frac{1}{2}\tau^2 + \frac{\theta}{2}\varepsilon^2 + cZ \quad (Z = 1 \;\; \textit{if} \;\; \varepsilon \neq 0, \; Z = 0 \;\; \textit{otherwise}), \qquad [12]$$

rather than Equation 6. In Figure 4 I have calculated how the original loss function (Equation 6) rises with the nominal interest rate under the *purely discretionary* regime analyzed so far, in which ε is given by Equation 11, and under a *fixed* exchange rate, in which ε is constrained to be zero. (The parameter settings are the same as in Figure 3.) Given the expectations embodied in the period 1 interest rate i, the loss under discretion is below that under a fixed rate, and the relative disadvantage of maintaining a fixed rate rises with i. Once the excess loss of a fixed exchange rate exceeds c, the government will find it optimal to devalue. The figure shows a value of c such that two distinct outcomes are possible. The first is that the bond market expects no devaluation, in which case the nominal interest rate is set at i* and, indeed, no devaluation occurs.

The second possibility is a direct consequence of the existence of two equilibriums under pure discretion. Suppose the market expects the currency to be devalued at the rate ε_2 shown in Figure 3 and sets the nominal interest rate at the corresponding level i_2. Then the government will be induced to carry out the anticipated devaluation, the realignment cost c notwithstanding. This is a first example of a self- fulfilling speculative attack: there exists an equilibrium in

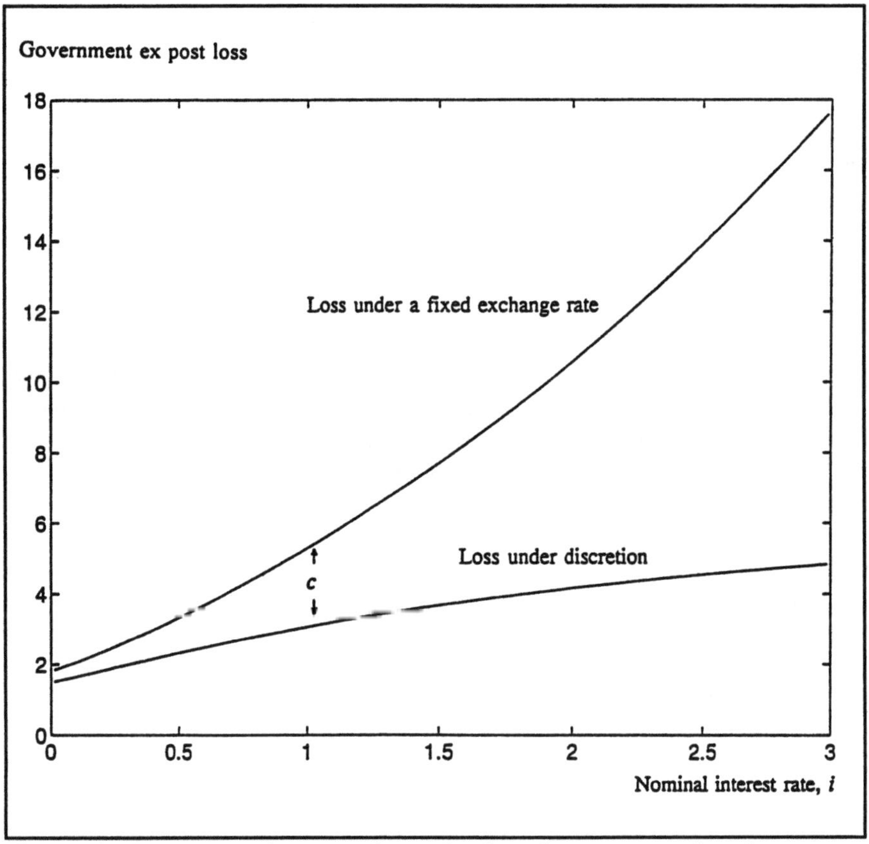

Figure 4: Government losses under a fixed exchange rate and under *ex post* discretion

which the exchange parity is viable, but the government is nonetheless led to change the parity simply because private expectations of a change make it too costly not to. Clearly, a sharp fall in c from a previously high level--as may have occurred, for example, after the Danish vote on Maastricht in June 1992--could allow a devaluation equilibrium to emerge where none existed before.

Equations 9 and 11 show that the lira interest rate i enters the government's period 2 reaction function *only* via ${}_1d_2$, the new debt incurred in period 1; this new debt would in turn be absent (see Equation 9) if the condition

$$ {}_0d_1 + g_1 - {}_0f_1 + \frac{{}_1f_2}{1 + i^*} = 0 \qquad [13] $$

held true--that is, if the government had a zero total cash flow on date 1. If equality (Equation 13) holds, the government reaction function in Figure 3 will be horizontal.

Abstract for the moment from mark assets and liabilities. Then the government will have no reason to fear self-fulfilling devaluation expectations if ${}_0d_1 + g_1 = 0$, that is, if no domestic-currency debt needs to be issued or rolled over in period 1. The government will be closer to this happy state, as Giavazzi and Pagano (1990) stress, if ${}_0d_1 = 0$, so that all the government's debt is long term. But, as explained in Obstfeld (1990a), this is not enough: debt management should try to match total short-term expenditure commitments to net short-term cash receipts, including repayment of principal (and, in general though not in this model, tax receipts).[19]

So far little has been said about reserve losses, which are at center stage in Krugman's (1979) story. Indeed, the assumption of interest-inelastic money demand in Equation 5 means that period 1 expectations do not influence international reserves--a highly unrealistic feature of the model that, if relaxed, would make self-fulfilling attacks more likely. Nonetheless, international reserves--more generally, any government positions in foreign currencies--can play a strategic role in the model. This point is seen by abandoning the temporary assumption that the foreign-asset terms in Equation 13 are zero.[20]

In principle, the option of official mark borrowing can eliminate the possibility of multiple equilibriums even when the government has a substantially negative lira cash flow on date 1. As Equation 13 shows, any foreign-currency receipts (principal or interest) due in period 1 will mitigate cash-flow needs then. But by setting ${}_1f_2/(1 + i^*) = -({}_0d_1 + g_1 - {}_0f_1)$, that is, by borrowing enough marks to entirely cover payments due, the government can sidestep the domestic bond market altogether and thus head off a domestic funding crisis that could lead to devaluation.[21]

This defensive foreign-currency borrowing would have to be huge if, as in the case of Italy, floating interest rates on public debt mean that most of it must effectively be refinanced each period. Most observers would judge such borrowing to be infeasible. Yet if the debt can be rolled over in domestic currency, it should be possible to roll it over in foreign currency: in equilibrium the government faces the same intertemporal budget constraint under either choice.

While sufficient mark borrowing can remove the multiplicity problem in this model, and thus the possibility of a self-fulfilling attack on the lira, a small amount of foreign-currency borrowing can make matters worse by lowering the depreciation tax base in period 2 but not radically reducing the government's incentive to devalue. Figure 5 shows how a relatively small amount of borrowing shifts the government reaction function downward but does not flatten it enough to avoid a high interest rate equilibrium worse than the original one.[22] Foreign-currency borrowing insufficient to eliminate a potential second equilibrium makes the government worse off if that potential is realized.

The model set out above captures aspects of the Italian crisis in September 1992, when the government was forced to rely heavily on Bank of Italy financing to cover sharply higher cash-flow requirements. The model applies equally to other situations, such as Britain's in the 1950s and 1960s, when authorities sought to avoid the "twin disasters of internal and external collapse of the value of the pound sterling" (Goodhart, 1973, p. 513) in the face of a large and increasing public debt.

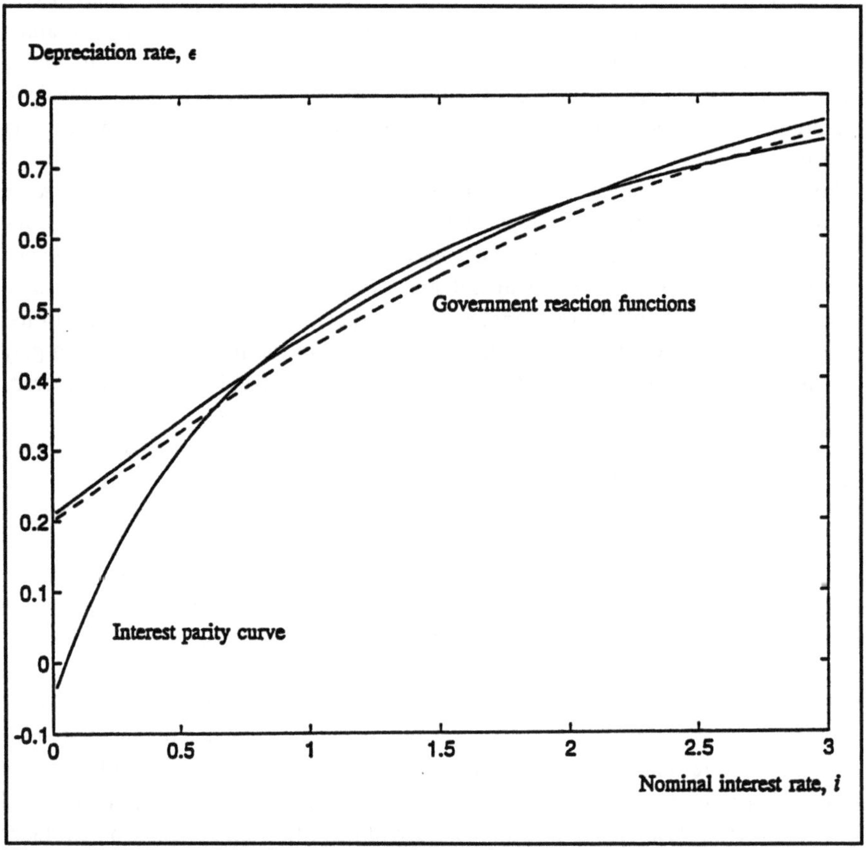

Figure 5: Effects of foreign-currency borrowing

3.2 The Role of Aggregate Demand Shocks

A second model, based on closed-economy models by Barro and Gordon (1983) and Kydland and Prescott (1977), shows that a regime of fixed but adjustable parities can engender multiple equilibriums. In some equilibriums, the economy may be worse off than under irrevocably fixed exchange rates, as nominal wage-growth expectations erode competitiveness and make devaluations more frequent.[23] In this model, devaluations are triggered by the government's desire to offset negative output shocks, but a sudden shift in market sentiment regarding the government's willingness to tolerate unemployment can trigger a devaluation that would not have occurred under different private expectations.

In this model, lowercase variables denote natural logarithms and purchasing power parity holds, so that e, the (log) home-currency price of foreign exchange, equals p, the (log) money price of domestic output, given that p*, the (log) foreign-currency price level, is constant and normalized to zero. Domestic output y given by

$$y_t = \alpha(e_t - w_t) - u_t \ , \qquad [14]$$

where w is the money wage and u is a mean-zero, *serially independent* shock dependent on foreign interest rates, private and government demand shifts, and so on. Workers and firms agree to set period t wages w_t on date t - 1 so as to maintain a constant *real* wage,

$$w_t = E_{t-1}(e_t), \qquad [15]$$

where $E_{t-1}(\bullet)$ is a conditional expectation based on date t - 1 information. This information does not include u_t, and the wage is not indexed to the value of u_t that occurs.

While period t wages cannot adjust to period t demand shocks, the government *can* respond to them by changing the contemporaneous exchange rate.[24] This assumption gives stabilization policy a role. Assume temporarily, as in the last model, that the exchange rate can be freely managed, and that the government's wishes to minimize the loss function

$$\mathcal{L}_t = \sum_{s=t}^{\infty} \beta^{s-t}\ell_s = \sum_{s=t}^{\infty} \beta^{s-t}[\theta(e_s - e_{s-1}) + (y_s - y^*)^2], \qquad [16]$$

where β, 0 < β < 1, is the government's discount factor. (Later a fixed cost of realignment will be introduced.) The loss function (Equation 16) penalizes deviations of inflation rates from a target of zero. It also penalizes deviations of output from a target y*. The target y* could be zero, which happens to be the rational-expectations equilibrium output level when u is at its mean value of zero. I will assume, however, that the government targets a strictly positive y*. Such targeting could reflect, for example, entrenched distortions in the labor market that lead to equilibrium output below the efficient level.[25]

The government's *flow* loss for period t can be expressed as

$$\ell_t = \frac{\theta}{2}(e_t - e_{t-1})^2 + \frac{1}{2}[\alpha(e_t - w_t) - u_t - y^*]^2 \qquad [17]$$

with the help of Equation 14. Under a regime with credible precommitment, the government would choose the path of the exchange rate once and for all in some initial period; this choice, in turn, would tie down expectations and the path of nominal wages. As in the previous section, however, the model assumes that such precommitments are not possible. Instead, the government chooses the home currency's exchange rate e_t each period to minimize ℓ_t *given* the nominal wages agreed in period t - 1. (There is no intertemporal dimension to the government's exchange-rate decision, which does not affect the policy problem to be faced in later periods.[26])

Minimization of Equation 17 over e_t (for given w_t) requires that

$$\frac{\partial \ell_t}{\partial e_t} = \theta(e_t - e_{t-1}) + \alpha[\alpha(e_t - w_t) - u_t - y^*] = 0.$$

Define λ to be $\alpha^2/(\theta + \alpha^2)$. Then the above derivative condition gives the government's reaction function:

$$e_t - e_{t-1} = \lambda(u_t/\alpha) + \lambda(w_t - e_{t-1}) + \lambda(y^*/\alpha). \qquad [18]$$

According to Equation 18, the government uses the exchange rate partially to offset shocks u_t to output. Since wages were set in period t - 1, however, the government also finds it optimal after the fact to attempt a "surprise" depreciation whenever wage inflation risks eroding competitiveness. Similarly, the government will attempt to drive output above its "natural" level by devaluing. Only as $\theta \rightarrow \infty$, so that inflation becomes infinitely undesirable, does a fixed exchange rate become optimal ex post ($\lambda \rightarrow 0$).[27] In general, λ measures the government's willingness to accommodate.

Of course, workers and firms understand the strategy in Equation 18 and set wages accordingly. Equation 15 therefore implies that in a rational-expectations equilibrium,

$$w_t = e_{t-1} + \lambda E_{t-1}(u_t/\alpha) + \lambda(w_t - e_{t-1}) + \lambda(y^*/\alpha),$$

or, since $E_{t-1}(u_t) = 0$,

$$w_t = e_{t-1} + \frac{\lambda}{1 - \lambda}(y^*/\alpha). \qquad [19]$$

Combining Equations 18 and 19 shows that the equilibrium depreciation rate is

$$e_t - e_{t-1} = \lambda(u_t / \alpha) + \frac{\lambda}{1 - \lambda}(y^*/\alpha). \qquad [20]$$

Notice that unless $\lambda = 0$, the economy is afflicted by a systematic inflation bias proportional to the deadweight output loss y^*. This bias results from the government's (in equilibrium, futile) attempts to exploit the potential short-run Phillips trade-off due to the predetermination of nominal wages. A fixed exchange rate would eliminate this inflation bias, but it would also prevent the government from responding to unpredictable output shocks. Whether a fixed rate is advisable in light of this trade-off is an empirical question.

In practice, governments cannot credibly commit to fix exchange rates between national currencies in all circumstances. A more realistic assumption, as in the last model, is that domestic policymakers face a fixed cost c of realignment, making the period loss function in Equation 17

$$\ell_t = \frac{\theta}{2}(e_t - e_{t-1})^2 + \frac{1}{2}[\alpha(e_t - w_t) - u_t - y^*]^2 + cZ_t, \qquad [21]$$

where Z is defined as in Equation 12.

How does the government behave under the loss function (Equation 21)? Remember that the government faces a preset nominal wage w_t when it decides its exchange rate for period t, and so a predetermined expected rate of price inflation, $\pi_t = w_t - e_{t-1} = E_{t-1}(e_t) - e_{t-1}$. If the government maintains a fixed exchange rate (thus setting $e_t - e_{t-1} = 0$), then Equation 21 shows that its loss is

$$\ell_t^F = \frac{1}{2}(\alpha\pi_t + u_t + y^*)^2.$$

If the government realigns instead, it sets the exchange rate by Equation 18 and incurs the fixed cost c, so its loss is

$$\ell_t^R = \frac{1}{2}(1 - \lambda)(\alpha\pi_t + u_t + y^*)^2 + c.$$

Clearly a realignment will occur whenever

$$\ell_t^F - \ell_t^R = \frac{1}{2}\lambda(\alpha\pi_t + u_t + y^*)^2 - c > 0,$$

that is, when

$$\frac{1}{2}\lambda(\alpha\pi_t + u_t + y^*)^2 > c. \qquad [22]$$

Treating Equation 22 as an equality and solving for its two roots, one finds upper and lower values for the shock u, $\underline{u} < \bar{u}$, such that the government devalues whenever $u > \bar{u}$ and revalues whenever $u < \underline{u}$. In either case, the government will set the new exchange rate at the ex post optimal level given by Equation 18.[28]

In principle, an escape-clause arrangement of this sort (such as the one present in Stage Two of the plan for European Monetary Union) can raise welfare. It allows exchange-rate flexibility in those extreme situations where it is most needed, while restraining inflationary proclivities otherwise; and this effect provides a potential rationale for imposing a realignment cost c. In practice, however, a beneficial escape clause may be hard to implement. The reason for this difficulty, as Equation 22 shows, is that the trigger points $\underline{u}$ and $\bar{u}$ at which the escape option is exercised depend on prior expectations of depreciation π_t, and these, in turn, depend on market perceptions of where the realignment trigger points lie. This element of circularity creates the potential for multiple equilibriums, and a sudden shift in equilibriums can trigger a crisis for an exchange rate that previously appeared to be strong on the basis of fundamentals.

To illustrate this possibility, it simplifies matters to assume temporarily that devaluation requires policymakers to pay a cost c, but that *revaluations* are not possible at all. (The validity of this presumption will be verified later for a particular example.) For concreteness, the disturbance u_t is assumed to be uniformly distributed over the interval $[-\mu,\mu]$. I suppose that market participants believe the domestic currency will be devalued whenever a shock more severe than a threshold level $\bar{u}$ occurs (i.e., when $u_t > \bar{u}$). In an equilibrium, the market assessment of $\bar{u}$ equals the highest value of the shock at which the government still finds it optimal to defend the exchange parity.

Identification of equilibriums requires two steps: (1) calculation of market depreciation expectations given an anticipated devaluation threshold $\bar{u}$ and (2) calculation of the actual threshold given market expectations.

When market participants believe on date t - 1 that the date t exchange rate will be changed if $u_t > \bar{u}$, they expect the date t depreciation rate to be

$$\pi = Prob\{u_t \leq \bar{u}\}\cdot 0 + Prob\{u_t > \bar{u}\}\cdot E\{e_t - e_{t-1} \mid u_t > \bar{u}\}, \qquad [23]$$

where the last expectation is a date t - 1 expected value of what depreciation will be next period conditional on u_t exceeding $\bar{u}$. (π is not a function of time because the shock u_t is serially independent.) Under the assumed uniform probability distribution for u_t,

$$Prob\{u_t > \bar{u}\} = \frac{\mu - \bar{u}}{2\mu}, \quad E\{u_t \mid u_t > \bar{u}\} = \frac{\mu + \bar{u}}{2}.$$

Given the devaluation reaction function (Equation 18),

$$E\{e_t - e_{t-1} \mid u_t > \bar{u}\} = \lambda\left[\frac{\mu + \bar{u}}{2\alpha}\right] + \lambda\pi + \lambda(y^*/\alpha).$$

Thus, Equation 23 implies that

$$\pi = \left[\frac{\mu - \bar{u}}{2\mu}\right]\left[\lambda\left(\frac{\mu + \bar{u}}{2\alpha}\right) + \lambda\pi + \lambda(y^*/\alpha)\right],$$

which reduces to

$$\pi = \delta(\bar{u}) = \lambda\left[\frac{\mu - \bar{u}}{2\mu}\right]\left[\left(\frac{\mu + \bar{u}}{2\alpha}\right) + (y^*/\alpha)\right] \div \left[1 - \lambda\left(\frac{\mu - \bar{u}}{2\mu}\right)\right]. \qquad [24]$$

The government takes the expectations in Equation 24 as given and minimizes its loss. Equation 22 implies that the largest shock consistent with a continuing fixed exchange rate is a solution $\tilde{u}$ to the equation $(1/2)\lambda[\alpha\delta(\bar{u}) + \tilde{u} + y^*]^2 = c$. Since $\bar{u}$ must equal $\tilde{u}$ in equilibrium, and since, moreover, we are interested only in devaluation situations such that $\alpha\delta(u) + u + y^* > 0$,[29] the condition for $\bar{u}$ to be an *equilibrium* devaluation threshold is that

$$\sqrt{\lambda}\,[\alpha\delta(\bar{u}) + \bar{u} + y^*] = \sqrt{2c}. \qquad [25]$$

Figure 6 illustrates the possibility that there are multiple equilibrium thresholds. In the figure, there are two intersections of the function $\sqrt{2}[\alpha\lambda(u)+u+y^*]$with the (transformed) devaluation cost $(2c)^{1/2}$. (The parameters underlying the figure are $\alpha = 1$, $\theta = .15$, $y^* = .01$, and $\mu = .03$.[30]) One threshold occurs at $\bar{u} = .0099$, and at it, the associated expected depreciation rate is $\delta(.0099) = 1.23\%$ per period. The second equilibrium threshold is at $\bar{u} = -.0234$. There, expected depreciation is $\delta(-.0234) = 5.71\%$ per period. At this high expected depreciation rate, wage inflation creates a competitiveness problem and unemployment so painful that a devaluation will occur unless the output shocks hitting the economy are quite favorable. Thus, the relatively low credibility of the authorities in the second equilibrium is self-validating.[31]

Economists so far have little to say about which particular equilibrium will occur in a situation where several are possible. In this model, however, any random event could trigger a shift from an equilibrium in which markets view devaluation as unlikely to one in which they view it as very likely. Figure 6 shows that the shift could even be from a situation where devaluation is viewed as *impossible* to one in which it is viewed as a near certainty. Such a shift would be accompanied by a sharp rise in domestic interest rates and a loss in foreign reserves, and unless subsequent economic conditions turned out exceptionally favorably, a devaluation would likely ensue.

This scenario captures aspects of the EMS crisis that erupted in September 1992. Notice that reserve losses certainly accompany a crisis, but they are not the factor that triggers it, nor are they the factor that ultimately leads the authorities to devalue. Even a version of the model without multiple equilibriums suggests that negative output shocks can trigger devaluations. If such shocks are persistent (contrary to the assumption made above), higher interest rates and reserve losses

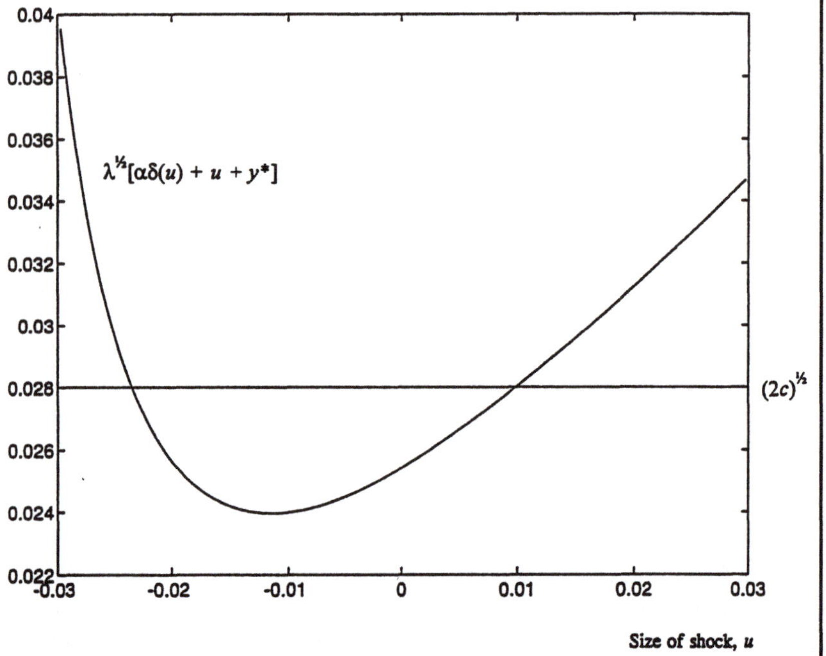

Figure 6: Multiple equilibrium realignment thresholds

will tend to precede realignment.[32] Persistent output shocks can also throw the economy from a configuration with a sole equilibrium into one with several.

4. Concluding Remarks

If speculative currency crises are a manifestation of possible multiple equilibriums, an obvious barrier to understanding them is the lack of any convincing account of how and when market expectations coordinate on a particular self-fulfilling set of expectations.

More generally, we have no more than an inkling of the factors that cause speculative attacks to occur on some days rather than on others. Obvious economic and political tensions can endure for some time before an attack occurs, with the proximate cause of the attack some seemingly trivial event that takes on significance only when viewed as the culmination of a series of signals concerning the economies involved and the resolve of their authorities. Thus, one can make cogent arguments as to why uncertainty over the Maastricht treaty's future led to currency turbulence in the second half of 1992, but why was Black Wednesday not Black Tuesday or Black Thursday? To explain this timing (if indeed there is an explanation), one must postulate a model in which the market's response to a series of informative signals ultimately precipitates a crash. Caplin and Leahy (1994) explore such a model in the context of industry investment, but their heavy reliance on private information makes a direct extension to the foreign-exchange market context problematic. More work on this problem is needed and under way.

The models developed above raise the basic question of whether the crises they portray result from "fundamentals" or from "purely" self-fulfilling expectations. This dichotomy is a false one. The fundamental factors in these models are the dynamic-consistency problems implied by the preferences and constraints of governments. The constraints themselves are endogenous through their dependence on market expectations, and this critical endogeneity, combined with the authorities' inability to adhere to preordained rules, leads to multiplicity. Institutions that tie authorities' hands can eliminate the multiplicity problem. Absent such institutions, however, and given official objectives, the danger always exists that expectations produce equilibriums in which the authorities prefer to abandon their prior exchange-rate targets.

Endnotes

1. This abridged and slightly modified version of an article that appeared in *Cahiers Économiques et Monétaires* no. 43, 1994, appears here with the permission of the Banque de France. I thank Matthew Jones and Dennis Bacsafra for excellent research assistance. Camilla Sommarmo, Lars Hörngren, and Lars E. O. Svensson generously helped me obtain data. Comments from Jeffry Frieden, Lars Hörngren, Kerstin Mitlid, André Orléan, Henri Pagès, and Lars E. O. Svensson led to improvements in the article, as did the discussions at a Banque de France conference and at presentations sponsored by New York University's C. V. Starr Center and the Séminaire d'Économie Monétaire Internationale chaired by Daniel Cohen, Jacques Mélitz, and Charles Wyplosz. Any errors and all interpretations are my own. Financial support was provided by the Center for German and European Studies at the University of California, Berkeley; by the Ford Foundation (through a grant to Center for International & Development Economics Research at Berkeley); and by the National Science Foundation of the United States.

2. Agénor, Bhandari, and Flood (1992) and Blackburn and Sola (1993) survey the large literature growing out of Krugman's (1979) article. The basic reason for rational speculative attacks on price-fixing schemes was first set out by Salant and Henderson (1978) in the context of the gold market.

3. Under perfect capital mobility, a central bank whose *only* reason for departing from a currency peg is reserve inadequacy could simply sell domestic assets from its portfolio and attract an equal reserve inflow. This action, which amounts to borrowing reserves with domestic currency, leaves unchanged both the public sector's net debt to the private sector and the national net foreign wealth position. If the peg is in question for reasons other than reserve adequacy, however, the transaction can have strategic implications. Buiter (1987) analyzes a model in which domestic debt issue is more costly than foreign-currency borrowing, so that an open-market sale of domestic debt worsens the public finances.

4. In two earlier articles (1986, 1988), I presented models in which speculative attacks trigger government responses that effectively validate those attacks. Dellas and Stockman (1993) build on my 1986 analysis to show how the possibility that a government will introduce capital controls in a crisis can generate self-fulfilling attacks. These articles do not, however, derive official responses from models of optimal government behavior, as I do here. Probably the earliest attempt formally to analyze the realignment decision in a strategic context is in a neglected chapter of a book by Gale (1982, chapter 3). Gale concluded, as I do below in more fully specified models, that devaluations could be self-fulfilling phenomena.

5. Ozkan and Sutherland (1993) and Bensaid and Jeanne (1993) explore models in which higher nominal interest rates depress output, so that governments abandon pegged exchange rates if nominal interest rates reach too high a level. Both models produce realistic interest-rate dynamics prior to a collapse: those in the first model come from the stochastic evolution of foreign interest rates, those in the second come from the market learning about the fixed cost policymakers incur when they realign. A similar fixed cost figures in the models below; the Bensaid-Jeanne model shares with those models the prediction that self-fulfilling attacks may occur. In earlier work, Gros (1992) studies a dynamic model in which realignment is driven by interest rates, and self-fulfilling attacks are possible. While Gros did not explicitly cast his model in a setting of policy optimization, it would not be hard to rationalize his assumptions in terms of policy objectives like those assumed by Ozkan and Sutherland and by Bensaid and Jeanne.

6. On general theoretical grounds, however, there is no presumption that this must always be so. For an excellent analytical discussion of how dynamic inconsistency and international coordination problems can interact with electoral rivalry, see Persson and Tabellini (1995).

7. Hörngren and Lindberg (1993) present an excellent review of recent Swedish currency experience.

8. Reserve data come from the Riksbank's *Assets and Liabilities: Weekly Statement*, various issues. Forward position data are reported in the Riksbank's *Quarterly Review* 1993:4, table 28; they do not appear on the bank's balance sheet. Note that an official forward sale of foreign currency effectively reduces the net supply of domestic-currency bonds in private hands while increasing that of foreign-currency bonds; there are no monetary-base effects. The forward sale thus is equivalent to a *sterilized* spot sale of foreign reserves. Forward positions can be rolled over upon maturity through a swap of domestic for foreign currency.

9. Hörngren and Lindberg (1993) recount that the Riksbank sold over 160 billion kronor in six days. The krona magnitudes in Figure 4 have not been revalued to reflect the currency's depreciation starting on November 19.

10. Figure 2 gives the impression that the sum of the Riksbank's foreign reserves and net forward position was around zero when the krona collapsed in November--an apparent confirmation of Krugman's (1979) assumption that total reserves are driven to zero in a collapse. This appearance is an artifact of intragovernment accounting conventions. Offsetting the Riksbank's large foreign-reserve acquisition in early September was a corresponding balance-sheet liability to Sweden's National Debt Office, which itself borrowed intervention reserves for the Riksbank in the foreign-exchange market. The resulting "domestic" liability on the Riksbank's balance sheet thus reflected a foreign liability of the Swedish

government. Arguably, Sweden's foreign reserves were below zero at the end of November 1992.

11. The model develops ideas sketched by Obstfeld (1990a). Giavazzi and Pagano (1990), as I do here, built on Calvo's (1988) important analysis of dual equilibriums in markets for domestic-currency public debt. (See also Alesina, Prati, and Tabellini, 1990.)

12. Formal models of government behavior incorporating these factors were introduced by Lucas and Stokey (1983), Persson and Svensson (1984), and Persson, Persson, and Svensson (1987). Milesi-Ferretti (1993) explores political motivations for debt management in a monetary model.

13. The terminology comes from Persson and Svensson (1984).

14. The tacit assumption in Equation 1 is that no seigniorage revenue is available in period 1 because the exchange rate must remain fixed until period 2.

15. In Equation 2, it would be more appropriate to take private-sector income as the tax base, but this would only introduce inessential complications. Notice, however, that since y excludes interest payments on government debt held by the domestic public, a tax rate τ on y in excess of 1 is not excluded.

16. Adding a traditional interest-rate response of money demand would only raise the likelihood of the multiple equilibriums shown below.

17. The figure is obtained by setting $y = 1$, ${}_0d_1 = 1.0$, ${}_0d_2 = 0.2$, ${}_0f_1 = 0$, ${}_0f_2 = 0$, ${}_1f_2 = 0$, $g_1 = g_2 = 0.35$, and $i^* = .05$.

18. De Kock and Grilli (1993) formalize the credibility costs of realigning through a trigger-strategy model. They also find a possibility of multiple equilibriums. I do not explore in detail *why* policymakers found it optimal to institute the fixed rate and subject themselves to the realignment cost. Particularly if we ignore the possibility of strategic debt management (taken up below), it is entirely possible that a realignment cost has the potential to improve economic welfare by preventing excessive currency depreciation.

19. This is not a balanced-budget prescription, since principal repayments are included in cash flow. Notice that if the government is exposed to the period 1 lira interest rate, there is always an asymptotic intersection at which $i = +\infty$ and $\varepsilon = 1$: the government's nominal commitments then are infinite and the only way to meet them is to eradicate their real value entirely through a confiscatory inflation. I do not consider this intersection at infinity to be an equilibrium.

20. In Obstfeld (1990b) I discuss this strategic role of reserve use in the context of sterilized foreign-exchange intervention. Calvo (1991) presents a model that illustrates a related point, that sterilization of reserve inflows in the course of inflation stabilization may raise inflationary expectations by increasing the outstanding stock of domestic-currency government debt.

21. In essence, the government is issuing consumption-indexed debt in this case.

22. The broken reaction function comes from keeping all the settings of Figure 3 except that for ${}_1f_2$, which is lowered from 0 to -.25.

23. For a more detailed discussion of a similar model, see Obstfeld (1991).

24. I assume capital mobility and perfect asset substitution, so realignment is the only form monetary policy can take.

25. Serial dependence in the employment shock u_t works like predictable time variation in y*.

26. This property would not hold if current government behavior influenced market expectations of its future behavior, as in the trigger-strategy equilibriums analyzed by De Kock and Grilli (1993). Here, instead, market expectations are assumed to be history-independent.

27. If the government could precommit its exchange-rate reaction function, it would choose the function $e_t - e_{t-1} = \lambda(u_t/\alpha)$, that is, it would forswear accommodating wage shocks as well as any attempts to offset predictable real distortions through currency depreciation. See Obstfeld (1991).

28. There is no point in setting it at a different level, because any new rate is fully incorporated into date t + 1 money wages.

29. When this quantity is negative, devaluation is never optimal but revaluation (which has been excluded) is.

30. The choices $\alpha = 1$ and $\theta = .15$ make $\lambda = .87$, which corresponds to a rather accommodative government. With distributions for u more complicated than the uniform, however, multiple equilibriums (sometimes more than two of them) can arise under much less accommodative governments. See Obstfeld (1991).

31. For the chosen parameters, note that when the public expects discretion to be exercised at u = -.03 and above, the monetary authority has a substantial incentive to devalue, not revalue, even when u = -.03. (Apply Equations 24 and 25.) Thus, there was no loss of generality in assuming from the outset that revaluations never occur.

References

Agénor, Pierre-Richard, Bhandari, Jagdeep S., and Flood, Robert P. "Speculative Attacks and Models of Balance-of-Payments Crises." *International Monetary Fund Staff Papers* 39 (June 1992): 357-394.

Alesina, Alberto, Prati, Alessandro, and Tabellini, Guido. "Public Confidence and Debt Management: A Model and a Case Study of Italy." In Dornbusch, Rudiger, and Draghi, Mario (eds.), *Public Debt Management: Theory and History.* Cambridge, England: Cambridge University Press, 1990: 94-118.

Barro, Robert J., and Gordon, David B. "A Positive Theory of Monetary Policy in a Natural Rate Model." *Journal of Political Economy* 1983, 91: 589-610.

Bensaid, Bernard, and Jeanne, Olivier. "The Instability of Fixed Exchange Rate Systems when Raising the Nominal Interest Rate Is Costly." Paris: Banque de France and Ecole Nationale des Ponts et Chausées-CERAS, December 1993.

Blackburn, Keith, and Sola, Martin. "Speculative Currency Attacks and Balance of Payments Crises." *Journal of Economic Surveys* 1993, 7 (June): 119-144.

Brock, William A. "A Simple Perfect Foresight Monetary Model." *Journal of Monetary Economics* 1975, 1 (April): 133-150.

Buiter, Willem H. "Borrowing to Defend the Exchange Rate and the Timing and Magnitude of Speculative Attacks." *Journal of International Economics* 1987, 23 (November): 221-239.

Calvo, Guillermo A. "Servicing the Public Debt: The Role of Expectations."American Economic Review 1988, 78: 647-661.

Calvo, Guillermo A. "The Perils of Sterilization." *International Monetary Fund Staff Papers* 1991, 38: 921-926.

Caplin, Andrew, and Leahy, John. "Business as Usual, Market Crashes and Wisdom After the Fact." *American Economic Review* 1994, 84: 548-565.

De Kock, Gabriel, and Grilli, Vittorio. "Fiscal Policies and the Choice of Exchange Rate Regime." *Economic Journal* 1993, 103: 347-358.

Dellas, Harris, and Stockman, Alan C. "Self-Fulfilling Expectations, Speculative Attacks, and Capital Controls." *Journal of Money, Credit and Banking* 1993, 25: 721-730.

Drazen, Allan, and Masson, Paul R. "Credibility of Policies Versus Credibility of Policymakers." *Quarterly Journal of Economics* 1994, 109: 735-754.

Eichengreen, Barry, and Wyplosz, Charles. "The Unstable EMS." *Brookings Papers on Economic Activity* 1993, 1: 51-143.

Gale, Douglas. *Money: in Equilibrium.* Cambridge Economic Handbooks. Cambridge, England: Nisbet/Cambridge, 1982.

Giavazzi, Francesco, and Pagano, Marco. "Confidence Crises and Public Debt Management." In Dornbusch, Rudiger, and Draghi, Mario (eds.), *Public Debt Management: Theory and History.* Cambridge, England: Cambridge University Press, 1990, 125-143.

Goodhart, Charles A.E. "Monetary Policy in the United Kingdom." In Holbik, Karel (ed.), *Monetary Policy in Twelve Industrial Countries.* Boston, MA: Federal Reserve Bank of Boston, 1973, 465-524.

Gros, Daniel. "Capital Controls and Foreign Exchange Market Crises in the EMS." *European Economic Review* 1992, 36: 1,533-1,544.

Guidotti, Pablo, and Végh, Carlos. "Losing Credibility: The Stabilization Blues." Working Paper No. 92/73, International Monetary Fund, September 1992.

Hörngren, Lars, and Lindberg, Hans. "The Struggle to Turn the Swedish Krona into a Hard Currency." Arbetsrapport No. 8, Sveriges Riksbank, April 1993.

Krugman, Paul. "A Model of Balance-of-Payments Crises." *Journal of Money, Credit and Banking* 1979, 11: 311-325.

Kydland, Finn E., and Prescott, Edward C. "Rules Rather than Discretion: The Inconsistency of Optimal Plans." *Journal of Political Economy* 1977, 85: 473-491.

Lucas, Robert E., Jr., and Stokey, Nancy L. "Optimal Fiscal and Monetary Policy in an Economy Without Capital." *Journal of Monetary Economics* 1983, 12 (July): 55-93.

Milesi-Ferretti, Gian Maria. "Do Good or Do Well? Public Debt Management in a Two-Party Economy." International Monetary Fund, August 1993.

Obstfeld, Maurice. "Rational and Self-Fulfilling Balance-of-Payments Crises." *American Economic Review* 1986, 76: 72-81.

Obstfeld, Maurice. "Competitiveness, Realignment, and Speculation: The Role of Financial Markets." In Giavazzi, Francesco, Micossi, Stefano, and Miller, Marcus (eds.), *The European Monetary System*. Cambridge, England: Cambridge University Press, 1988: 232-247.

Obstfeld, Maurice. "Discussion." In Dornbusch, Rudiger, and Draghi, Mario (eds.), *Public Debt Management: Theory and History*. Cambridge, England: Cambridge University Press, 1990a: 146-152.

Obstfeld, Maurice. "The Effectiveness of Foreign-Exchange Intervention: Recent Experience, 1985-1988." In Branson, William H., Frenkel, Jacob A., and Goldstein, Morris (eds.), *International Policy Coordination and Exchange Rate Fluctuations*. Chicago: University of Chicago Press, 1990b: 197-237.

Obstfeld, Maurice. "Destabilizing Effects of Exchange Rate Escape Clauses." Working Paper No. 3603, National Bureau of Economic Research, January 1991.

Ozkan, F. Gulcin, and Sutherland, Alan. "A Model of the ERM Crisis." University of York, December 1993.

Persson, Mats, Persson, Torsten, and Svensson, Lars E.O. "Time Consistency of Fiscal and Monetary Policy." *Econometrica* 1987, 55: 1,419-1,431.

Persson, Torsten, and Svensson, Lars E.O. "Time-Consistent Fiscal Policy and Government Cash-Flow." *Journal of Monetary Economics* 1984, 14 (November): 365-374.

Persson, Torsten, and Tabellini, Guido. "Strategic Aspects of International Macroeconomic Policy." In Grossman, Gene M., and Rogoff, Kenneth S. (eds.), *Handbook of International Economics*, vol. 3. Amsterdam: North-Holland, 1995.

Portes, Richard. "EMS and EMU After the Fall." *World Economy* 1993, 19(January): 1-16.

Salant, Stephen W., and Henderson, Dale W. "Market Anticipations of Government Policies and the Price of Gold." *Journal of Political Economy* 1978, 86: 627-648.

Stein, Ernesto, and Streb, Jorge. "Political Stabilization Cycles in High Inflation Economies." University of California at Berkeley, November 1993.

Velasco, Andrés. "Are Balance of Payments Crises Rational? A Dynamic Game Approach." New York University, July 1993.

Macroeconomic and Political Determinants of Realignment Expectations: Some European Evidence

Andrew K. Rose and Lars E.O. Svensson[1]

Realignment expectations are analyzed for European exchange rates using daily financial data since the inception of the European Monetary System. It is difficult to find strong meaningful relationships between realignment expectations and macroeconomic variables, although there are linkages between realignment expectations and inflation differentials. It is also hard to find strong signs that political events consistently affect realignment expectations. For instance, the political uncertainties associated with the 1992 Danish referendum on the Maastricht treaty do not appear to have had a strong affect on realignment expectations. Indeed, there were few indications of poor Exchange Rate Mechanism credibility before late August 1992; the dimensions of the currency crisis of September 1992 appear to have taken both policymakers and private agents largely by surprise.

1. Introduction

This article presents empirical analysis of macroeconomic and political determinants of expectations of European exchange rate realignments. Since the inception of the European Monetary System (EMS) in early 1979, 11 governments have linked their exchange rates through formal participation in the Exchange Rate Mechanism (ERM); a number of other countries (such as Austria, Norway, and Sweden) have participated in a more informal, unilateral manner. The objective of this article is to characterize empirically the perceived credibility of these exchange arrangements. More precisely, the objective of this research is to understand better the causes, effects, and behavior of European exchange rate realignment expectations under the EMS. Special attention is paid to the ERM in the period preceding the currency crisis of autumn 1992.

Our research is motivated by the generally poor level of understanding of the empirical causes and characteristics of credibility. This gap in knowledge may have profound consequences; if policymakers are to be able to manipulate the level of credibility, they must first have a clear view about the determinants of realignment expectations. Whereas researchers have developed precise methods of measuring realignment expectations, they have been able to shed only a little light on the actual causes of realignment expectations. See Lindberg, Svensson, and Söderlind (1991) and Koen (1991) or the complementary and independent studies by Chen and Giovannini (1994) and Caramazza (1993), the last of which provides somewhat more positive results.

On a different note, we would like to understand realignment expectations in the European currency crisis that began in September 1992. Were macroeconomic divergences the ultimate causes of poor credibility and the currency crisis? For instance, had the underlying problems been clearly brewing because of the loose fiscal and tight German monetary policy experienced since reunification (as some have alleged) or because of slow persistent real exchange rate divergence since the last general ERM realignment of 1987? Such explanations seem intuitively plausible, yet are worth examining since it is notoriously difficult to link macroeconomic conditions to flexible exchange rates with statistical criteria. Alternatively, was either the imminent prospect of European Monetary Union (EMU) or its possible deferral (as a result of the Danish and French referenda on the Maastricht treaty) an important source of the problem? In this case, we might expect news about the outcomes of the referenda to be manifest in credibility measures. Or was the crisis more financial and speculative in nature (as suggested in the popular press), largely independent of underlying political and economic fundamentals, and therefore less susceptible to correction by official policy?

We find that the credibility of European exchange rate pegs varies significantly over time, mostly for reasons that cannot be well-explained by standard macroeconomic variables. There are signs that higher inflation differentials (vis-à-vis Germany, the center of the EMS) reduce credibility. However, exchange rate realignment expectations generally appear to be relatively disconnected from macroeconomic phenomena to a degree that is disconcerting from an economist's point of view. Realignment expectations, like typical floating exchange rates, move dramatically over time, frequently reacting to economic nonevents and not moving consistently in response to events that would appear to be relevant from a theoretical viewpoint. Perhaps the most dramatic illustration of the latter point is the relatively high level of ERM credibility that persisted until late August 1992, despite a variety of pieces of relevant economic and political news. That is, the currency crisis of 1992 does not appear to have been anticipated by financial markets. Both private-sector agents as well as policymakers appear to have been taken by surprise by the events and aftermath of mid-September.

In the next part of the article, we discuss how to measure expectations of exchange rate realignments, that is, credibility. After a brief discussion of our data set in the following section, we present our measures of realignment expectations. Then we analyze the macroeconomic determinants of realignment expectations using nonstructural econometric techniques. The next section draws out certain implications of our analysis for the currency crisis.

2. Measuring Realignment Expectations

We will only briefly discuss a variety of different ways to measure realignment expectations since these methods have been used extensively; the reader is referred to Rose and Svensson (1993), Lindberg, Svensson, and Söderlind (1991), and Svensson (1993) for further analysis.

We use two measures of realignment expectations in our study: raw interest differentials and interest differentials adjusted for expected exchange rate drift (the drift-adjustment method). Clearly these measures are closely related; reassuringly, they also typically deliver the same message.

We let δ_t denote the differential between the domestic currency interest rate (on Euro-deposits of a given maturity Δt) and the deutsche mark (DM) interest rate on a similar security. If the (natural logarithm of the nominal) spot price of a DM in domestic currency at time t is denoted s_t, then uncovered interest parity (UIP) can be expressed as:

$$\delta_t = E_t(\Delta s_t)/\Delta t, \tag{1}$$

where E_t denotes the expectations operator conditional upon information available at time t, and $\Delta s_t \equiv s_{t+\Delta t} - s_t$. Thus interest rate differentials reflected the total rate of expected depreciation of the domestic currency.[2]

The total rate of expected depreciation can be separated into two parts:

$$E_t(\Delta s_t)/\Delta t \equiv E_t(\Delta x_t)/\Delta t + E_t(\Delta c_t)/\Delta t \tag{2}$$

where x_t denotes the deviation of the log of the spot rate from c_t, the log of the central parity, and thus $s_t \equiv c_t + x_t$. The object of interest to us is $E_t(\Delta c_t)/\Delta t$, the expected rate of change of the central parity (i.e., the expected rate of realignment), which we also denote by g_t.[3] We think of a high value of g as indicating poor credibility, low (or even negative) values being manifestations of high credibility.

We measure realignment expectations in two ways. The easier method is simply to use the interest rate differential, δ; this strategy makes sense under the assumption $E_t(\Delta x_t)/\Delta t = 0$. Since no estimation need be undertaken, this measure has the advantage of simplicity. It has the disadvantage that it ignores potentially nontrivial expected changes in x, which may be relevant if there is substantial mean-reversion and volatility in x, the exchange rate within the band. Thus, our second and preferred measure of credibility relies on g, that is, adjusting δ_t for expected exchange rate drift by subtracting an estimate of $E_t(\Delta x_t)/\Delta t$, the drift-adjustment method. The price to be paid for a more precise estimate of g is the set of complications arising from the fact that the adjustment term, $E_t(\Delta x_t)/\Delta t$, is unknown and must therefore be estimated.

Rose and Svensson (1993) and Lindberg, Svensson, and Söderlind (1991) review a variety of methods of estimating $E_t(\Delta x_t)/\Delta t$; our results will typically be quite insensitive to the exact choice of estimation technique. Our default technique relies on ordinary least squares (OLS) estimation of:

$$(x_{t+\Delta t}-x_t)/\Delta t = \Sigma_i\alpha_i + \beta x_t + \gamma\delta_t + u_{t+\Delta t} \tag{3}$$

where $u_{t+\Delta t}$ is a forecast error realized at time $t+\Delta t$, assumed to be orthogonal to information available at time t (but certainly not serially independent, so that a corrected covariance matrix must be used); and the different intercepts correspond to the periods between realignments vis-à-vis the DM. This equation should be interpreted as a statistical projection, rather than as anything structural.[4]

3. Data

Our chief database consists of daily observations of exchange and interest rates collected at the end of October 1992. The data set begins with the start of the EMS on March 13, 1979, and ends on October 26, 1992; it is discussed in further detail in Rose and Svensson (forthcoming). The exchange rate data are mid-ecu-rates recorded at 2:30 pm Swiss time. The interest rates are annualized Euro-interest bid rates (which should be relatively free of political risk) recorded at 10:00 am Swiss time. So as to sharpen our focus on short-term realignment expectations, we use one-month and three-month maturities for our interest rates. In practice, we typically focus on the period since November 1981, since the Irish interest rate data are available only after that date. We collected data for Germany and the six long-term participants in the ERM: Belgium (which maintains an exchange peg of unity to Luxembourg), Denmark, France, Holland, Ireland, and Italy. For some purposes, we also use comparable data for the more recent ERM participants (Portugal, Spain, and the United Kingdom). To compare ERM participants with unilateral pegs, we also collected data for Austria, Norway, and Sweden. Throughout, Germany is treated as the base country, both because of its role as the traditional anchor of the ERM and to emphasize the special role of German macroeconomic shocks in the events leading up to 1992.

We checked the data set in a number of ways, including visual assessment of both the levels and growth rates of the series, as well as checking for outliers (defined as observations lying outside three sample standard deviations of the sample mean on a year-by-year basis) by comparing our data with independent figures in *The Financial Times*. On the basis of these filters, we have identified a number of potentially questionable observations, which we treat as missing for the purpose of our analysis.

The raw exchange rate data are plotted (along with nominal ERM bands) in Figure 1. Figure 2 contains analogous time-series plots of three-month interest differentials.

We also use a number of macroeconomics series in our study. These series were extracted from the International Monetary Fund's *International Financial Statistics* (IFS) compact disk. The data are monthly and are available from March 1979

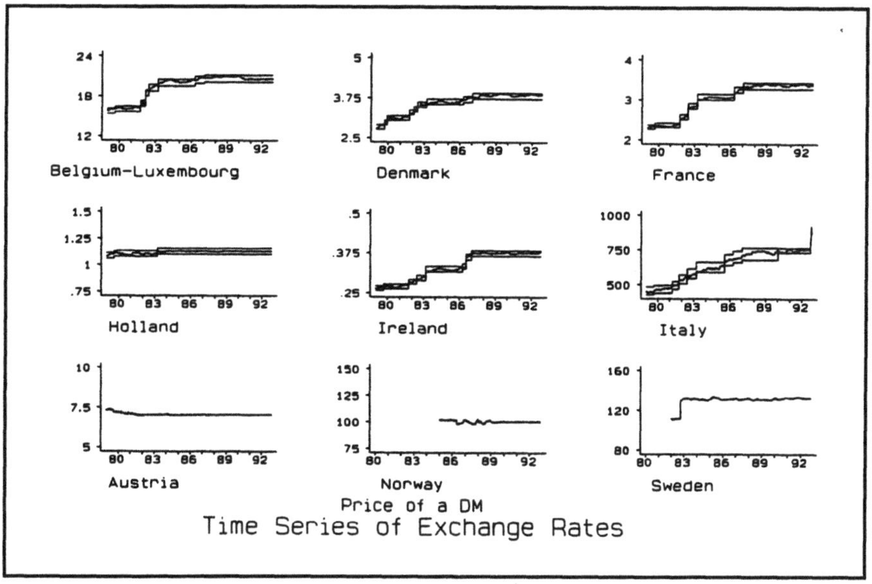

Figure 1: Raw Exchange Rates

through September 1992 (with a few exceptions, which are available somewhat later).

The "real exchange rate" is an effective multilateral exchange rate index number (1985 = 100) based on relative normalized unit labor costs in manufacturing (IFS mnemonic ..reu); "money" is Reserve Money (IFS line 14); "inflation" is the rate of change of the consumer price index (IFS line 64..x); "output" is an index of industrial production (IFS line 66..b or 66..c); the "trade balance" is exports divided by cost, insurance, and freight (CIF) imports (IFS line 70 divided by IFS line 71); and "reserves" is total reserves minus gold (IFS line 11.d). These series have also been checked and corrected where necessary. With thc exception of the inflation rate, all of the macroeconomic variables have been transformed by taking deviations of natural logarithms of domestic values from (logs of) German values.

4. Measures of Realignment Expectations

Table 1 contains estimates of Equation 3, estimated with daily data divided by the entire available sample since the beginning of the ERM (the Irish sample is shorter than that of the other currencies, since the Irish interest rate data are available only after late 1981). Observations that overlap an actual realignment are excluded, as described in Rose and Svensson (1993). The equation is estimated with OLS, but the standard errors have been corrected for heteroscedasticity and the serial correlation that necessarily results from the "overlapping observations" problem, with a Newey-West covariance estimator. Results are tabulated for the one-month market; results are similar for the three-month maturity.

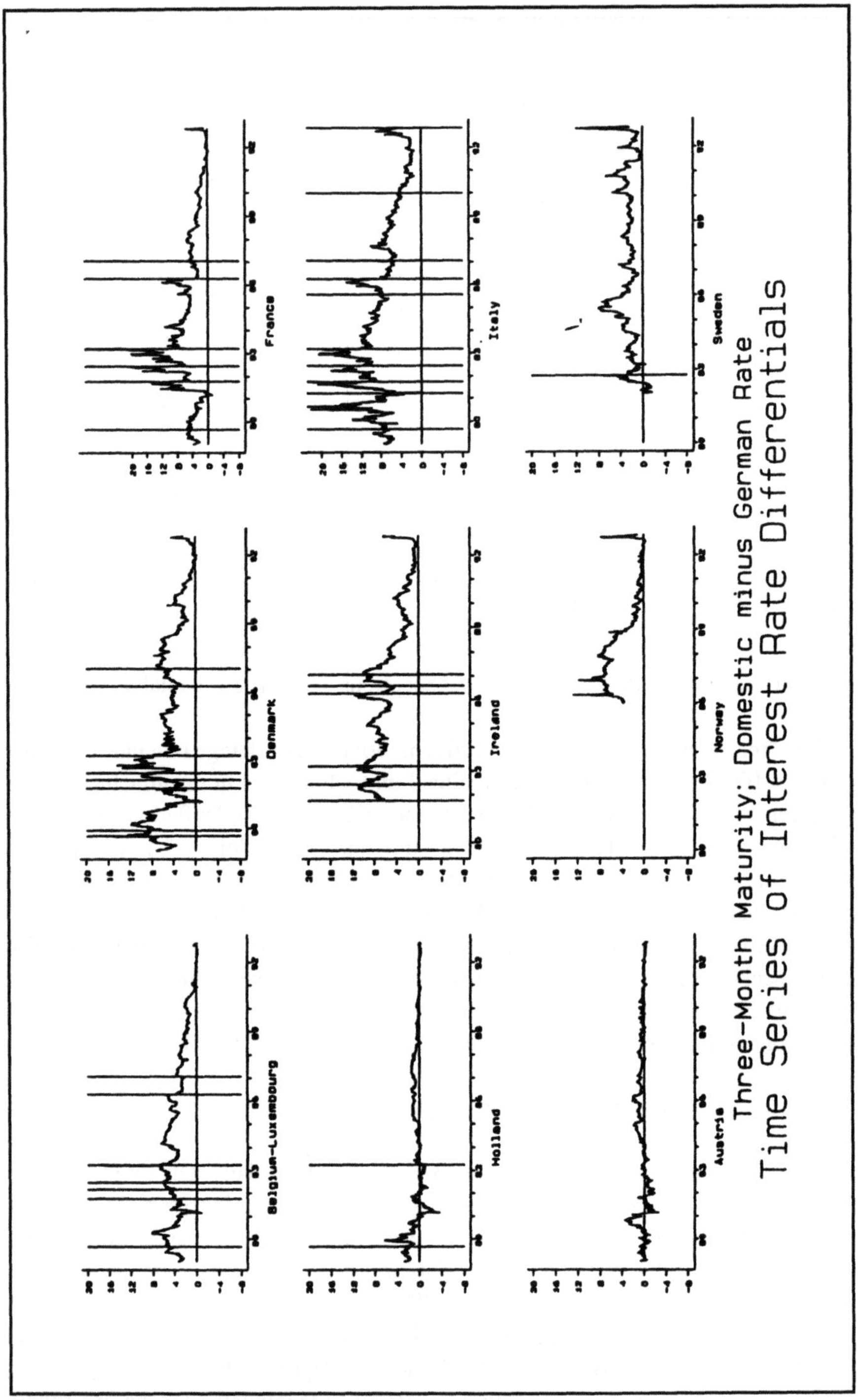

Figure 2: Raw Interest Differentials

Table 1: Estimates of Equation 3 -- Expected Rate of Depreciation Within Band (1-month horizon)

Variable	Country					
Coefficients:						
	Denmark	Belgium	France	Holland	Italy	Ireland
x	-2.41	-1.62	-1.82	-3.03	-1.10	-1.21
	(.43)	(.35)	(.47)	(.81)	(.25)	(.48)
δ	-.74	-.56	-.15	-1.16	-.35	-.54
	(.17)	(.25)	(.16)	(.33)	(.25)	(.15)
Intercept 1	8.92	5.76	2.20	8.01	-.98	n/a
	(3.12)	(1.96)	(1.20)	(1.46)	(2.88)	
Intercept 2	12.93	2.83	-1.66	-1.65	6.63	n/a
	(1.76)	(1.42)	(1.76)	(.71)	(2.66)	
Intercept 3	.60	5.27	4.55	.65	6.72	6.86
	(1.46)	(1.46)	(3.01)	(.22)	(3.37)	(2.90)
Intercept 4	.06	12.67	2.22	n/a	9.64	7.78
	(1.85)	(5.38)	(2.27)		(3.99)	(2.53)
Intercept 5	7.00	6.47	-1.26	n/a	7.73	2.78
	(3.55)	(1.85)	(1.25)		(4.35)	(1.29)
Intercept 6	5.32	3.40	2.31	n/a	3.50	7.41
	(2.43)	(1.09)	(2.10)		(2.92)	(3.76)
Intercept 7	-.67	4.43	2.16	n/a	4.39	2.99
	(1.17)	(1.06)	(.73)		(2.57)	(1.47)
Intercept 8	5.07	1.85	n/a	n/a	1.72	2.07
	(1.59)	(.53)			(1.75)	(.56)
Intercept 9	4.51	n/a	n/a	n/a	4.16	n/a
	(.85)				(1.96)	
Intercept 10	n/a	n/a	n/a	n/a	1.09	n/a
					(1.23)	
Diagnostic						
N	3151	3179	3207	3286	3027	2482
$\hat{\sigma}$	5.75	4.65	5.74	3.46	8.47	4.98
$\sigma(\Delta x/\Delta t)$	6.66	5.24	6.23	3.94	8.81	5.57
Significance Levels for Hypothesis Tests of Exclusion Restrictions						
Lags	.52	.79	.29	.41	.00**	.13
Nonlinear	.42	.11	.28	.03*	.22	.28
Limits	.01**	.16	.00**	.28	.16	.30
Joint	.18	.17	.00**	.03*	.01**	.23

Note: OLS estimates with Newey-West standard errors (computed with 22 off-diagonal bands) in parentheses; one-month interest maturity; sample excludes periods one month before actual realignments. All variables scaled by 100. *p<.05. **p<.01.

The results indicate substantial mean-reversion in the x process for each of the ERM currencies; the estimated β coefficients of x are large in both economic and statistical terms, soundly rejecting the hypothesis that x has a unit root for each currency except the Irish punt (which is a more marginal case, possibly resulting from the shorter sample). The coefficients of the interest rate differential are negative and frequently significant; a high domestic interest rate relative to the German rate is associated with appreciation. Intercepts vary substantially across regimes.

Three diagnostics follow the coefficients tabulated in Table 1: N, the sample size; $\hat{\sigma}$, the estimated residual standard error; and $\sigma(\Delta x/\Delta t)$, the sample standard deviation of the regressand. It should be noted that the standard error of the estimated residual is typically close to (but obviously always less than) the standard deviation of the dependent variable. That is, the equations predict relatively poorly the actual change in the exchange rate within the band. This is of no importance in itself, since our objective is to estimate the *expected* change in the exchange rate within the band, $E_t(\Delta x_t)/\Delta t$, not the *actual* change in the exchange rate within the band, $\Delta x_t/\Delta t$.

Equation 3 is also compared to a more general specification that includes: five lags of x, quadratic and cubic powers of x, and deviations from effective bilateral ERM upper and lower limits.[5] The significance levels for four hypothesis tests are tabulated: (1) "lags" tests the null hypothesis that the five daily lags of x are jointly nonsignificant; (2) "nonlinear" tests for significance of the higher-order x terms; (3) "limits" tests whether effective ERM limits matter; and (4) "joint" tests the first three jointly. In Table 1 the reader can see significant and highly significant rejections of the null hypothesis. The joint test is rejected for France, Holland, and Italy for three different reasons. We stick to Equation 3 for uniformity and simplicity, especially since the estimates of this equation are not intrinsically interesting.

Figure 3 contains time-series plots of 95% confidence intervals for the resulting (three-month) estimates of g from March 1979 through October 1992 (one-month results are similar). Again, actual realignments are marked with a vertical line. The units of g measure expected realignment rates and should be interpreted as the product of the expected realignment *size* times the expected realignment *frequency*. Thus a value of 10% per annum indicates that a realignment of 5% (a typical ERM realignment size) has an expected frequency of 2 p/a (=10% annually/5%), or a .5 (=2/4) probability of realignment in the subsequent *quarter*.

Figure 3 shows that ERM exchange arrangements clearly lacked perfect credibility in the sense that realignment expectations were typically nonnegligible throughout the sample. The positive values indicate expectations of devaluation against the DM, although there are occasionally signs of expected DM devaluation. This result is quite consistent with the literature (Svensson, 1993). A downward drift in the series (indicating increasing credibility) is also noticeable from the 1987 realignment until the late summer of 1992.[6] Many movements appear to be common across currencies, both trends and individual episodes. There is also an

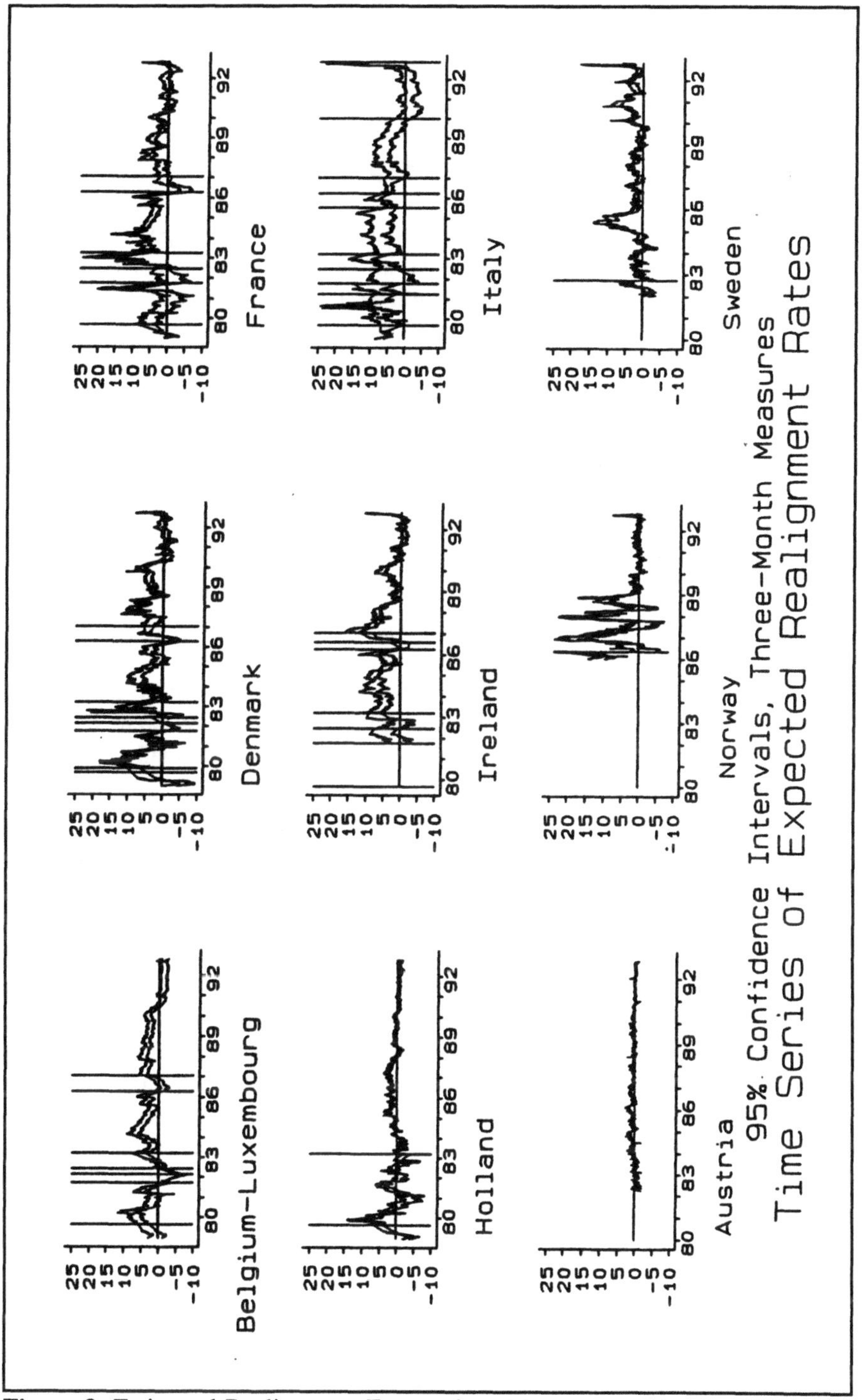

Figure 3: Estimated Realignment Expectations Measures

unsurprising similarity between the measures of realignment expectations in Figure 3 and the raw interest rate data in Figure 2. This similarity also extends across maturity; for all countries, the levels and first differences of the four measures (δ and g for two maturities) are highly positively correlated.

5. Determinants of Realignment Expectations

In this section, we investigate the determinants of realignment expectations using reduced-form techniques. We are interested in seeing whether there is a tight link between macroeconomic variables and our measures of realignment expectations. The set of macroeconomic variables that we investigate is relatively broad and includes most plausible candidates that are either implied by theoretical work or have been mentioned in the popular press.

Traditional monetary models of exchange rate determination with flexible prices imply that the fundamentals driving exchange rates are linear combinations of money and output; thus money and output are obvious candidates for macroeconomic variables worthy of inclusion. Comparable monetary models with sticky prices are augmented by additional terms involving inflation, which is therefore also included. Flood and Rose (1992) provide references and details. As Eichengreen and Wyplosz (forthcoming) show, various models of balance-of-payments crises assign key roles to actual or expected levels of international reserves, trade balances, and the real exchange rate. The last variable is particularly important insofar as it measures the cumulative impact of different trends in competitiveness. We therefore treat all of these as potentially important determinants of credibility.

We are also interested in investigating the link between implicit bandwidth, monetary independence, and realignment expectations. One of us has argued that exchange rate bands give central banks some degree of monetary independence even with free capital mobility (Svensson, forthcoming). This monetary independence can be used, for example, to smooth the domestic interest rate response to shocks in foreign interest rates or realignment expectations by allowing counteracting exchange rate fluctuations within the band. However, a few countries (Austria since 1982, Holland since 1983, Belgium since 1990, and Sweden during part of 1992) have conspicuously abstained from exploiting any monetary independence within the band and instead pegged their exchange rates very closely to the central parity. Some time after this occurred, realignment expectations all but vanished, with the exception of Sweden. Hence, we are led to the hypothesis that not exploiting potential monetary independence improves credibility. Toward that end, we therefore investigate the linkages between our measures of realignment expectations and the amount of monetary independence exploited within the band. The latter is measured by the standard deviation of expected future exchange rate drift within the band. The notable exception to our list of potential credibility determinants stems from our inability to find a reliable measure of fiscal policy at the monthly frequency.

We begin our investigation by temporally aggregating our daily observations of realignment expectations to the monthly frequency in order to be able to compare our measures with macroeconomic data. We then stack the monthly observations for our six ERM countries into a panel. (We focus on the ERM countries both because of EMS-specific institutional features like the short-term financing facilities and because of the general agreement that Germany acts as the center country for the system, implying that our macroeconomic variables can be expressed as deviations from German values. Countries with their own currency baskets like Norway and Sweden should be compared with an appropriately country-weighted average of macroeconomic variables.) We choose not to use quarterly frequency, even though that would enable us to use national accounts and balance-of-payments data, since one of the most striking features of our credibility measures is their volatility, a feature that might be lost with further temporal aggregation.

We begin our exploration by running contemporaneous regressions of our realignment expectations measures on the six macroeconomic variables and our measure of exchange rate volatility *in levels*. The estimated coefficients clearly cannot be interpreted as being structural in any sense, since credibility may feed back to macroeconomic performance or exchange rate volatility.[7] The panel regressions are augmented by country and year dummies. Thus we estimate the following equation:

$$g_{it} = \Sigma_i \alpha_i + \Sigma_\tau \alpha_\tau \mathrm{Year}_{\tau t} + \beta^\sigma \{\sigma_{it}[E(\Delta x)/\Delta t]\} + \beta^m m_{it} + \beta^r r_{it} + \beta^q q_{it} + \beta^p p_{it} + \beta^y y_{it} + \beta^b b_{it} + v_{it} \qquad (4)$$

where g_{it} is the mean of g (at a given maturity) for country i during month t; $\{\alpha_i\}$ is a set of country-specific dummies that control for time-invariant institutional features etc. of our countries; $\{\mathrm{Year}_{\tau t}\}$ is a set of year-specific dummies that can account for oil shocks etc. that affect countries similarly; $\sigma_{it}(E(\Delta x)/\Delta t)$ denotes the standard deviation during month t of the expected drift in exchange rate i within the band, derived from estimates of Equation 3, and is our measure of monetary independence; m is the difference between the natural logarithms of a country's and German values of the money supply; r denotes reserves; q is the real exchange rate; p is the inflation rate; y is output; b is the trade balance; and v_{it} is a disturbance that we assume to be well-behaved, that is, orthogonal to the regressors. Equation 4 is estimated with OLS; standard errors are computed with autocorrelation- and heteroscedasticity-consistent covariance estimators.

The results of estimating Equation 4 with our ERM panel are presented in Table 2. The individual coefficients of the macroeconomic variables are tabulated, as are the standard errors (which are estimated with the Newey-West correction). The estimates are not especially encouraging in the sense that there do not appear to be tight links between realignment expectations and most of their posited determinants. Inflation has a large and precisely estimated impact on credibility;

Table 2: Estimates of Equation 4 -- Contemporaneous Effects of Macrovariables on Realignment Expectations

Maturity	Money	Real Exchange Rate	Inflation	Output	Trade	International Reserves	Monetary Independence
One month: Mean of g (N = 784, σ = 2.64)							
Coefficient	-1.73	.83	.61	6.21	-.82	-4.31	1.54
(s.e.)	(1.16)	(3.97)	(.10)	(3.33)	(1.31)	(.91)	(.45)
Three month: Mean of g (N = 732, σ = 2.09)							
Coefficient	-1.15	-.47	.46	4.32	.84	-3.84	1.34
(s.e.)	(1.04)	(3.54)	(.09)	(3.15)	(1.05)	(.81)	(.41)

Note. OLS estimation of panel of monthly data for six ERM currencies; autocorrelation- and heteroscedasticity-consistent standard errors (computed with 12 lags) in parentheses. Country and year dummies included. Variables scaled by 100.

an increase in a country's inflation rate relative to the German rate is associated with a significant increase in realignment expectations (i.e., a decrease in credibility), holding all else constant. Similarly, decreases in international reserves are also correlated with increased realignment expectations. Increases in exchange rate variability and therefore the degree of exploited monetary independence are also associated with significant increases in realignment expectations. These results seem perfectly sensible and reasonable. However, there do not appear to be clear links between realignment expectations and money, output, real exchange rates, or the trade balance. Similar results are obtained (1) if interest rate differentials are used as regressands or (2) if the standard deviation of either the exchange rate within the band or its first difference is used in place of the standard deviation of expected future exchange rate drift as a measure of exploited monetary independence.

The results of Table 2 are suspect for a number of reasons, chiefly associated with simultaneity bias and nonstationarity of the regressors. In the absence of a structural theory of realignment expectations, we continue our exploration by estimating a VAR, which incorporates the variables of interest to us; we focus on the realignment expectations equation of the VAR. We do not attempt to restrict our VAR so as to be able to interpret the coefficients in a structural way (or to improve efficiency). While positive results would not indicate the structural interpretation of our findings, it is more difficult to explain away negative results. Moreover, our exercise is close in spirit to the exercises that participants in financial markets may go through if they attempt to understand exchange rate credibility by projecting realignment expectations on an information set consisting of lagged values of macroeconomic variables. This rational expectations interpretation is pursued further by Chen and Giovannini (1994).

The VAR links exchange rate realignment expectations to our six macroeconomic variables as well as exploited monetary independence; the VAR is also conditioned on a number of other factors. The equation of greatest interest to us is:

$$g_{it} = \Sigma_i \alpha_i + \Sigma_\tau \alpha_\tau \mathrm{Year}_{\tau t} + \Sigma_j \phi_j g_{it-j} + \Sigma_j \beta_j^{\sigma} \sigma_{it-j}[E(\Delta x)/\Delta t] + \Sigma_j \beta_j^{r} r_{it-j}$$
$$+ \Sigma_j \beta_j^{m} m_{it-j} + \Sigma_j \beta_j^{q} q_{it-j} + \Sigma_j \beta_j^{p} p_{it-j} + \Sigma_j \beta_j^{y} y_{it-j} + \Sigma_j \beta_j^{b} b_{it-j} + v_{it}. \qquad (5)$$

We use $j = 1,...,6$ monthly lags as our default, but we check our estimates by also reporting the case with only three lags. We are most interested in the null hypotheses $\Sigma_j \beta_j^z = 0$ for $z = r, m, q, p, y, b, \sigma$. That is, we seek to discover whether (permanent) changes in the macroeconomic variables are associated with (permanent) changes in the level of realignment expectations, that is, whether there are potentially important macroeconomic determinants of realignment expectations.[8]

Table 3 presents some results derived from estimation of Equation 5 using both the one- and three-month measures of g. The statistics tabulated are the significance levels for a variety of hypothesis tests concerning the effects of individual macroeconomic variables. A low figure indicates that the null hypothesis -- of no significant cumulative effect on realignment expectations of, for example,

Table 3: Estimates of Equation 5 -- Tests of Effects of Macroeconomic Variables on Realignment Expectations

Maturity	Money	Real Exchange Rate	Inflation	Output	Trade	International Reserves	Monetary Independence
Effects on Mean of g: (Six Lags)							
One month: (N = 749, $\hat{\sigma}$ = 1.67)	.953	.298	.000**	.735	035*	.606	.168
Three month: (N = 569, $\hat{\sigma}$ = .92)	.067	.235	.000**	.643	.221	.018*	.842
Three Lags:							
One month: (N = 769, $\hat{\sigma}$ = 1.82)	.084	.124	.000**	.896	.940	.136	.700
Three month: (N=646, $\hat{\sigma}$=1.09)	.110	.256	.011*	.833	.968	.081	.984
δ as regressand: (Six Lags)							
One month: (N=749, $\hat{\sigma}$=1.48)	.148	.384	.100	.652	.221	.083	.727
Three month: (N = 586, $\hat{\sigma}$ = .63)	.191	.718	.028*	.055	.034*	.018*	.034*

Significance levels for test of null hypothesis of no cumulative effect of variable on the mean of g (or δ) in Equation 4. OLS estimation of panel of monthly data for six ERM currencies; heteroscedasticity-consistent standard errors. Country and year dummies and lags of the dependent variable are also included.

six lags of the logarithm of domestic money relative to German money -- can be rejected with great confidence.

The close link between inflation divergence and realignment expectations found in the contemporaneous regressions carries over to a dynamic model. Moreover, the coefficients consistently sum to a positive number, indicating that higher inflation is associated with higher realignment expectations and therefore with reduced credibility, as seems sensible. However, the other results of Table 3 are more negative. There do not appear to be statistically significant links between realignment expectations and up to six lags of the other hypothesized variables, including reserves and exploited monetary independence (the variables that were significantly related to realignment expectations contemporaneously). While individual coefficients on, for example, particular lags of money are statistically significant, they are canceled out by coefficients on other lags so that there are typically no significant cumulative effects. Apparently significant findings of linkages between macroeconomic variables and realignment expectations are also not robust in the sense that they vary with the number of lags chosen in the VAR, the maturity used to estimate credibility, and the choice of g rather than δ as a measure of credibility.[9]

The sensitivity of the results in Table 3 has been explored extensively; the finding of no significant and consistent relationship between the set of macroeconomic variables and realignment expectations characterizes a number of different perturbations of the basic methodology. For instance, if Equation 5 is estimated either country by country (that is, using only the time-series variation in the data) or year by year (using only the pure cross-sectional variation), a variety of different links between the mean of g and the macroeconomic variables can be found; however, the coefficient sums vary dramatically in sign and significance from country to country and year to year.[10] To take one example, the ties between inflation and realignment expectations are significant at the .05 level for four of the six countries when the three-month maturity is used for credibility and the VARs are estimated with six lags. However, only one of the six countries has a significant relationship using the one-month measure of credibility, and none of the estimates is significant when the VARs are estimated with three lags (using either maturity to measure credibility). Further, either first differencing the data or using alternative measures of exchange rate volatility does not change the basic conclusion of no apparent relationship between macroeconomic variables and credibility.[11,12]

Finally, it is also of interest to investigate the effects of realignment expectations on the macroeconomic variables in the VAR. Table 4 is an analogue to Table 3 in that it reports significance levels for a series of hypothesis tests that assume under the null hypothesis there is no cumulative effect of (six lags of) the mean of g on the other variables of the VAR. There are few convincing indications that realignment expectations have an important effect on either the six macroeconomic variables or the volatility of exchange rate drift. Results vary with the maturity of the credibility measure; they also vary with the lag length used for VAR

Table 4: Hypothesis Tests of Effects of Realignment Expectations on Macrovariables

Maturity	Money	Real Exchange Rates	Inflation	Output	Trade	International Reserves	Monet. Independence
Effects of Mean of g: (Six Lags)							
1 month	.15	.07	.20	.40	.27	.06	.09
3 mths	.26	.12	.96	.82	.91	.01**	.31

Note: Significance levels for test of null hypothesis of no cumulative effect of the mean of g on variable in VAR analogue to Equation 5. OLS estimation of panel of monthly data for six ERM currencies; heteroscedasticity-consistent standard errors. Country and year dummies and lags of the dependent variable are also included.

estimation. There are some indications that a sustained rise in g lowers the level of reserves.[13]

To sum up, with the exception of a strong link from inflation differentials, there are few clearly significant channels of macroeconomic influence on realignment expectations. We are not very surprised at this result, given the well-known difficulties of linking exchange rates to macroeconomic phenomena (Flood and Rose, 1992). Still, it makes us uncomfortable to realize that countries that have achieved closer macroeconomic convergence with Germany (in dimensions other than inflation) do *not* appear to have been consistently rewarded by financial markets with higher credibility and, thus, a lower interest rate differential (given the level of the exchange rate). Stated alternatively, the data do not show that high-credibility ERM countries like Holland have acquired their reputations as a result of significantly different macroeconomic behavior compared with countries like Italy.

6. A Partial Characterization of the Currency Crisis

In this section, we describe the behavior of ERM credibility during 1991 and 1992, focusing on the period preceding the currency crisis that erupted in September 1992. In particular, we search for indications that the currency crisis was associated with macroeconomic phenomena (which typically have long gestation periods, e.g., real exchange rate divergence or the impact of German reunification) or with developments concerning EMU.

Figure 4 consists of nine multiple time-series graphs for 1991 and 1992. The top six graphs depict the time-series behavior of (95% confidence intervals for) realignment expectations for the long-term ERM participants. Individual months in 1992 are marked on the x-axis; vertical lines mark the Danish referendum of June 2, 1992, and Black Wednesday, September 16, 1992. Black Wednesday, four days before the French referendum on the Maastricht treaty, is generally considered to be both the beginning and the peak of the currency crisis. The lower three graphs depict the average level of one-month interest rates and extracted common factors (Rose and Svensson, forthcoming) for both the one- and three-month measures of g.

The currency crisis was not preceded by a gradual deterioration in ERM credibility. Indeed, realignment expectations were essentially constant through the period after German reunification. There were few indications of decaying ERM credibility after 1990, despite the increasingly dire *economic* news from both Germany (e.g., concerning the fiscal cost of reunification and the tight monetary policy that followed) and the other ERM participants (including the British recession, the cumulative deterioration in Italian public finances, and competitiveness problems in both Italy and the United Kingdom). It seems surprising that ERM realignment expectations did not change in reaction to these important economic factors. However, it is consistent with the negative results of the previous section, which found few consistent responses of credibility to macroeconomic factors. The absence of strong linkages between macroeconomic factors and credibility is also consistent with the fact that several targets of the speculative attacks of later September 1992 had apparently strong macroeconomic fundamentals (France is the most frequently cited example).

Realignment expectations also did not change dramatically in response to *political* news about the prospects of EMU. For instance, interest differentials and g fell after the Maastricht summit of December 1991 and did not move dramatically in response to the Danish and Irish referenda in June 1992.[14] (The small responses are unsurprising, since the outcomes of both polls were close to expectations.[15]) The potential exception is the case of Italy, but even the Italian data were comparable to what had been previously experienced during the so-called New EMS.[16] For these reasons, it seems hard to believe that doubts about EMU were very important in causing the problems in the EMS. If doubts about Maastricht ratification generated turbulence in the EMS, these doubts might be expected to have been manifest in realignment expectations that rose with the polls preceding the Danish and French referenda for a number of ERM currencies; but there is little evidence of this in the data.

Nevertheless, the polls probably had some effect on realignment expectations. By late August 1992, there were growing (but still weak) indications from the financial markets that a general revaluation of the DM against other European currencies was called for; this realignment certainly seems to be consistent with the underlying macroeconomic fundamentals from a theoretical viewpoint. Indications of rising realignment expectations can be measured using the data in Figures 4 and 5. After months of relatively low realignment expectations, around August 25 (the date of the first polls showing a slight majority against French ratification of the

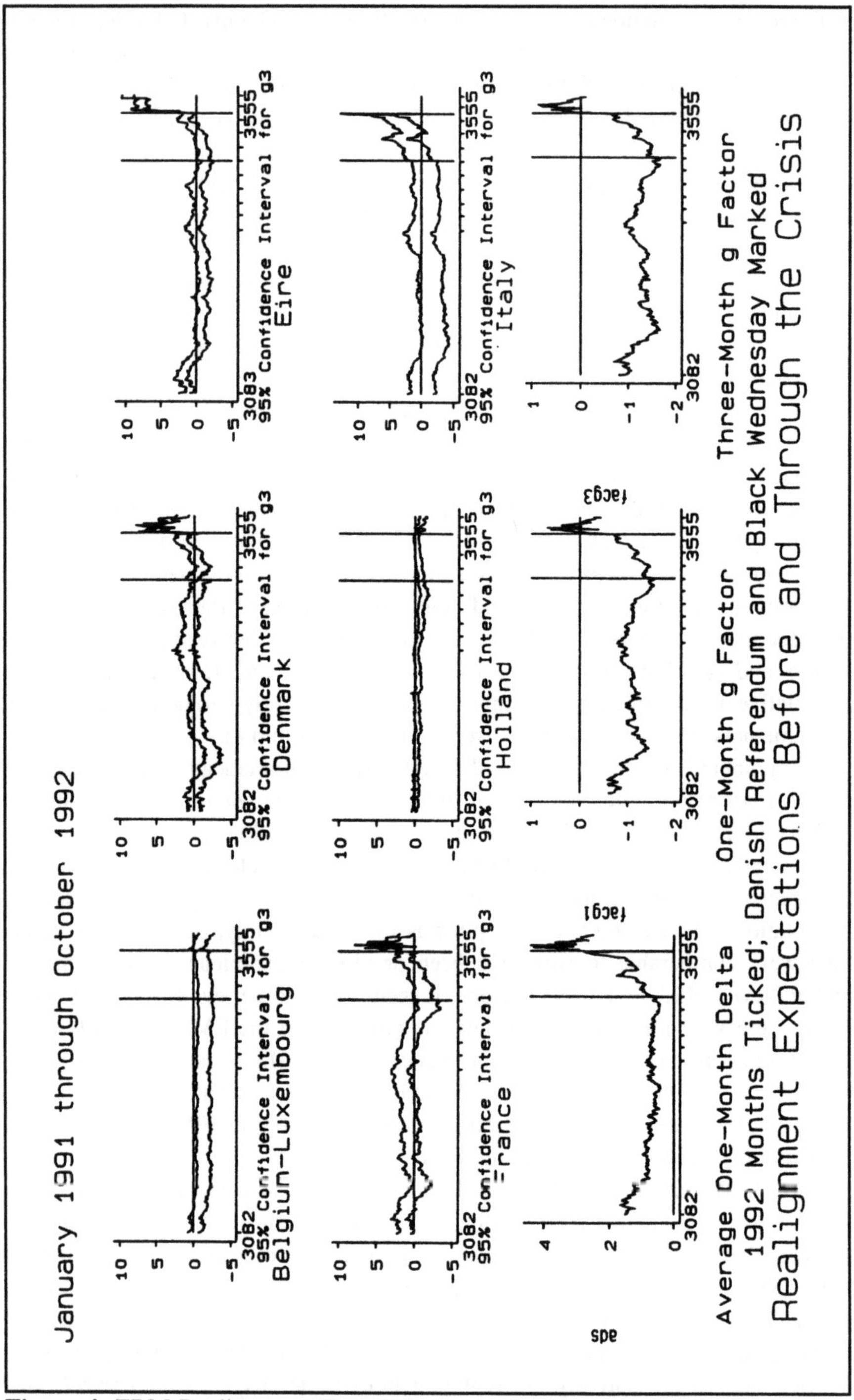

Figure 4: ERM Realignment Expectations and the Currency Crisis

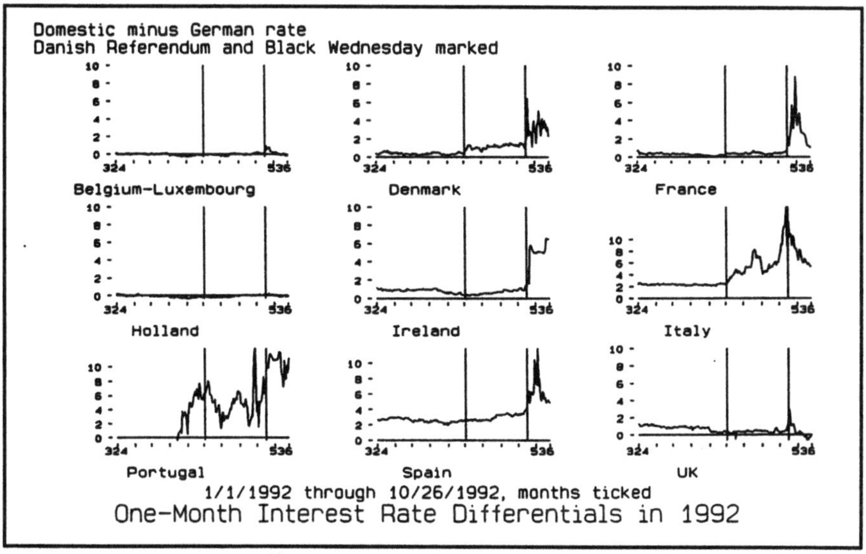

Figure 5: Short Interest Differentials in 1992

treaty) realignment expectations rose, indicating worsening credibility.[17] However, the movement was only a modest increase and was not without historical precedent. These reasonable realignment expectations remained stable through the Italian devaluation of September 14, before finally rising dramatically on Black Wednesday, two days later, when the lira and the pound sterling dropped out of the ERM altogether. Detailed evidence on this issue is presented in Figure 5, which is a set of time-series graphs of the 1992 measures of interest differentials for the one-month market for all nine partners of Germany in the ERM. It is striking that interest differentials remained low throughout the ERM until shortly before the currency crisis. Eichengreen and Wyplosz (forthcoming) show similar results. It is also important to realize that neither the increase in realignment expectations in late August 1992 nor their level thereafter was without historical precedent. Figure 3 clearly indicates that the EMS had previously weathered comparable credibility crises. Thus the data appear to indicate that *financial markets (as well as policymakers) were surprised by the events of mid-September.* Financial market participants may not have been very forward-looking, although this seems hard to believe at the time of events like the various referenda on the Maastricht treaty. Alternatively, the currency crisis may have been caused by phenomena without long, detectable gestation lags.

We attribute some of the chaotic conditions of European exchange markets during mid-September to the tactical decision not to revalue the DM against most or all European currencies, but instead to devalue the lira in a piecemeal fashion, when similar pressure was being experienced by other currencies (especially sterling). The fear among policymakers that an EMS realignment would substantially induce realignment expectations seems to have been excessively high.

Nevertheless, it is striking that indications of a pending crisis did not emerge until late August 1992. Even then, our measures indicate that the movements and levels of realignment expectations were similar to those experienced in the period since 1987. There was remarkably little discussion in the popular press of an incipient European currency crisis before the very late summer of 1992. The September 5 issue of *The Economist* did not cover recent currency developments;[18] neither did *Euromoney* in its August issue. While the minutes of the American Federal Open Market Committee indicate that the committee discussed the impact of the European currency crisis in its meeting of October 6, the EMS is not even mentioned in the minutes of the August 18 meeting, despite concerns about the dollar. Indeed, most of the popular financial press in the late summer of 1992 focused on the weakness of the dollar, not the weakness of the EMS.

It is easy to claim ex post facto that traditional macroeconomic analyses of exchange rate developments indicated (even before German reunification) that a DM revaluation was warranted. On the other hand, the old parities had stood up well, weathering a variety of events since 1987 that might have been expected to result in realignments. These included: the removal of all capital controls, German reunification, the Persian Gulf crisis, entry of three new currencies into the ERM, dramatic British and Italian elections, and the onset of the recession of the early 1990s. The new EMS had weathered these situations well with constant or enhanced credibility and did not appear to be very well-described by traditional models. Given this set of circumstances, it is perhaps understandable that neither European monetary authorities nor financial markets anticipated the crisis.

7. Conclusion

Our examination of ERM realignment expectations has shown that they are only weakly related to standard macroeconomic phenomena. Of the variables that we examine, only inflation differentials vis-à-vis Germany affect ERM realignment expectations in a systematic way. Further, abstaining from the exploitation of monetary independence within ERM bands also seems not to reduce realignment expectations. On the other hand, the common nature of ERM credibility is a stylized fact in search of a theory. Perhaps our most striking result is that financial markets do not seem to have anticipated the currency crisis of September 1992.

The dramatic events of the 1992 currency crisis certainly seem to be consistent with standard economic theories. For instance, the combination of loose fiscal and tight monetary policy in Germany would be expected in a variety of models to lead to a real DM appreciation in the early 1990s, much as the same combination of American policy implied a real dollar appreciation a decade earlier. However, a note of caution is warranted about even this result, since standard exchange rate models generally have a dismal empirical performance (Meese, 1990).

Nevertheless, a real DM appreciation does not necessarily imply a nominal depreciation; it can also be achieved through lower inflation in the rest of the ERM compared with Germany. Ex ante, the latter appeared to be a more difficult route to follow than the former; ex post, both alternatives were used. On balance then, a nominal DM appreciation appears to have been a likely result of German reunification, though not a complete necessity. Also, the underlying tension among national monetary policies, fixed exchange rates, and capital mobility had long been well-noted and led to doubts about the sustainability of the ERM, all aided by uncertainty about EMU. It remains a mystery that the deepest financial markets in the world yielded so remarkably few indications of an imminent crisis. As noted above, realignment expectations rose significantly after the Danish referendum only for the Italian lira. That is, there were few indications of a pending widespread currency crisis that would affect currencies with strong economic fundamentals like France and Denmark.

What did cause the ERM's fall from grace? There are two standard explanations: either doubts about EMU or the unwillingness of policymakers to react to the shock of German reunification with a general realignment of the ERM. These explanations may seem convincing now; nevertheless, neither financial markets nor policymakers seem to have been convinced before the crisis.

Endnotes

1. We thank Sveriges Riksbank for assistance with the data set and Magnus Dahlquist for research assistance. For hospitality and research support during the course of this research, Rose thanks: Federal Reserve Bank of San Francisco; H. M. Reasury; Institute for International Economic Studies; and the International Monetary Fund; Svensson thanks the Swedish Council for Research in the Humanities and Social Sciences. For comments, we also thank: Bill Branson; Robert Gordon; Guido Tabellini; and paticipants at the June 1993 London School of Economics Financial Markets Group Conference, the 1993 International Seminar on Macroeconomics; and the Fall 1993 Meeting of the Study Group of the Political Economy on European Integration. This article is an abbreviated version of our unpublished manuscript "European Exchange Rate Credibility Before the Fall." The views expressed here are those of the authors alone.

2. We rely on UIP holding at least approximately, despite the evidence against this hypothesis in floating exchange rate regimes (Froot and Thaler, 1990). The UIP hypothesis works well for France during the ERM period, but worse for the other countries, typically being rejected at reasonable significance levels. A discussion of the relevant deviations from UIP can be found in Rose and Svensson (1993). A small time-varying exchange risk premium that might account for the deviations from UIP will not significantly affect our results unless its movements coincide with changing realignment expectations for some mysterious reason.

3. If x jumps at realignments, then the devaluation of the spot exchange rate that occurs at realignments will not coincide with the size of the central parity realignment; see Rose and Svensson (1993) and Svensson (1993) for further discussion.

4. This estimation procedure does not guarantee that expected future exchange rates within the band are constrained to lie within the band limits. Chen and Giovannini (1992) have suggested that this issue be handled by a logistic transformation of the exchange rate within the band, using the explicit bandwidth. However, the underlying (target-zone) exchange rate theory does not suggest such a transformation, which may also work badly in practice since it prevents predicted future exchange rates from reaching the edges of the band. In addition, the procedure relies on explicit maximal bandwidths, which may be irrelevant in practice because of either implicit bands or more narrow effective limits that result from the multilateral nature of the ERM. Lindberg, Svensson, and Söderlind (1991) and Rose and Svensson (1993) have compared this technique to the method used above and found very similar results. In any case, reasonable confidence intervals of expected future exchange rates within the band for our estimates almost never lie outside the band.

5. The ERM is a multilateral peg, so that effective bilateral limits are sometimes much more narrow than notional bilateral limits. Thus the pound might be much

more constrained in its movements vis-à-vis the DM if the peseta is close to its ERM limit, since the pound is constrained vis-à-vis the peseta.

6. The gradual improvement in credibility that characterizes the post-1987 era also characterizes the three shorter-term ERM participants, Portugal, Spain, and the United Kingdom.

7. While the hypothesis of a unit root cannot typically be rejected at standard significance levels for the six macroeconomic variables we consider (in log-differential form), this is not true of either the mean of g or the degree of exploited monetary independence. Thus conventional cointegration techniques cannot be used to investigate the relationships between macroeconomic variables and credibility. Still, any *steady-state* relationship between g and the regressors should be easy to detect with this quasi-cointegrating regression.

8. If the covariance matrix were estimated with an instrumental variables technique to take account of any generated regressor effects, our negative results would almost surely be strengthened.

9. This finding is consistent with the less formal work of Eichengreen and Wyplosz (forthcoming), who show that Italy was the only clear case of an EMS country that suffered a decline in competitiveness before the currency crisis.

10. This indicates that our use of a panel data set may reconcile our results with the more positive findings of Caramazza (1993), who analyzes an analogue to Equation 4 with French time-series data.

11. As mentioned in Footnote 10, the macroeconomic variables appear to have unit roots; in fact, they also typically appear to be close to individual random walk processes. Thus, first differencing the data roughly transforms the data from levels to innovations. The negative results of the first-differenced VAR can thus be interpreted as an absence of strong links between credibility and macroeconomic news.

12. As suggested by Chen and Giovannini (1994), we also included (lags of) the time from the latest realignment in our regressions. The null hypothesis that the cumulative impact of (lags of) time from the latest realignment is zero cannot be rejected in our panel regressions at even the .1 significance level.

13. The volatility of expected exchange rate drift also appears to have few statistically significant cumulative effects on the six macroeconomic variables.

14. Eichengreen and Wyplosz (forthcoming) argue that the currency crisis stemmed in part from doubts about the likelihood of EMU, as do the Commission of the European Communities (1993) and the Group of Ten (1993). However,

Froot and Rogoff (1991: 270) contend that faster transition to EMU is *more* likely to destabilize the EMS, stating "Intra-EMS interest-rate differentials might begin rising sharply as union draws closer."

15. On page 64 of the April 4 issue, *The Economist* stated, "The biggest threat to [Maastricht] ratification comes from Denmark. Opinion polls suggest that a slight majority will vote no in the June referendum." Much closer to the referendum date, the same magazine stated on page 58 of the May 23 issue, "Ordinary Danes will have their own chance to vote on the treaty in a referendum on June 2nd. Opinions polls show them equally divided for and against."

16. Economist Intelligence Unit. *Country Report: Italy* 1992, 3: 7. On August 24, 1992, the Economist Intelligence Unit wrote:

> Exchange rate stability will be maintained -- The lira is currently overvalued against the Deutschemark on purchasing parities and there have been constant rumours of a lira devaluation. Pressure on the lira, which was trading close to its floor with the Deutschemark in July, was relieved, as investor confidence was restored. The Bank of Italy is committed to exchange rate stability as the cornerstone of its general economic policy . . . the government remains committed to maintaining its central rate within the ERM and will allow interest rates to rise if it shows signs of further decline. . .
>
> A devaluation is extremely unlikely. In this context, a devaluation would be resisted by the central bank, as well as by the government. . . . A positive result in the French Maastricht referendum would give a new fillip to monetary integration and diminish fears that Italy will renege on its convergence commitments. However, if the European project is derailed by popular opposition, then a new run on the lira can be expected, reviving the devaluation option, but only, in that event, within an EMS realignment.

In its *Country Report: France* (1992, 3: 7) issued on July 17, the Economist Intelligence Unit (EIU) stated: "The EIU foresees no marked weakening of the franc against the Deutschemark in 1992 and 1993, provided German monetary policy is tightened no further." In its *Country Report: Germany* (1992, 3: 12) issued August 4, the same institution claimed that through the fact that the Lombard rate was unchanged on July 16, "the Bundesbank has offered the prospect of stability in money market rates and within the Exchange Rate Mechanism, at least in the short term."

17. Even a week earlier, there was little comment in the public press about European currencies; the Foreign Exchange section of the *Wall Street Journal* on August 18 stated that "a lack of news kept most major currency players sidelined." The Group of Ten (1993) lists eight events from June 2, 1993 (the beginning of the chronology) to August 27, compared with over 70 afterward.

18. But *The Economist*'s "Economic Focus" column tackled the subject of exchange market efficiency. Even more ironically, on May 16 the same magazine wrote an article asking "could sterling aspire to replace the D-mark as the ERM's anchor currency?" (page 29).

References

Caramazza, Francesco. "French-German Interest Rate Differentials and Time-Varying Realignment Risk." *International Monetary Fund Working Paper Series* 1993, 1.

Chen, Zhaohui, and Giovannini, Alberto. "Estimated Expected Exchange Rates Under Target Zones." *National Bureau of Economic Research Working Paper Series* 1992, 3, 995.

Chen, Zhaohui, and Giovannini, Alberto. "The Determinants of Realignment Expectations Under the EMS: Some Empirical Regularities." *London School of Economics Financial Markets Group Discussion Paper* 1994, 184.

Commission of the European Communities. *XXVIth General Report on the Activities of the European Communities 1992.* Brussels: European Community, 1993.

"Denmark's Maastricht Vote." *The Economist* May 23, 1992, 58.

"Dollar Ends Lower as Yen Remains in Demand for Repatriation of Assets." *Wall Street Journal,* August 18, 1992, C15 (E).

"Economics Focus: Currency Markets." *The Economist* September 5, 1993, 81.

Economist Intelligence Unit. *Country Report: France* 1992, 3.Economist Intelligence Unit. *Country Report: Germany* 1992, 3.

Economist Intelligence Unit. *Country Report: Italy* 1992, 3.

Eichengreen, Barry, and Wyplosz, Charles. "The Unstable EMS." *Brookings Papers on Economic Activity* (forthcoming).

"Eurobuzz: Post Maastricht Tension." *The Economist* April 4, 1992, 64.

Flood, Robert A., and Rose, Andrew K. "Fixing Exchange Rates: A Virtual Quest for Fundamentals." *Institute for International Economic Studies Seminar Paper* 1992, 529.

Froot, Kenneth A., and Rogoff, Kenneth. "The EMS, the EMU, and the Transition to a Common Currency." *National Bureau of Economic Research Macroeconomics Annual* 1991, 6: 269-317.

Froot, Kenneth A., and Thaler, Richard H. "Anomalies: Foreign Exchange." *Journal of Economic Perspectives* 1990, 4 (3): 179-192.

Group of Ten. *International Capital Movements and Foreign Exchange Markets.* Included in, "A Report to the Ministers and Governors by the Group of Deputies." April 1993, unpublished.

Koen, Vincent R. "Testing the Credibility of the Belgian Hard Currency Policy." *International Monetary Fund Working Paper Series* 1991, 79.

Lindberg, Hans, Svensson, Lars E.O., and Söderlind, Paul. "Devaluation Expectations: The Swedish Krona 1981-1991." Institute for International Economic Studies Seminar Paper 1991, 495.

Meese, Richard A. "Currency Fluctuations in the Post-Bretton Woods Era." *Journal of Economic Perspectives* 1990, 4 (1): 117-134.

Rose, Andrew K., and Svensson, Lars E.O. "Expected and Predicted Realignments." *Scandinavian Journal of Economics* 1995, 97(2).

Rose, Andrew K., and Svensson, Lars E.O. "European Exchange Rate Credibility Before the Fall." *European Economic Review* 1994, 38(6).

"Sterling Stuff." *The Economist.* May 16, 1992, 29.

Svensson, Lars E.O. "Assessing Target Zone Credibility." *European Economic Review* 1993, 37: 763-802.

Svensson, Lars E.O. "Why Exchange Rate Bands? Monetary Independence in Spite of Fixed Exchange Rates." *Journal of Monetary Economics* 1994, 33: 157-199.

Political Biases in Fiscal Policy: Reconsidering the Case for the Maastricht Fiscal Criteria

Giancarlo Corsetti and Nouriel Roubini[1]

This paper reconsiders the arguments for binding fiscal and budget rules such as those implied by the Maastricht Treaty fiscal criteria for a monetary union in Europe. Given the concern in Europe about "excessive" budget deficits caused by political biases in fiscal policy, we consider in a theoretical framework the trade-off between rules and discretion in fiscal policy in the presence of politically motivated fiscal deficits. We discuss the role of a political bias when deficits are motivated by economic shocks such as recessions and in economies which are open to international trade in assets and goods. We find that endowing politically biased governments with the ability to respond to economic shocks with deficit finance will not exacerbate the existing political biases. In an open economy, the ability to borrow abroad will significantly increase the deficit. However, restrictions to public foreign borrowing will not reduce the political bias as long as the private sector has access to international capital markets at the same terms as the government. The analysis suggests that a certain degree of fiscal discretion might be beneficial and that Maastricht type of rules might impose excessive constraints on the behavior of fiscal authorities.

1. Introduction

The emergence and persistence of large public sector budget deficits in many industrial and developing countries has generated a widespread concern that policy makers may be too keen on resorting to "excessive" deficit financing without good economic reasons. The concern is grounded in many historical examples when large fiscal deficits have occurred in the absence of transitory cyclical downturns (such as recessions) or transitory spending shocks (such as wars or natural disasters), examples which are difficult to reconcile with traditional theories of optimal fiscal borrowing. Moreover, a growing body of literature, at both theoretical and empirical levels, argues that political biases in fiscal policy are at the root of the tendency of governments to run "excessive" fiscal deficits.

In Europe, the framers of the Maastricht Treaty on monetary union were so concerned with the possibility of "excessive deficits" that they introduced strict rules limiting the size of national debt and deficits, to be satisfied as precondition for the admission of a country to the monetary union. The so called "fiscal convergence" criteria limit the budget deficit to be below 3% of GDP and the gross public debt to be below 60% of GDP. Considering that public investment expenditures average 3% of GDP in the EC, the deficit criterion implicitly amounts to a current balanced budget rule, i.e. the current revenues should equal current expenditure.

Another dimension of the concern about excessive government borrowing regards the external balance implications of fiscal deficits. In the United States, large fiscal deficits in the 1980s have been financed through foreign borrowing. Budget deficits have been associated with current account deficits that turned the U.S.A. in a debtor country. In Europe, the concern that the growing liberalization of international capital markets might increase the governments' incentive to borrow led the Delors Committee to recommend limits to the ability of governments to finance fiscal deficits through foreign borrowing. While such a recommendation was not explicitly included among the Maastricht fiscal convergence criteria, there are indirect references to it in the Treaty. The Treaty implicitly suggests that countries found to be having "excessive deficits" might be restricted in their ability to borrow from abroad.[2]

As discretion in policy making may lead to public debt and deficits in excess of what is desirable, should policy makers be subject to rules constraining their ability to borrow? Specifically, do rigid fiscal rules such as those imposed by the Maastricht Treaty (that severely restrict the ability of governments to run budget deficits and may potentially limit their ability to finance them in international markets) make economic sense?

This paper re-considers the case for fixed versus flexible fiscal rules, reflecting on the main issues at stake in this fiscal version of the on-going debate between supporters of rules versus discretion. Our analytical framework is a model of political bias in fiscal deficit and debt appropriately developed to allow for a tax-smoothing motivation for fiscal deficits; we consider both a closed economy and an cconomy open to external trade in goods and financial assets, and carry out some numerical simulations of our model.

Our main results are the following:

1. Allowing politically biased governments the flexibility of running budget deficits for tax-smoothing purposes will not lead to an exacerbation of the already existing deficit bias.
2. As long as politically biased governments do not default on their debt, the will behave as tax-smoothers in the presence of output shocks.
3. The size of the deficit due to a political bias towards current spending increases significantly in an open economy relative to a closed one. What drives this result is the slope of the supply curve in the capital markets.
4. The larger budget deficits in an open economy will be matched, almost one to one, by current account deficits and external debt accumulation.
5. When the private sector has access to international capitals under the same conditions as the public sector, limiting the ability of the government to borrow abroad has no effects on the deficit bias of the government.

6. If there are interest differentials penalizing private international borrowing, the political bias of a partisan benevolent government is reduced, but to a very limited extent.

The scheme of the paper is the following. In section 2 we present a survey of the theoretical and empirical literature on the economic and political determinants of fiscal deficits. In section 3 we contrast political equilibria and tax smoothing equilibria in a model of partisan fiscal deficits and debt. We allow for the public endowment to vary over time, so that a benevolent government would have an incentive to smooth tax rates and run fiscal deficits or surpluses. Since closed form solutions to the government non-linear problem are not available, we resort to numerical simulations to measure the size of these political biases. Next, in section 4, we look at a small open economy. In this case, we are interested in the size of the deficits when we allow intertemporal trade with the rest of the world as opposed to a closed-economy; we derive again some numerical results. Section 5 will present some concluding normative remarks.

2. Survey of the Theoretical and Empirical Literature on the Economic and Political Determinants of Fiscal Deficits

What are the determinants of fiscal deficits and public debt? Are fiscal deficits determined mostly by economic factors or are there any political biases in fiscal policy? In this section we will present a brief survey of the literature on the determinants of fiscal deficits as a way to motivate the theoretical model presented in the next section.

Keynesian theories of output stabilization advocate the use of deficit financing as an instrument of demand management, thus predicting a strongly countercyclical behavior of the deficit. Neoclassical theories of public sector deficits, such as tax smoothing, see government borrowing as the outcome of optimizing decisions by benevolent policy-makers trying to minimize the efficient cost of distortionary taxation over time. According to this approach, it is not optimal to raise tax rates when revenues are temporarily low because of a recession or when spending is temporarily high. Rather, tax rates should be smooth over time, allowing for public deficits to emerge in case of temporary output and spending disturbances.

The neoclassical view of budget deficits has been recently challenged by a body of empirical and theoretical work. For example, the theory has a hard time in explaining the large and persistent U.S. deficits since 1982. Additional empirical studies fail to find evidence of tax smoothing and optimal seigniorage for a number of OECD countries in the 1970s and 1980s: in particular, there often occur sizable deficits which cannot be explained by transitory shocks to output or spending.

An indirect argument against tax smoothing is also given by the finding that, in a number of European countries, the present path of fiscal policies does not seem to be consistent with long term solvency of the public sector. The results of formal econometric testing of solvency (see Corsetti and Roubini, 1991 and 1993) are reinforced by indicators of fiscal stance such as "primary gaps", which give an assessment of the size of fiscal adjustment required to avoid a rising debt to GDP ratio (Blanchard, 1990; Buiter, Corsetti and Roubini, 1993). In several European countries, these primary gaps are very large.

Faced with a growing evidence that deficits are often too large with respect to their optimal level from either a Keynesian or a neoclassical perspective, many authors have started to explore the role of political distortions in explaining actual fiscal policy making. A recent yet growing literature elaborated the idea that political distortions may lead governments to follow systematic policies of excessive borrowing. There are at least five classes of political models of fiscal deficits: 1. the public choice approach (Buchanan); 2. models of government weakness and decentralized government; 3. distributional conflicts models; 4. models of strategic public debt choice; 5. political business cycle models.[3]

The findings of the empirical literature testing the above models are very encouraging. Using a panel of 15 OECD countries, Roubini and Sachs, 1989a and 1989b, find that political instability, as proxied by variables such as average duration and government weakness (including dummy variables for single party majority, presidential, presidential with divided government, multi-party coalition and minority governments), leads to higher real inflation-adjusted budget deficits. Following up the study by Roubini and Sachs, 1989a and 1989b, Alesina, Cohen and Roubini, 1992 and 1993, also include in the regression model electoral factors (such as those stressed by the political business cycle theory) and partisan variables. They find evidence that, after controlling for economic factors and political 6instability, the deficit is indeed affected by partisan and electoral factors: left-wing governments tend to run larger fiscal deficits than right-wing ones and deficits are larger in electoral years.

Grilli, Masciandaro and Tabellini, 1991 have tested the effects of both government strength and the duration of political coalitions on fiscal deficits in European countries, while Von Hagen, 1993, shows the role of legislative fiscal rules in contributing to fiscal policy biases in several European countries. Concerning the United States, Poterba, 1993, finds evidence of partisan biases in fiscal deficits at the level of U.S. states. Moreover, the large U.S. deficits of the last 12 years have been partly imputed to the effects of "divided government" (see McCubbins, 1990, Fiorina, 1990). Finally, a political bias towards excessive deficits and its external balance implications appear to be very relevant for developing countries. Evidence provided by Edwards and Tabellini, 1991, and Roubini, 1991, for a sample of developing countries suggests that political instability is associated with excessive fiscal deficits in the 1960-1982 period. In this respect, if the bias towards excessive deficits is exacerbated by the ability to borrow internationally: the internationalization of the world capital markets in the 1970s might have caused part of the excessive accumulation of foreign debt that eventually resulted in the debt crisis of the eighties.

Regarding seigniorage revenues and inflation rates, Alogouskoufis and Philippopoulos, 1991, find partisan government effects on the inflation rates in

Greece, which contribute to explain the high level of nominal deficit in that country. Similarly, Alesina and Roubini, 1992, and Alesina, Cohen and Roubini, 1992 and 1993, find partisan and political business cycle effects on inflation rate for a large set of OECD countries. Cukierman, Edwards and Tabellini, 1992, find significant effects of political instability on seigniorage revenues while Ozler and Roubini, 1993, find evidence of two-way causality between political instability and inflation in a large panel data set.

In summary, the available empirical evidence stresses the importance of political factors in explaining the size of the deficits (as well as seigniorage and inflation rates) for many industrial and developing countries. The growing awareness of the fiscal aspects of political distortions has led to the normative suggestion that fiscal policy should be subject to rules restraining the ability of governments to run budget deficits.

As the strong evidence on the presence and the effects of a political bias towards excessive borrowing gets more and more attention in both the scientific and the political arenas, it is important to assess the case for the most frequently proposed solutions to the problem, namely constitutionally mandated balanced budget rules and rigid limits to deficits such as those contained in the Maastricht Treaty. In this paper we will therefore re-consider, within a theoretical framework, the case for rules versus discretion in fiscal policy making in the presence of political distortions. Rigid rules prevent policy makers from responding to political incentives to run deficits; however, they also eliminate the possibility of using an important tool to stabilize output (according to the Keynesian view) and/or to smooth tax distortions over time. The model that we will present in the next section will focus on the second motive for deficit financing, developing the analytical framework by Alesina and Tabellini, 1990, so as to allow for a non-smooth endowment and international trade of goods and assets. In the original formulation of their model, these authors consider a closed deterministic economy with a constant opportunity set over time. Under these conditions, a benevolent non partisan government would balance the budget and 8spend on the whole spectrum of public goods in every period. Compared to this solution, the political equilibrium in the presence of partisan governments with uncertain perspectives of re-election is characterized by an initial fiscal deficit. This is because, when the probability of re-election decreases, the party in power will increase current expenditure on its preferred public goods so as to leave less room for future public spending on less preferred public goods.

Our model considers an economy where the opportunity set varies deterministically over time, thus providing an important motive for the optimal use of fiscal deficits and surpluses to smooth tax-related distortions over time. As a benevolent non partisan government will smooth taxes and spending balancing the budget in average, will the bias towards excessive borrowing of a partisan policy-maker be exacerbated by its ability to borrow for tax smoothing purposes? Within our framework of analysis, provided that the public sector is always solvent, a politically biased government will also smooth taxes, and the deficits will move counter-cyclically around a positive average. We will also argue that the degree of tax smoothing will not be significantly affected by the degree of the political bias.

Given that most European countries are very open and able to borrow in international capital markets, it is important to analyze whether the bias towards fiscal deficits is increased in an open economy. Therefore, we also consider the open economy implications of a model with "excessive deficits". Compared to a political equilibrium in a closed economy, we will analyze two issues: first, how the ability of governments to borrow from abroad affects the bias towards deficits; second, whether limitations to the governments' ability to borrow internationally such as those advocated by the Delors Committee might affects the deficit bias.

In the following section, we address both positive and normative questions in a closed economy with a non-smooth endowment; the open economy issues are next addressed in section.

3. Politically Biased Fiscal Deficits in a Closed Economy

The first issue we address is the behavior of a partisan government with uncertain perspective of re-election when the economy opportunity set is not constant over time. For the sake of simplicity, we consider deterministic variations of the economy-wide endowment, instead of shocks to productivity or tastes - the basic insight will nonetheless be the same as in a stochastic model.

We begin by looking at the simplest possible amendment to the two-period model by Alesina and Tabellini, 1990, hereafter AT, in the form of some initial government endowment, not necessarily positive, known by the players. The two periods are defined time 0 and time 1.

The economy is populated by a large number of atomistic individuals, all born at the beginning of the period zero and all sharing the same time-horizon. They are endowed with one unit of labor-time per period, which can be transformed in one unit of non-storable output. Utility is derived by consuming a private good C, leisure X and two kinds of public goods, g and f. Agents differ uniquely in their preferences regarding the optimal composition of public goods. As their utility is time separable, the i-th agent's maximization problem can be written as maximizing its lifetime utility subject to its intertemporal budget constraint:

$$\max_{C_0, X_0, X_1} \left[U(C_0) + V(X_0) + a^i h(g_0) + (1-a^i) h(f_0) \right] + \delta \left[U(C_1) + V(X_1) + a^i h(g_1) + (1-a^i) h(f_1) \right] \tag{1}$$

subject to

$$C_0 + qC_1 = (1-\tau_0)(1-X_0) + q(1-\tau_1)(1-X_1) \tag{2}$$

where q=1/(1+r) is the discount factor, with the real interest r endogenous in equilibrium, and τ_0 and τ_1 are tax rates on labor income. Equation (1) represents the intertemporal budget constraint: the present discounted value of lifetime consumption (left hand side of the equation) must be equal to the present discounted value of after-tax labor income.

The government is constrained to use a flat rate tax on labor income, identical for all agents but not across periods. It obviously decides the level and composition of public spending in terms of g and f, goods which can be transformed into each other at no cost. Deficits are financed by issuing a one-period discount bond, at the price q, paying b unit of output at the beginning of the following period. These bonds are not risky, i.e. the government will always honor its liabilities. We also assume that the initial stock of debt is zero, i.e. b = 0.

In this section of the paper, and differently from AT, we assume the existence of some initial public endowment, in the form of government resources exogenously given only at time 0 ($\varepsilon_0 = \varepsilon$). As in period 1 the exogenous endowment is zero (i.e. $\varepsilon_1 = 0$), we have the simplest framework to generate a tax-smoothing motive for the government. As shown below, such an initial endowment will imply that a social planner would find optimal to run a budget surplus in the first period, i.e. a balanced budget in each period would not be optimal.

Two parties compete for power. They are both concerned with private agents' utility stemming from consumption of the private good and leisure. However, they hold different views regarding the desirability of each particular public good. One party, hereafter R, is concerned only with spending on f; the other party, D, is concerned with spending on g. The party in office in the first period, say the party D, faces a probability of re-election equal to P, exogenously given. Thus the probability that the other party, R, come to power in the second period is (1-P).

Under the assumption that the objective function of the party in office is time-separable, we can separate out the maximization problem into two steps: the first step (intra-temporal problem) solves the problem of choosing tax-rates as well as level and composition of spending for a given deficit; the second step (intertemporal problem) looks at the problem of choosing an optimal borrowing pattern. Since we are more concerned with the intertemporal pattern of borrowing, we will only sketch the intra-temporal problem and focus on the optimal borrowing decision. Regarding the first problem, it should be clear that, since both parties hold extreme views about public spending, party D will spend uniquely on the good g, party R only on good f. Thus, for a given deficits, both parties will choose the same tax rate and the same level of spending, although on different public goods. In particular, the party in office will maximize its single period utility subject to a market allocation constraint, the resource constraint and its own flow budget constraint.

In order to consider the intertemporal borrowing problem, we first define the one period indirect utility for the party in office as R^e $(b_t, b_{t+1}, \varepsilon)$ and the one period indirect utility for the party not in office as R^n $(b_t, b_{t+1}, \varepsilon)$. These indirect utilities will be a function of both the initial and the end-of-period stock of debt (b_t and b_{t+1}), as well as the government endowment ε. They give the maximum level of utility that a government can achieve, for a given pattern of deficit and endowment. The indirect utility $R^e(.)$ is increasing in the level of end-of-period debt b_{t+1}, decreasing in the initial debt b_t. Intuitively, running a higher deficits allows the party in office to achieve a higher level of utility by increasing spending on its own preferred public good without generating tax-related distortions. Conversely, for any given level of end-of-period debt, a larger initial debt b_t will reduce the utility of the party in office, since the need to service the debt will force the government to spend less and/or tax more.

Then, by making use of the one-period indirect utility function, the policy problem faced by the incumbent party can be written as the problem of choosing the optimal end-of-period debt level so as to maximize its own expected utility over the relevant time horizon. In a two period model where $b_0 = 0$ (by assumption) and $b_2 = 0$ (by public sector solvency: the economy cannot end with positive public debt), we have:

$$V^e(b_1) = \underset{b_1}{Max} \{R^e(0, b_1, \epsilon) + \delta[PR^e(b_1, 0, 0) + (1-P)R^n(b_1, 0, 0)]\} \tag{3}$$

Intuitively, in deciding how much debt b_1 to leave to the next government, the incumbent party will consider the likelihood of still being in power in the future - with probability P. This probability is important in assessing the disutility stemming from a current deficit, in terms of future higher distortionary taxation and/or reduced spending on g_1. The optimal b_1 is chosen so that the incumbent government is indifferent, at the margin, about leaving or not an extra dollar of debt. The first order conditions of this problem can be conveniently rewritten as follows:

$$(\lambda_0-\lambda_1)U'(C_1)+\lambda_0 U''(C_1)\frac{dC_1^*}{db_1}b_1 = (1-P)h'(g_1^*)\frac{dg_1^*}{db_1} \tag{4}$$

where λ_0 and λ_1 are the Lagrange multipliers associated with the government budget constraint at time 0 and 1, respectively - which are the shadow prices of resources in public hands in the two periods. Consider first the case of a party which will be reappointed with probability one (P=1). The optimal debt condition (4) becomes

$$(\lambda_0-\lambda_1)U'(C_1)+\lambda_0 U''(C_1)\frac{dC_1^*}{db_1}b_1 = 0. \tag{5}$$

In a smooth environment, i.e. $\varepsilon = 0$, this condition would be satisfied with $\lambda_0 = \lambda_1$ and $b_1 = 0$. The government would keep tax and spending rate constant across periods. With a non smooth endowment (i.e. $\varepsilon \neq 0$) the solution just described does not apply. With a balanced budget, the lagrange multipliers associated with the government budget in the two periods will differ. For example, if $\varepsilon < 0$, the lagrange multiplier will be larger in the first period ($\lambda_0 > \lambda_1$). It follows that condition (5) cannot be satisfied by $b_1 = 0$. Instead, in the presence of a negative endowment shock, it will be optimal to run a budget deficit ($b_1 > 0$) of the appropriate size.

This argument makes it clear that, even without uncertainty about re-appointment, a negative initial public endowment will lead the party in office to run a deficit, while a positive initial public endowment will induce a budget surplus. The tax smoothing behavior of the policy makers implies that a fiscal balance in each period is not optimal whenever output and endowment shocks occur.

In the presence of electoral uncertainty, we know from AT that parties representing extreme constituencies, i.e. interested only in good g or in good f, tend to use debt strategically when facing uncertain re-appointment: the size of the budget deficit at the end of the first period is decreasing in the probability of re-appointment. The presence of a non-smooth endowment poses two additional questions. First, there is the question of whether all governments, regardless of their reelection probability, will smooth tax rates when facing a variable endowment. In other terms, will all governments, regardless of their reelection probability, respond to a positive endowment shock with a larger surplus (or a smaller deficit)? Second, there is the question of how the propensity to tax-smoothing changes for parties with different probability of re-election. Would a government with a lower re-election probability have a smaller incentive to smooth tax rates and spending in the presence of endowment/output disturbances?

The first question implies considering the effect on the end-of-period debt of a change in the government endowment, regardless of the probability of re-appointment (i.e. $db_1/d\varepsilon$). The second question implies considering how the derivative $db_1/d\varepsilon$ changes as the probability of reelection P changes. An unambiguous analytical answer to these questions would involve very strong restrictions on the parameters of our problem. In order to sign $db_1/d\varepsilon$ and its derivative with respect to P, we therefore resort to a numerical simulation, where the single period utility is assumed to be quadratic and additive in public and private consumption and leisure.

The simulation results, shown in Table 1, compare the fiscal deficit (in level and as a share of GDP) that would be chosen by partisan governments facing different probabilities of re-election, under two circumstances: one where the initial public endowment is equal to zero and the other when the initial endowment ε is positive and equal to 0.1. There are three main sets of results. First, consider the political bias towards excessive borrowing. Regardless of ε, columns (a) through (d) show that, as the probability of reelection P is falling, the government will choose to increase its first period fiscal deficit (or reduce its fiscal surplus) both in absolute terms and as a share of GDP. For example when $\varepsilon = 0$, (column (a)), the fiscal balance goes from zero to a deficit of 0.053 (13.09 % of GDP) as the reelection probability falls from 1 to 0.83.

Second, the table shows that when the initial public endowment ε is positive, the government runs larger initial budget surplus (or lower deficits) compared to the case where ε is zero. This can be seen by reading the table along its rows. The result implies that an increase in the initial endowment of the party in office will lead to an increased surplus (or reduced deficit), regardless of the probability of reappointment. This result is intuitive because, while a government with reelection probability lower than one might have an overall deficit bias, it will still smooth taxes in the presence of output disturbances. It might be helpful to point out that the problem faced by a government uncertain about its reelection is equivalent to the problem faced by an optimizing government with a higher rate of time preferences relative to future public spending.

Third, in columns (e) and (f), we show the response to a fall in the probability P of the difference between the fiscal balance for a zero and a positive ε. This difference can be read as a measure of the extent of tax smoothing as P is falling. The absolute difference between the two fiscal balances (column (e)) is relatively insensitive to changes in P: as P falls from 1 to 0.83, the difference in absolute deficits increases marginally from 0.0326 to 0.0337. Conversely, column (f) shows that the difference in fiscal balances as a share of GDP is actually falling as the probability of reelection is reduced: it goes from 9.05% of GDP for P=1 to 8.00% for P=0.83. The different results in columns (e) and (f) are due to the movement of GDP vis a vis a change in the endowment and government policies. The results in columns (e) and (f) are also presented in Figure 1. Both columns (e)-(f) and Figure 1 suggest that, in our example, the deficit differential is quite flat and insensitive to the value of the re-election probability. In other words, two governments with very different reelection probability will respond to changes in endowment ε in a similar way: they will both improve (worsen) their fiscal balance by a similar amount if they observe a positive (negative) endowment shock. Allowing governments that have a political bias to use deficits to smooth taxes is not going to exacerbate such a political bias: government with different P will respond similarly to an endowment shock.

How general are these results, i.e. is it likely that the derivative $db_1/d\varepsilon$ is insensitive to changes in P in more general functional specifications? In other terms, is the magnitude of tax-smoothing in the presence of endowment/output shocks likely to be affected by the re-election probability in more general setups? While this probability affects the average level of the deficit, the analysis above suggests that politically biased governments will also smooth taxes. The extent to which the deficit will fluctuate around the positive politically-rooted average will depend on the intertemporal elasticity of substitution characterizing the utility function. As this decreases, the tax-smoothing component of the deficit (surplus) becomes less sensitive to the probability of re-election.

4. Small Open Economy

An important equilibrium characteristic of the model discussed in the preceding section is the presence of an upward sloping supply curve faced by the ruling government in the capital market. In a closed economy, any attempt by the

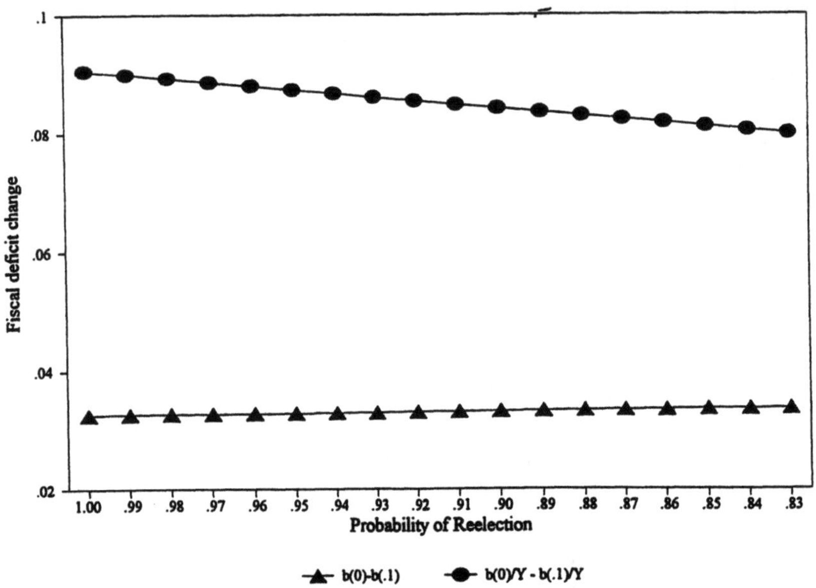

Figure 1: Fiscal deficit and election probability

government to finance current public consumption by borrowing must necessarily modify the intertemporal price of private consumption, changing the interest rate. An interesting question is then what would be the implications of a flatter supply curve in the capital market, as the economy opens up to trade in financial assets and commodities. Would the deficit bias be greater? The major change in the analysis consist of replacing the period by period resource constraints with an intertemporal one, for both households and the government sector. Also, as a convenient benchmark case is that of a country which is small in the world economy (infinite supply elasticity), the interest rate can be taken as exogenously given at some level r equal to the private sector discount rate ($1/\delta$ -1).

Define b_t as the public debt held by domestic agents, b_t^g as the public debt held by foreigners and b_t^p as the foreign liabilities of the private sector. The resource constraint of the economy is:

$$1-X_t+\epsilon_t-(C_t+g_t+f_t) = -(q_t b^p_{t+1}-b^p_t)-(q_t b^g_{t+1}-b^g_t), \quad t = 0,1. \tag{6}$$

This expression is the familiar national income identity: the income produced by the country ($1 - X_t + \varepsilon_t$) minus private and public consumption ($C_t + g_t + f_t$) must be equal to the accumulation of net foreign assets of the country (i.e. the current account of the balance of payments). We assume that initial stocks of debt are zero ($b_0^p = b_0^g = 0$) and that the country is solvent so that $b_2^p = b_2^g = 0$.

The consumer problem is identical to that in the closed economy but now the discount factor $q = 1/(1+r)$ is constant at the exogenously given world rate of interest. As we assume that r is equal to the domestic rate of time preference, so that $q = \delta$, the private sector will always and fully smooth consumption of goods and leisure over time ($C_0 = C_1$ and $X_0 = X_1$).

Since the effect of uncertain perspectives of re-election is that of increasing the discounting of future spending on the public good preferred by the ruling party, the intertemporal problem faced by the government can be written as follows:

$$\max_{C,X,g} \{U(C_0) + V(X_0) + h(g_0)\} + \delta\left\{U(C_1) + V(X_1) + Ph\left[\frac{1+\epsilon-X_0-C_0-g_0}{\delta} + (1-C_1-X_1)\right]\right\} \quad (7)$$

subject to

$$C_0U'(C_0) + \delta C_1U'(C_1) = V'(X_0)(1-X_0) + \delta V'(X_1)(1-X_1) \quad (8)$$

where tax rates do not appear explicitly among the set of choice variables because we substituted the first order conditions for the consumer problem in the government budget constraint, and we used the resource constraint to eliminate g1. It is worth recalling that the competitive equilibrium with no borrowing constraint implies $C_0 = C_1$ as well as $X_0 = X_1$, i.e. complete smoothing over the lifetime of private consumption and leisure.

How would the access to international capital markets affect the deficit bias relative to the case of a closed economy? In a small open economy, the supply of capital in the financial markets is flat at the prevailing interest rate. Additional borrowing by the government affects the level of private consumption by increasing the magnitude of tax-related distortions implied by the service of the debt, but has no second order effects on the intertemporal profile of the competitive allocation. So, how does P affect the deficit bias in an open economy? The results of our numerical simulations are presented in Table 2, where the exercise in Table 1 has been extended to a comparison between a closed and an open economy. Consider first the first two columns of the table. Abstracting from the composition if spending, the first column illustrates the benchmark case of a non partisan benevolent government in a closed economy (P=1). With a constant opportunity set ($\varepsilon = 0$), both public consumption and tax rates are smooth over time and the deficit is zero. However, when the probability of re-election shrinks from 1 to .95, as shown in the second column, the intertemporal profile of public consumption tilts in favor of the first period while tax rates just do the reverse. The government now runs a deficit equal to 3.86% of GDP. Correspondingly, the interest rate raises from 5.26% in the first column to 6.46% in the second column. When the probability of re-election falls from 1 to .95, the tilt in public consumption is much more pronounced in the case of an open economy, as shown in columns 5 and 6. The budget deficit now becomes as high as 12.7% of GDP, which is three times the corresponding number in column 2 (3.86%). It should also be noticed that the public deficit (12.7% of GDP) almost completely translates into the current account deficit (12.3% of GDP).

The positive implication of the exercise is therefore that the access to international capital markets, by reducing the financial constraint of the government, increases the size of the deficit. It is important to stress that it is the slope of the supply schedule for capital, not the level of the interest rate, which produces this result. Consider a closed economy with partisan government. The political equilibrium implies a positive deficit and an interest rate higher than the discount rate. Suppose that by chance the prevailing interest rate in the international market is equal to the domestic equilibrium rate. What would be the effect of letting the economy borrow in the world capital market? An additional numerical simulation (not shown in table 2) confirms our intuitive conjecture: as the profile of private consumption becomes smooth over time, we have a sharp increase in the deficit corresponding to a more pronounced tilt in the intertemporal profile of public consumption. For the same parameter values of the second column in table 2, the deficit increases from 3.86% to more than 12% of GDP. Therefore, even if the interest rate in a closed economy partisan equilibrium is identical to the one in the open economy, the mere ability to borrow abroad leads to a much higher fiscal deficit in an open economy.

Another interesting question refers to the effects of limiting international borrowing by the government. Is the political bias towards excessive deficits lowered by such a rule? If both private agents and the public sector have access to international market at the same conditions, it is irrelevant whether the public sector borrow directly or through the private sector. This is the case implicitly considered in Table 2; in particular, we could restrict the government behavior by allowing it to borrow only domestically ($b^g = 0$). As long the private sector is allowed to borrow abroad, restricting the public sector ability to borrow externally does not affect at all the fiscal deficit bias of the government: the government would just borrow domestically the same amount and let the private sector borrow internationally whatever is needed. In this sense restrictions to external borrowing by the government, such as those recommended in the Delors Report and implied by the Maastricht sanctions, would be completely ineffective in a context where the ability of private agents to borrow internationally is not restricted.

The above observation is correct under the assumption that private and public agents borrow in international markets at the same rate. If this is not the case, a positive interest differential on private borrowing can effectively discourage the issue of public debt if the government is concerned with private sector utility, since it amounts to an implicit tax on private agents. Suppose that the public sector is not allowed to borrow internationally and suppose that there is a positive interest differential of about 2% between foreign private borrowing rates and domestic government borrowing rates. Then, simulation results suggests that the political equilibrium deficit shrinks very little, from 12.7% to 11% of GDP. In other terms, even after restricting the government to borrow at home only and allowing for a differential between private and public borrowing rates, the deficit bias of a government is not significantly affected in an open economy.

To sum up, we have argued that the size of the deficit due to a political bias towards current spending increases in an open economy with respect to a closed one. What drives this result is the slope of the supply curve in the capital markets. When the private sector can have access to international capitals under the same conditions of the public sector, limiting the ability of the government to borrow abroad has no effects on the political equilibrium allocation. If, however, there are interest differential penalizing private borrowing, the political bias of a partisan benevolent government is reduced, but to a very limited extent. The above results, while obtained by using numerical simulations, are quite general and robust to different parameter choices.

There are several caveats to the results we have illustrated above. First, the model we considered rules out the possibility of default on debt, both in open and closed economy; i.e. the commitment to honor debt obligations is perfectly credible. One might argue that governments, in particular governments subject to political bias, indeed consider default as a viable policy option. A formal model of default would require the consideration of a number of issues: the correct pricing of the default risk, the possibility of rationing in the capital markets, how parties representing different economic constituencies may have different attitudes towards using the default option (i.e. resorting to the taxation of capital and wealth) etc. The implications of the default option for the deficit bias is not trivial. On the one hand such an option increase the bias when shocks hit the economy since the government might be tempted to rely on greater deficit financing in the anticipation of a future default. On the other hand, rational agents and markets will price the default risk, making the access to credit more costly and/or more difficult.

Second, in the presence of a default risk, a government may be rationed in the international capital markets even without formal rules restricting its ability to borrow abroad. In the case of endogenous market rationing, it is likely that the private sector would also be credit-constrained at the international level. It might then not be realistic to assume that governments are unable to borrow while private agents are. If both the public and the private sectors are credit constrained in the international markets, the situation reverses to the above case of a closed economy in the presence of a default risk.

5. Conclusions

The analysis in the paper allows us to reconsider the arguments in favor of rigid constraints to the ability of solvent governments to borrow in order to finance fiscal deficits in closed and open economies. These arguments are at the core of the current policy debate in Europe on the validity of the rigid fiscal rules required by the Maastricht Treaty as preconditions for a monetary union.

In the presence of political biases, fiscal deficits and government debt will be positive even when it would be optimal to run zero fiscal balances. However, if there are shocks to output, tax-smoothing considerations imply that government surpluses/deficits would be optimal even if the government is not otherwise politically biased in its fiscal policy.

What are then the advantages and disadvantages of binding fiscal rules, such as a balanced budget amendment compared to a world where fiscal policy is completely discretionary? In the presence of output shocks, a discretionary political equilibrium leads to excessive deficits but allows governments to smooth tax rates. Compared to this discretionary political equilibrium, a binding balanced budget rule will avoid the political bias towards budget deficits that would occur with partisan governments but this rigid rule would not allow the smoothing of taxes that is optimal in the presence of transitory shocks and is feasible in the discretionary equilibrium. In fact, compared to the balanced budget regime, the discretionary political equilibrium allows for the possibility of smoothing tax rates in the presence of real transitory shocks, something ruled out by the balanced budget rule.

One of the common concerns expressed in Europe about allowing politically biased governments the flexibility of running deficits and smoothing tax rates in the presence of output shocks is that this would lead to an exacerbation of the already existing fiscal bias. One of the results of our analysis suggests that this should not be a concern: as long as politically biased governments do not default on their debt, they will behave like tax smoothers in the presence of output shocks. While deficits will be positive in the presence of a fiscal bias, the amount of deficit spending due to an output shock would not be different between a politically biased government and one that it is not; for a given interest rate, the two types of government would react to an output shock in the same way.

Our analysis also suggests that the political fiscal bias would be much larger in an open economy where the government is allowed to borrow internationally. In this sense the concerns expressed by the Delors Report regarding international financing of fiscal deficits are legitimate. Even if the interest rate in the world economy were identical to the equilibrium interest rate in a politically distorted closed economy, opening up the economy to international trade in assets would increase the political bias of the government. This is so because, in a closed economy the political bias is kept in check by the effects that a larger deficit has on the real interest rate and therefore on the tax distortions created by the deficit. In an open economy, instead, the real interest rate effects will not occur, the biased government will know that a deficit will create less tax distortions than in the case of a closed economy and will therefore be more prone to run fiscal imbalances.

Moreover, in a open economy, the larger fiscal deficits will be matched, almost one to one, by current account deficits. This result is consistent with evidence about the 'twin' fiscal and trade deficits in the U.S. and several European countries in the 1980s and the large fiscal and current account deficits and external debt accumulation observed in many developing countries in the 1970s and up to the onset of the debt crisis in 1982.

The concern that the ability to borrow internationally might lead to an exacerbated fiscal bias whenever there are political distortions has led to the policy suggestion (namely in the case of the debate about EMU) that governments should be restricted in their ability to borrow internationally. Our analysis, however, suggests that any such limits would be ineffective in reducing the fiscal bias if the private sector is allowed borrow internationally at the same terms as the government. Limits to international borrowing by a government would lead a biased government to borrow more domestically and let the private sector to smooth its consumption with foreign private borrowing. In the case in which the private sector cannot borrow internationally at the same rate as the public sector, the government fiscal bias would be reduced, but by an insignificant amount.

The analysis in the paper does not provide easy policy prescriptions. There are obvious tradeoffs between rules and discretion: the benefits of tax smoothing at the cost of a persistent political bias in a discretionary political equilibrium; the benefits of tying the hands of deviant governments with a balanced budget fiscal rule versus the cost of not allowing tax smoothing. In the absence of political biases, the presence of transitory output shocks implies that the optimal fiscal rule followed by a social planner would be one of full tax smoothing. This fully state contingent tax-smoothing rule would be first best and dominate both the discretionary political equilibrium and the balanced budget rule. Under certain conditions, such a first best rule might be enforceable through a reputational equilibrium in a world with alternating partisan parties. However, such a first best cooperative equilibrium might not be enforceable in a political equilibrium when the realization of the shock is subject to observational errors and potential cheating on the part of the ruling governments. In this case, a second best equilibrium might take the form of a "fiscal rule with an escape clause" (a flexible rule). Such a rule would impose a fiscal balance whenever the real shock is below a certain threshold and allow for tax-smoothing and fiscal deficits if the transitory disturbance is large enough.[4] However, the complexity of such a rule, in face of the need of simple, unambiguous and clearly understood fiscal rules, might also render this compromise between rules and discretion politically unfeasible. We leave to future analysis a formal treatment of the optimal degree of fiscal discretion.

Endnotes

1. We thank Barry Eichengreen, Jeffry Frieden, Andres Velasco and participants to the NYU Conference on Political Economy for helpful comments and suggestions.

2. In fact, one of the treaty sanctions against deviant countries would be the cutoff from loans made by the European Development Bank. Moreover, while the assessment of excessive deficits would be initially kept confidential, persistence in fiscally deviant policies would lead the European Community to make public its assessment of excessive deficits. This action would have the aim and effect of reducing the international rating of the debt of the deviant countries and therefore increase their cost and ability to borrow in international financial markets.

3. See Buchanan, Rowley, and Tollison (1986), Roubini and Sachs (1989a and 1989b), Cukierman and Meltzer (1989), Alesina and Drazen (1991), Alesina and Tabellini (1990), Tabellini and Alesina (1990), Nordhaus (1975), Rogoff (1990), Rogoff and Sibert (1989), Aghion and Bolton (1990), and Alesina, Ozler, Roubini, and Swagel (1992). Open Economy formulations of these models include Alesina and Tabellini (1989) and Velasco (1993). For a more systematic survey of this literature, see Corsetti and Roubini (1993) and Alesina and Perotti (1994).

4. For a more detailed discussion of these points, see Corsetti and Roubini (1993).

References

Aghion, P. and P. Bolton, "Government Debt and the Risk of Default: A Political Economic Model of the Strategic Role of Debt", in R. Dornbusch and M. Draghi eds. *Public Debt Management: Theory and Practice,* Cambridge University Press, 1990.

Alesina, A., G. Cohen and N. Roubini, "Macroeconomic Policy and Elections in OECD Economies", *Economics and Politics,* March, 1992.

Alesina, A., G. Cohen and N. Roubini, "Political Business Cycles in Industrial Economies", *European Journal of Political Economy,* 1993.

Alesina, A. and A. Drazen, "Why Are Stabilizations Delayed? A Political-Economic Model", *American Economic Review,* 1170-1188, 1991.

Alesina, A., S. Ozler, N. Roubini and P. Swagel, "Political Instability and Economic Growth", NBER W.P. No. 4173, September, 1992.

Alesina, A. and R. Perotti "The Political Economy of Budget Deficits", NBER W.P. No. 4637, February, 1994.

Alesina, A. and N. Roubini, "Political Cycles in OECD Economies", *Review of Economic Studies,* October, 1992.

Alesina, A. and G. Tabellini, "A Political Theory of Fiscal Deficits and Debt in a Democracy", *Review of Economic Studies,* July, 403-414, 1990.

Alesina, A. and G. Tabellini, "External Debt, Capital Flight and Political Risk", *Journal of International Economics,* 27: 199-220, 1989.

Ames, B, *Political Survival: Politicians and Public Policy in Latin America,* Berkeley: University of California Press, 1987.

Barro, R., "On the Determination of Public Debt", *Journal of Political Economy,* October, 87, 940-971, 1979.

Barro, R., "Government Spending, Interest Rates, Prices and Budget Deficits in the United Kingdom, 1730-1918", *Journal of Monetary Economics,* 1987.

Blanchard, O., "Suggestions for a New Set of Fiscal Indicators", OECD, Department of Economics and Statistics Working Papers, No.79, April, 1990.

Buchanan,.J.M., C.K. Rowley and R.D. Tollison, *Deficits,* New York: Basil Blackwell, 1986.

Buiter, W., G. Corsetti and N. Roubini, "Excessive Deficits: Sense and Non-Sense in the Treaty of Maastricht", *Economic Policy,* Spring, 1993.

Buiter, W. and K. Kletzer, "Reflections on the Fiscal Implications of a common currency", in Alberto Giovannini and Colin Mayer eds., *European Financial Integration,* Cambridge University Press, Cambridge, pp. 221-244, 1991.

Committee for the Study of Economic and Monetary Union (Delors Committee), *Report on Economic and Monetary Union in the European Community,* Luxembourg, 1989.

Corsetti, G. and N. Roubini, "Fiscal Deficits, Public Debt and Government insolvency: Evidence from OECD Countries", *Journal of Japanese and International Economies,* 5, 354-380, 1991.

Corsetti, G. and N. Roubini, "The Design of Optimal Fiscal Rules for Europe after 1992"; in Francesco Giavazzi and Francisco Torres (eds.) *Adjustment and Growth in the European Monetary Union,* Cambridge University Press, 1993.

Cukierman, Edwards and Tabellini, "Seigniorage and Political Instability", *American Economic Review,* 1992.

Cukierman, A. and Meltzer, "A Political Theory of Government Debt and Deficits in a Neo-Ricardian Framework", *American Economic Review,* 4, 713-732, 1989.

Fiorina, M., "An Era of Divided Government", in G. Peele et al. eds. *Developments in American Politics,* Oxford: Oxford University Press, 1990.

Grilli, V. D. Masciandaro and G. Tabellini, "Political and Monetary Institutions and Public Finance Policies in the Industrial Democracies", *Economic Policy,* 13, 342-392, 1991.

Hamilton, J.D. and M.A.Flavin, "On the Limitations of Government Borrowing: A Framework for Empirical Testing", *American Economic Review,* 76, 808-819, 1986.

Lucas, R. Jr. and N. Stokey, "Optimal Monetary and Fiscal Policy in an Economy without Capital", *Journal of Monetary Economics,* 12:55-94, January, 1983.

Mankiw, G., "The Optimal Collection of Seigniorage", *Journal of Monetary Economics,* 20, 1987.

McCubbins, M, "Party Governance and U.S. Budget Deficits: Divided Government and Fiscal Stalemate", in Alesina, A. and G. Carliner eds. *Politics and Economics in the 1980s.* Chicago: University of Chicago Press, 83-111, 1991.

Nordhaus, W., "The Political Business Cycle", *Review of Economic Studies,* 42, 169-190, 1975.

Ozler, S. and N. Roubini, "Economic and Political Determinants of Inflation Rates: An Empirical Investigation using a Panel Data Set", mimeo, Yale University, 1993.

Persson, T. and L. Svensson, "Why a Stubborn Conservative Would Run a Deficit: Policy with Time Inconsistent Preferences, *Quarterly Journal of Economics,* May, 325-346, 1989.

Poterba, J., "State Responses to Fiscal Crises: "Natural Experiments for Studying the Effects of Budgetary Institutions", mimeo, MIT, 1992.

Rogoff, K., "Equilibrium Political Budget Cycles", *American Economic Review,* 80, 21-36, 1988.

Rogoff, K. and A. Sibert, "Elections and Macroeconomic Policy Cycles" *Review of Economic Studies,* 55, 1-16, 1989.

Roubini, N., "Economic and Political Determinants of Budget Deficits in Developing Countries", *Journal of International Money and Finance,* 10, 549-572, 1991.

Roubini, N. and J. Sachs, "Political and Economic Determinants of Budget Deficits in the Industrial Democracies", *European Economic Review,* May, 903-933, 1989a.

Roubini, N. and J. Sachs, "Government Spending and Budget Deficits in the Industrial Countries", *Economic Policy,* 8, 99-132, 1989b.

Tabellini, G. and A. Alesina, "Voting on the Budget Deficit", *American Economic Review,* 80, 37-52, 1990.

Velasco, A. "Are Balance of Payments Crises Rational? A Dynamic Game Approach", mimeo, New York University, 1993.

Von Hagen, J., "Budgeting Procedures and Fiscal Performance in the European Communities", mimeo, May, 1992.

Fiscal Convergence Criteria, Factor Mobility, and Credibility in Transition to Monetary Union in Europe

Michael M. Hutchison and Kenneth M. Kletzer[1]

Economic efficiency considerations lead us to anticipate pressures for the development of a fairly extensive system of fiscal federalism under European Monetary Union. Given the divergent economic environments facing European Community members and the increasing degree of factor mobility, these pressures are likely to be significant. Fiscal unification could lead to sharing debt burdens for efficiency reasons when a portion of the shocks is permanent and taxes are distortionary. We argue that this expectation could undermine the credibility of "no-bailout" clauses of national government debts by the European Community-wide fiscal authority and central bank. Lack of credibility, in turn, provides an incentive to have excessive deficits. This points to the desirability of some form of fiscal convergence criteria as an entry condition to European Monetary Union.

1. Introduction

When the Maastricht summit was concluded in December 1991 with the signing of the Treaty on European Union by the 12 European Community (EC) members, enthusiasm for European unification was, at least temporarily, at its height. While the plan to reach full monetary union by the end of the 1990s has been jeopardized by subsequent events (notably the crisis in the Exchange Rate Mechanism), the timetable set out by the Maastricht treaty remains and a core group of EC members may indeed proceed. The Maastricht accord sets out several criteria of how monetary and fiscal policies should be coordinated in anticipation of the creation of a monetary union. Even if these particular criteria are modified, some conditions for entry into the European Monetary Union (EMU) will undoubtedly be entertained.

The fiscal convergence criteria are perhaps the most controversial of the EMU entry conditions. Criticisms or rationalizations for the constraints on public sector budget deficits and public debt agreed at Maastricht fall into three broad categories. The first is that deficit-financing and the issue of public debt by the government of one member affect interest rates and other relative prices for the entire union. This interdependence brought about by economic integration leads to efficiency and distributional reasons for fiscal policy coordination. The second is that with a single currency, the inflation costs of monetizing deficits are shared, and seignorage revenues for the entire union could potentially be spent to bail out a single member. This leads to a bias toward higher national deficits after creation of the EMU unless the new European central bank is truly independent of national fiscal authorities. One solution is to limit deficits outright, and another is to appoint central bankers known to care mainly about inflation. A third point is that a bias toward inefficiently large deficits may already exist for political reasons, and that monetary union is a convenient low-cost opportunity for adopting a constitutional limitation to counter these tendencies.

In this article, we argue that there are reasons based on economic efficiency considerations to anticipate pressures for the development of a fairly extensive system of fiscal federalism under EMU. Given the divergent economic environments facing EC members and the increasing degree of factor mobility, these pressures are likely to be significant. We argue that this expectation could undermine the credibility of "no-bailout" clauses of national government debts by the EC-wide fiscal authority and central bank. Lack of credibility, in turn, provides an incentive to have excessive deficits. This points to the desirability of some form of fiscal convergence criteria as an entry condition to EMU.

Our starting point is the observation that monetary union removes the ability of national governments to choose autonomous monetary policies to address asymmetric national or regional macroeconomic shocks. This places the burden for pursuing divergent macroeconomic stabilization policies on the national fiscal authorities. At the same time, the elimination of political, legal, and other institutional barriers to market integration reduces the ability of individual member governments to impose wide differences in future tax burdens by increasing the possibility of tax avoidance through factor mobility and accumulation. This restricts the scope for using deficit finance for tax-smoothing and stabilization when national incomes are subject to idiosyncratic shocks with permanent components. It also leads to potential efficiency gains using deficit-financed stabilization policies at the EMU level.

We show that national public debts outstanding at the time of fiscal unification generally influence the distributional impact of stabilization policies under a federal fiscal system. Further, fiscal unification might lead to sharing debt burdens for efficiency reasons when a portion of the shocks is permanent and taxes are distortionary. Finally, it is also possible that distributional concerns within the EMU could lead national governments to a priori anticipate that they alone will not repay the debts they incur. To many of its proponents, the creation of the EMU is a step toward the ultimate goal of the political unification of Europe, perhaps indicating greater concern over the income and wealth distribution among the EC member states.

Once governments anticipate that part of the debt they issue will probably be borne by other countries, they will tend to run deficits in excess of what is efficient. If this is the case, it means that the no-bailout clause of the treaty lacks credibility and the supplementary fiscal convergence criteria might make sense.

In the next section, we discuss the economic convergence criteria of the Maastricht treaty and the objectives they seem to reflect. In the following section, we critically review some of the rationalizations for the convergence criteria offered in the literature. In the next section, we give our argument for why there could be pressures for more fiscal federalism and the eventual sharing of preexisting debt repayment.

The argument we explore for why national governments might need to be restrained from running excessive deficits relies on the importance of asymmetric national or regional macroeconomic shocks in the EMU and of tax flight with the integration of European markets. Then we survey the empirical analysis of asymmetric versus symmetric aggregate supply and demand shocks for Europe. Next we discuss the empirical evidence on factor mobility, emphasizing labor mobility in light of the very high degree of financial capital mobility already achieved in Europe. The experience of labor mobility among the Nordic countries is discussed at length, since it offers an additional useful and interesting source of information to what is available in other surveys.

2. The Economic Convergence Criteria of the Maastricht Accord

The European governments agreed to four criteria of economic convergence across countries as conditions of entry into the EMU. These criteria were incorporated in the Maastricht accord out of the fear that the EMU may result in economic and social tensions without sufficient convergence of key macroeconomic quantities. The first of the four entry requirements stipulates that inflation rates among the member countries converge toward the inflation rates of the three members with the lowest inflation rates. The second condition is that nominal exchange rates be stable and without persistent pressure for realignment prior to formation of the EMU. The third is that nominal interest rates should converge. The fourth criterion imposes targets on the public sector budget deficits (at 3% of gross domestic product, GDP) and public debt (at 60% of GDP) of countries joining the EMU.

With respect to the fiscal criteria, the Maastricht treaty incorporated the recommendations of the Delors Report (1989) that formal binding rules should be imposed to limit the discretion of policymakers over the size of public sector deficits and debt and the manner in which they are financed. These recommendations were made because the Delors Commission worried that unless public sector budgetary policies were convergent, the EMU could lack economic and political stability. The Maastricht accord follows this spirit in setting out the principle, in Article 104c, that "Member States shall avoid excessive deficits," where the phrase, "excessive deficits," is defined in Article 2 of the protocol on the excessive deficit procedure (annexed to the treaty) as general government deficits exceeding 3% of GDP. Second, the protocol states that general government gross debt should not exceed 60% of GDP. The treaty also requires all members to honor the 3% budget deficit and 60% public debt reference values when the EMU is operating.

The fiscal reference values are not rigid, and the treaty allows a good deal of discretion in their application. Article 104c(a) states that a deficit might not be considered excessive if it has "declined substantially and continuously and reached a level that comes close to the reference value; or, alternatively, the excess over the reference value is only exceptional and temporary and the ratio remains close to the reference value." This caveat allows for the possibility of EMU entry by several EC member states that could not meet the rigid reference values in time without suffering significant contractions of domestic employment and incomes. This clause allows a country such as Italy to meet the entry criteria by reducing its deficit as a percentage of GDP over time at an "adequate" rate. What is "adequate" is not spelled out by the treaty and appears to be left to political negotiations within the EMU.

The requirement that the gross-public-debt-to-GDP ratio not exceed 60% can also be waived for entry. Article 104c(b) states that the level of government debt should not exceed 60% of GDP or must be "sufficiently diminishing and approaching the reference value at a satisfactory pace." Again, this allows an escape from the reference values for several countries with debt-to-GDP ratios well in excess of the benchmark, notably Belgium, Greece, Ireland, and Italy.

Article 104c also sets a formal procedure to be followed for determining if a country has an "excessive deficit." This is a fairly complex process that charges the European Commission with monitoring budget positions and writing a report for the European Council on a country failing to satisfy the debt or deficit reference values. This assessment takes into account the caveats of the treaty. A qualified majority of the European Council decides whether or not the country has an excessive deficit. If a country is found to be in violation after membership in the EMU, another complicated process for determining the penalties to be imposed is initiated.[2]

The criteria for inflation, exchange rates, and interest rates appear fairly well-accepted.[3] This may be because they are consistent with gradual transition to adopting a common currency and hence a smooth landing into the EMU. Prior convergence of inflation rates and stability of exchange rates are not necessary for inaugurating the EMU, but they do imply some smoothness in the process that may be consistent with maintaining the credibility of the EMU. The convergence of nominal interest rates is consistent with (1) the inflation and exchange rate criteria being met, (2) the very high degree of financial capital mobility within Europe already, and (3) the absence of differences in the default risk on government debt.

Eliminating differences in the default risk premia of public sector debt, implicit in the interest rate convergence criteria, implies some sort of constraints on the fiscal and financial plans of member governments. Even ignoring capital market imperfections and differences in the incidence of capital income taxes, nominal interest rate differentials may be large. They result from expected depreciation of the nominal spot exchange rate, currency risk, and sovereign default risk. The first two sources disappear after the country irrevocably fixes its exchange rate by joining the EMU. Since market participants might reduce the probability they place on a country joining the EMU if it has difficulty satisfying the fiscal convergence criteria, interest rate convergence could become difficult to attain as well. If the default risk premia on issues of public debt for a member state are large, then significant fiscal adjustment would be needed just to satisfy the interest rate convergence requirement.

The specific restrictions on public sector budget deficits and outstanding debt proposed, however, have been the subject of a number of criticisms.[4] Moreover, satisfying the three convergence criteria regarding the inflation rate, the nominal interest rate, and the exchange rate may make it more difficult to attain the deficit and debt entry conditions. In particular, meeting the inflation rate convergence criterion limits a country's ability to use seignorage to finance its fiscal deficit and reduce its debt ratio toward the reference value.

3. Is there a Motivation for Fiscal Convergence Criteria?

The Delors Report and the Maastricht treaty reflect a broad belief that, without binding fiscal rules, some or all of the member governments could be subject to a systematic bias toward excessive public sector borrowing. The argument that each member of a monetary union has an incentive to incur excessive deficits is based on the idea that a portion of the costs of large deficits would be borne by other member countries.

The costs of public sector deficit finance can be shared either indirectly or directly. Fiscal policies chosen by one government can have indirect welfare effects on other member states either by affecting international prices in an integrated economy or by influencing the policy decisions of the common central bank under monetary union. They are directly borne by other members when the possibility exists that some of the public debt of one country will be repaid by the other members. For example, when a country faces the prospect of having to default on part or all of its government debt, negative spillovers could lead other fiscal authorities or the central bank to bail it out.

3.1 Fiscal Spillovers and Externalities between Interdependent Economies

One set of arguments made in favor of imposing rules for fiscal discipline on member states of the EMU is based on the point that even if there is no risk of a government defaulting, national fiscal and financial policies create spillovers for other countries through international markets. Government expenditure, tax, and deficit-financing policies affect international prices (in particular, interest rates) through integrated goods and factor and financial markets. In an integrated international economy, when the government of one country borrows heavily to finance persistent public sector deficits, interest rates rise, adversely affecting all debtors. Rising world real rates of interest redistribute income and wealth from debtors to creditors. These spillovers are the consequence of fiscal policy interdependence in an integrated international economy. Efficiently coordinated national fiscal policies will take account of this interdependence and will generally differ from uncoordinated policies.

The literature on the fiscal consequences of European integration frequently refers to all of the effects of national budgetary policies on other countries through international interest rates and other relative prices as externalities (Bovenberg, Kremers, and Masson, 1991). Buiter and Kletzer (1991a, 1991b, 1992) systematically distinguish between spillovers of national government budgetary policies that are a consequence of general economic interdependence through market integration and those that are correctly labeled as externalities. That is, when national fiscal and financial policies affect international relative prices, in general both the distribution of welfare across countries and the efficiency of resource allocation are affected. Precisely identifying the sources of international spillovers of the fiscal and financial policies of solvent governments and distinguishing between their distributional and efficiency effects are helpful for an informative discussion of the need and place for policy intervention.

In the absence of Ricardian equivalence, an increase in the deficit for one country with no change in its path of public consumption and investment spending will tend to reduce national saving and put upward pressure on the world real interest rate. If all taxes and transfers are lump sum, then this shift in the timing of net taxes to provide for a given stream of public spending by one country does not impair allocative efficiency in a competitive equilibrium for an economy without preexisting distortions. The adverse impact on debtors and the benefit to creditors are purely distributional effects. Buiter and Kletzer (1991a) show that in a noncooperative equilibrium, governments will choose budgetary policies strategically in beggar-thy-neighbor fashion. They show that the coordination of national budgetary policies for solvent governments is unnecessary for achieving a Pareto optimum with respect to household welfare but is needed to attain an optimum with respect to national social welfare objectives when national authorities care about the distribution of welfare across households within their respective countries.[5]

If national governments impose distortionary (non-lump-sum) taxes (perhaps, because they are the only feasible taxes), then Ricardian equivalence still fails and deficit-financing by solvent governments affects the efficiency of resource allocation. This is a special case of redistribution with preexisting distortions. The general statement holds for lump-sum taxes and transfers as well when there are Keynesian market failures arising from insufficient or excessive effective demand, incomplete financial markets, externalities, or imperfectly competitive markets.

With preexisting distortions, Canzoneri and Diba (1991) and Buiter and Kletzer (1991a, 1991b, 1992) argue that coordination of national fiscal policies can lead to outcomes that are Pareto superior to those achieved in its absence. Canzoneri and Diba (1991) point out that if distortionary taxes are the only instruments available to the national fiscal authorities, then an increase in current deficits (without changing public consumption or investment spending on any date) implies higher future taxes with concomitant increases in the excess burden of taxation. With perfect international capital mobility, the increase in borrowing by one government leads to a rise in the real rate of interest paid by other governments to their creditors. In a noncooperative equilibrium, this leads to higher distortionary taxes in other countries and increases the excess burdens incurred by their residents. Because the individual country's residents do not suffer the entire efficiency loss of taxes at the margin, Canzoneri and Diba show that public debt and the excess burden of taxes are excessive when fiscal policies are uncoordinated. Allocative efficiency can be improved by selecting policies with lower deficits. Since empirical studies persistently find that relatively small fractions of GDP are lost to the excess burden of taxation, perhaps the redistribution of wealth brought about by the impact of deficit-financing on interest rates and other relative prices is of greater concern to policymakers.

The analysis of the spillovers and externalities caused by the fiscal policies of solvent national governments in an integrated economy implies the need for coordinating budgetary policies, distortionary tax rates, and levels of spending on public goods that provide benefits across borders (or on the reduction of international detrimental externalities).[6] But it does not yield any logical reason for setting the same fixed targets for public debt or deficits for all countries. Further, the presence of international spillovers or externalities does not imply that public debt and deficits are necessarily excessive when governments do not coordinate their policies. Deficit spending can just as well be insufficient as excessive in either competitive equilibrium or Keynesian models, so that upper limits on public sector borrowing are not an obvious way to implement a cooperative outcome. Cooperative fiscal policies in an integrated economy should be state-contingent and country-specific, but how depends on the objectives of coordination and the nature of shocks to the economy. The Maastricht treaty's opening for deviations from the debt and deficit reference values might be seen to allow for such contingencies but does not provide any guidance for the design or implementation of coordinated budgetary policies.

3.2 Central Bank Independence and Fiscal Spillovers in EMU

The effects of fiscal policies on interdependent economies through international prices arise because markets are integrated and do not depend on whether or not there is monetary union per se. One way in which formation of a monetary union itself creates the possibility of fiscal spillovers is through pressures by fiscal authorities on the common central bank (or federation of central banks) to monetize deficits.

In a monetary union, the inflation costs of generating seignorage to finance the deficits of one member are shared by the residents of all other members of the union. If the policies of the European central bank are influenced (or directed) by national fiscal authorities, then governments have the incentive to incur larger deficits than they would with independent currencies if they behave noncooperatively.

The Maastricht treaty addresses this concern by providing for the establishment of an independent European central bank with the explicit goal of price stabilization. However, statutory independence and real independence may not go hand in hand, as pointed out by many authors over the years. A European central bank would have effective independence if it cannot be forced by either member state governments or a central fiscal authority to monetize deficits, engage in open market operations, or undertake foreign exchange market interventions. If an independent central bank counts consumption and employment growth along with low inflation among its objectives, then faced with the choice of contractionary fiscal policy, bankruptcy of the treasury, or higher inflation, it may well choose the third as the best available outcome.

Even a central banker with a strong aversion to inflation may succumb to fiscal authorities that persistently collect less revenue than they spend. A legally independent central bank can be forced to monetize deficits in a game of chicken with an uncooperative fiscal authority insistent on perpetual deficit-financing. When fiscal authorities anticipate that the central bank will be willing to monetize deficits ex post, they can behave in a Stackelberg fashion, incurring deficits that induce the central bank to follow the monetary policy they prefer. Rogoff (1989), among others, argues that a solution to this problem of dynamic inconsistency is to appoint central bankers who are extremely averse to allowing inflation.

This problem exists without monetary union or fixed exchange rates, but it is exacerbated by monetary union. For example, Canzoneri and Diba (1991) extend their analysis of deficit finance through distortionary taxes to show how the optimal trade-off for national authorities between financing public spending through (distortionary) factor income taxes or by generating seignorage revenues through base money creation is changed by monetary union. Because part of the inflation costs of monetizing deficits are borne by the residents of other countries, national governments prefer that a relatively larger share of public spending be financed by money creation with monetary union than without. In their model, the central bank will inflate because it cares about allocative efficiency.
The alternative for solvent governments is greater taxation, creating larger deadweight losses. This implies that a common currency leads to an increase in national deficits.

3.3 Potential Fiscal Crises and Bailouts

An important concern of the Maastricht treaty and the Delors Report is that European unification might lead to the possibility that other member countries are asked to rescue an insolvent government from a fiscal crisis. In addressing this concern, the treaty adopts the no-bailout principle (Article 104b) that states that each member country will be responsible for servicing its own public debt and that there will be no bailout by the other members if it fails to do so. The principle of independence for the central bank also bears on this point, since it is intended to rule out fiscal bailouts using seignorage collected from the union as a whole.

In the presence of imperfect financial markets, a fiscal or financial crisis in one country can create welfare losses for other countries because of financial market integration or through contagion effects in the financial system. Faced with a crisis caused by an unsustainable debt burden for one country, the rest of the member states have an incentive to bail it out. For example, the EMU could take over part of the debt or the European central bank could react by increasing the rate of growth of base money using the seignorage revenue collected for the EMU to finance a bailout of the member government.

The incentives for the rest of the EMU to bail out a country facing a fiscal crisis imply that prior commitment to the no-bailout principle is needed. Otherwise, excessive national deficits would be dynamically consistent policies for individual member governments as a general case.

If central bankers will react to avoid the welfare consequences of a liquidity crisis sparked by a potential public sector default, then fiscal authorities anticipating this can force the central bank to monetize deficits even though it has de jure independence. The external effects mean that the union may not be credible forswearing never to monetize the deficits of a member government facing imminent or eventual default.

If the no-bailout clause is credible and the emergent European central bank is truly independent, then each member country would remain responsible for servicing its own public debt and paying any default risk premia. The fiscal convergence criteria may have been included in the treaty because the no- bailout provision was presumed to be dynamically inconsistent.

3.4 The Political Economy of Excessive Deficits

Another argument for imposing upper limits on public sector debt and deficits is that there are political distortions that lead some governments to systematically run fiscal deficits in excess of what would be considered optimal for economic reasons. Several studies find empirical evidence consistent with such a political bias toward deficits in a number of countries. These include Roubini and Sachs (1989a, 1989b), Roubini (1991), Cukierman, Edwards, and Tabellini (1991), Grilli, Masciandaro, and Tabellini (1991), Alesina, Cohen, and Roubini (1992, 1993), and Corsetti and Roubini (1993). These articles show that various measures of political instability, short durations of governments, electoral cycles, and the partisan nature of governments are all factors that help to explain excessive fiscal deficits.[7] Formal tests for sustainability of fiscal policies indicate that a number of member countries of the EMU may need to undertake significant realignments of their fiscal policies. Most notably, public sector solvency fails for Greece and Italy under the assumption that current fiscal policies remain in force.[8]

When national public sector deficits exceed what would be optimal for a country for political reasons, welfare improvements require some type of commitment mechanism to enforce fiscal austerity. It is not necessary that rules binding the hands of the government be imposed and enforced from the outside. Member countries could adopt legislation or amend their constitutions to achieve such prior restraint on fiscal authorities and elected representatives. In the case of some countries (e.g., Greece and Italy), it can be argued that deficits are politically motivated and are excessive from the perspective of domestic welfare alone. This suggests that it is costly or difficult to reach domestic agreement on the measures to be taken to restrict excessive national deficits, so that the Maastricht initiative might be seen by some as a convenient opportunity to impose mutually beneficial external constraints on the behavior of member governments with the least difficulty.

Tendencies toward excessive national government deficits for political reasons can give rise to an efficiency-based case for international fiscal policy coordination if there are important international spillovers or externalities. Once more, even if Maastricht-type restrictions on member government deficits and debt are useful for either reason, it is certainly unlikely that uniform upper limits on public debt or (even, if sensibly defined) deficits would be suitable for all countries in a monetary union.

4. Fiscal Federalsim and the Dynamic Inconsistency of No-Bailout Clauses

We have discussed three arguments for the adoption of fiscal constraints. The first is that economic integration creates a social welfare-improving coordination of national deficit-financing plans regardless of market imperfections or whether nondistortionary fiscal policies are available. The second is that monetary union can increase the importance of externalities associated with unsustainable debt levels for one country. Restrictions on current deficits, however, should not be needed if the provisions eliminating bailouts and setting price-level stabilization as the sole goal for the central bank are credible. The third is that the Maastricht treaty represents a convenient opportunity to restrain already existing political biases to run deficits that are excessive from a purely national point of view. Our argument, also lending support to some form of budget and debt constraints upon entry into a monetary union, is based on the expectation of an increased fiscal federalist structure in the EMU. The elimination of political, institutional, and legal barriers to the economic integration of Europe and adoption of a common currency will most likely create pressures for a more extensive system of fiscal federalism in Europe than is presently on the agenda. These pressures arise because allocative efficiency generally would be improved when a union-wide fiscal authority undertakes deficit-financing policies to stabilize incomes and price levels in the presence of asymmetric fluctuations in aggregate demands or supplies across member states when there are preexisting distortions. With only distortionary taxes available to government and a high degree of factor mobility, more efficient tax-smoothing across asymmetric regional or national macroeconomic shocks can be achieved by using federal budgetary policies to implement intra-union international insurance.

The pressure for budget policies at the federal level will also be increased because of market integration and the fact that efficiency is generally increased by harmonizing taxes on all mobile sources of revenue, for example, income accruing to nonfixed factors. For the sake of allocative efficiency, it may make sense to share the repayment of national debts acquired before fiscal unification with jurisdictions other than the issuing one. Dynamically consistent policies for national fiscal authorities anticipating sharing debt burdens involve excessive national deficits followed by inefficiently high taxes (and excess burdens) for the entire union.

Restrictions on borrowing by member governments can be justified under these circumstances because they allow welfare-improving policies to be implemented that would not be dynamically consistent without some prior restraints. Imposition of the fiscal convergence criteria of the Maastricht treaty may also reduce the political tensions created by the possible redistribution of the repayment costs of national public debts, thereby facilitating progress toward greater fiscal federalism in the EMU.

We will next discuss the efficiency case for fiscal federalism with deficit finance at the union level used to stabilize incomes against asymmetric macroeconomic fluctuations within the union. We then elaborate our tax-smoothing argument that sharing the tax burden of individual national debts can be welfare-improving in an integrated economy. We close this section by discussing the distributional implications of efficient tax-smoothing in the presence of market integration and dynamic inconsistency of optimal policies.

4.1 Regional Shocks and the Case for More Fiscal Federalism

The budget of the EC is very small relative to the public sector budgets of the member nations. At present the EC budget is no more than 5% of the consolidated government spending of member countries (a little over 1% of EC gross national product, GNP). Moreover, over half of the EC budget (53% as of July 1992) is devoted to the Common Agricultural Policy and about one-fourth to Structural Funds targeted at low-income regions (serving primarily an income equalization, rather than a coinsurance, objective). This falls far short of the 5% of EC GNP minimum budget thought to ensure a viable monetary union recommended by the MacDougall Report in 1977.[9] And, to date, there are no plans to significantly increase the fiscal role of the central government of the European Union beyond responsibility for the distribution of seignorage revenues collected by a common central bank, and these will comprise a small fraction of the total of national public expenditures. By contrast, the share of central government expenditures in consolidated public spending is much larger in countries with fiscal federal structures, such as Canada and the United States, where it is approximately 42% and 64%, respectively.

Systems of fiscal federalism with a significant budgetary role at the federal level historically grew over time in monetary unions that are nations, such as Canada and the United States. This has not been true for monetary unions lacking political union, for example, the Latin Union or CFA Franc Zone. Nevertheless, theory suggests that monetary unification might lead to potential gains from a larger fiscal presence of the central government of the European Union. And it is noteworthy that closer political cooperation has been a long-standing goal motivating much of the economic integration process in Europe. The Maastricht treaty, for example, calls for a common EC defense policy. Economic pressures, together with a high likelihood of closer political cooperation, could well lead to the expectation of a more centralized fiscal structure developing within EMU such as recommended by the MacDougall Report.

By joining a monetary union, a country gives up its ability to pursue independent monetary policies for stabilizing incomes and prices against aggregate supply and demand fluctuations. With national currencies, exchange rate adjustment allows countries to pursue different monetary policies in the face of asymmetric macroeconomic shocks. Country- or region-specific fiscal policies become necessary for stabilization when there are asymmetric national or regional macroeconomic shocks with a permanently fixed exchange rate. Under national fiscal autonomy, stabilization would entail asynchronous public sector budget deficits and surpluses across member countries. Countercyclical fiscal policies imply that a country suffering a localized recession will increase its deficit, thereby raising its debt-to-output ratio relative to that of other member states. This will tend to increase the future tax revenue it must raise from production, consumption, and trading activities within its borders relative to the other countries.

Sources of national tax revenue have a habit of moving across borders to avoid differences in effective marginal rates of taxation in excess of differences in the value of the public services provided. As Musgrave (1959) pointed out, a high degree of factor mobility within a federal union implies that subnational levels of government are restrained in their capacity to impose taxes beyond the value of the benefits they provide in local public services. For example, wealthier taxpayers tend to migrate from jurisdictions that tax for the purpose of redistributing income and wealth. In an equilibrium with perfect factor mobility, posttax factor payments, corrected for differences in the services they receive from local public expenditures, will be equalized. Market integration works to restrict the capacity of individual national governments to collect future tax revenue for the purpose of paying interest on or amortizing accumulated public debt. Therefore, economic integration of Europe tends to reduce the extent to which national governments can use deficit finance for stabilizing national incomes in the presence of asymmetric shocks to national aggregate supplies or demands. At the same time, monetary union eliminates the possibility that countries can counter country-specific or region-specific macroeconomic shocks by pursuing divergent national monetary policies.

In answer to this problem, Ingram (1959) argued that fiscal federalism replaces regional fiscal policies for stabilizing regional incomes in the face of differential aggregate supply and demand shocks. The federal fiscal authorities assume responsibility for stabilizing incomes through the deficit financing of public spending programs.

Simple models of tax-smoothing following Barro (1979) can make this argument concrete. Barro adopts a simple closed-economy model in which national income is the product of a decreasing function of the average tax rate and an exogenous component that follows a random walk. Under the optimal fiscal policy for a solvent government financing a given stream of government purchases of goods and services, the average tax rate follows a martingale. The general implication is that if countercyclical deficits are needed for raising efficiency because only distortionary taxes are available to the government, then national public debt and taxes as fractions of GDP can display permanent responses to cyclical fluctuations. This holds even in special cases such that the public sector budget is balanced over cycles in expectation, although there is no general theoretical result for optimal intertemporal taxation that the budget be balanced over real output cycles. Comparing across economies, this would imply international divergence of tax rates and of public debts.

International integration of factor markets reduces the ability of national governments to impose taxes as a share of GDP in excess of their neighbors. This limits the extent to which future taxes and, therefore, public-debt-to-GDP ratios can diverge across countries, so that fiscal and financial policies for national governments may not be able to diverge very much from each other in response to asymmetric macroeconomic shocks. By adding further constraints to the tax-smoothing problem for individual governments, international factor mobility restricts the ability to use countercyclical deficit-financing to smooth purchasing power over idiosyncratic aggregate shocks.

This idea can be extended to allow for endogenous output in models with factor accumulation. Start with a simple two-country neoclassical growth model in which production of aggregate output employs internationally mobile capital and immobile labor and displays constant returns to scale. If lump-sum taxes are infeasible and there is a desire for public goods provision, then constrained Pareto optimality requires that capital income taxes be levied at a common rate across the border. This is the Diamond-Mirrlees production efficiency theorem for optimal taxation. Increasing the rate of capital income tax in one country has the same effect on posttax returns to all owners of capital and reduces the returns to labor in that country.

Suppose that national income is subject to stochastic shocks with a permanent component, but that we extend the simple tax-smoothing model by assuming that national output is a function of internationally mobile and immobile factors of production. In the general case, the optimum will entail interregional insurance transactions (state contingent transfers) when governments are limited to using only factor income taxes. Welfare is lowered by adding the restriction that the public sector of each country must remain solvent relying on the taxation of income accruing to factors employed in its borders (or, possibly, to foreign factor income paid to its residents) even though it can run deficits. Quite simply, some of the benefits from mutual insurance across members of the monetary union are lost without a significant fiscal federalist structure, and this in turn reduces welfare.

This part of our argument is traditional: allocative efficiency can be improved under a system of fiscal federalism if regions experience asymmetric macroeconomic shocks. Deficit-spending at the federal level for the purpose of regional stabilization is potentially welfare-improving because the elimination of institutional barriers to market integration and migration increases the importance and potential costs of tax flight. By smoothing tax burdens through government borrowing at the federal level, countercyclical reductions in tax collections from regions, or increases in public spending in regions, add the possibility of interregional insurance to the fiscal instruments of the union. Efficiently coordinated national fiscal policies subject to the constraint that every country must finance its own deficits, even when policymakers can agree on how the economy works and on the distributional objectives of coordination, may be inadequate to compensate for the loss of autonomy in monetary policies. The importance of pressures toward greater fiscal federalism in the EMU rests on the strength of the empirical evidence on asymmetric supply and demand shocks and on factor mobility in Europe.

4.1 Capital Mobility, Migration, and Existing Debt Obligations

How a long-term move toward a significant fiscal role for the European Union central government in the stabilization of regional incomes affects the medium-term accumulation of national public debt depends on the expectations held by fiscal authorities about the treatment of national public debts in a fiscal union. If the tax base available to each country's government must be used to service debt acquired before fiscal unification, then the tax burden on economic activities in each country would vary positively with accumulated past public debt as a fraction of output.

With factor mobility, optimal tax-smoothing implies that allocative efficiency could be improved in general by imposing common marginal tax rates on mobile sources of revenue. Such optimal tax schemes imply that differences in the level of outstanding public debt as a fraction of factor incomes would lead to different levels of taxation of the returns to immobile factors or assets. With financial capital highly mobile, physical capital is also very mobile in the medium or long run even if existing capital stocks are fixed or there are adjustment costs to investing. The burden of unanticipated differentially higher taxes on capital income will be borne by the owners of existing capital but not by new investors. If future taxes are anticipated, then the existing capital stock was already chosen on the basis of the present value of the posttax net returns it generates. This point can also apply to the accumulation of human capital. With perfect foresight or rational expectations, the future fixed-asset income available to a government running large deficits may be relatively small.

Departures from efficient commodity and factor income taxes will be required if the public-debt-to-GDP ratio of a member state is large enough relative to other members that taxes on fixed-asset income are inadequate to pay the interest differential or temporary capital levies are insufficient to amortize the difference. Differential taxation of the returns to physical investment, human capital, and unskilled labor for existing debt payment will induce inefficient international or interregional patterns of accumulation of both kinds of capital and migration of labor.

In general, a move to a more efficient tax structure through tax harmonization will affect the distribution of welfare across households and countries. In the theory of optimal taxation, distortionary taxes and subsidies are insufficient to allow an efficiency-enhancing reform to yield a Pareto improvement in the general case with many consumers. The desire to raise allocative efficiency could conflict with the desire to maintain the status quo distribution of welfare by trying to assure that each country service its own debt.

The political economy of sharing the tax burden of debt service across borders would depend on the specifics of the chosen model. Efficiency-improving moves toward uniform taxation of mobile factor incomes will tend to raise the posttax returns to some factors wherever they work. In lower debt countries, this could lead to political pressures for bailouts. We can easily envision a situation in which the burden of repaying debt is shifted across the owners of different factors as it is shifted across borders. An interesting line of conflict might arise between labor of different educational attainments. Economic integration could well lead to convergence of the returns to education within the union, while unskilled labor continues to adjust slowly to unemployment and real wage differences.

4.2 Debt Limits and Distribution

The potential for efficiency considerations and distributional conflicts to result in a redistribution of public debts can give rise to excessive deficits. Imposing a common limit on the debt-to-GDP ratio for each member is one way to assure that tax distortions to the dynamic and static allocation of productive resources are minimized without having to redistribute any of the debt burden. Since GDP is endogenous, this approach is not without problems. Further, setting a uniform goal may not be necessary from the point of view of achieving efficient tax systems without encouraging excessive deficits. In fact, imposing common limits constrains the policies for affecting the intragenerational and intergenerational distribution of welfare within countries and disregards differences in factor endowments, technologies, industrial structures, and so on.

Distributional conflict does suggest a way that Maastricht-type uniform limits on debt-to-output ratios might make sense. If a system of fiscal federalism with redistributional policies conducted at the federal level evolves, the outstanding national public debts could be absorbed into a single European debt without changing the debt-to-GDP ratio for any member state. This might keep significant distributional conflicts from interfering with the development of a more efficient assignment of fiscal responsibilities in a monetary union. It would require, however, some care adjusting for all of the obligations of national governments, for example, the differences in public sector pension funding at present.

Lastly, another possible motivation for the Maastricht treaty fiscal convergence criteria may be based on the politics of income distribution. Suppose that Ricardian equivalence fails and deficits redistribute income toward the current old generation away from the young and yet to be born. In this case, differential future public debt burdens imply future differences in per capita consumption growth rates, with declining growth rates in countries presently running large deficits. If political and fiscal unification occur, then social policies might be made at the union level to redistribute incomes to reduce differences across households in consumption and consumption growth. Such policies could tend to redistribute income toward countries with higher tax burdens due to the accumulation of debt.

If hopes for political union are so well-realized that citizens of Europe are considered European first, then divergent consumption levels and rates of growth across regions due to the selfishness of ancestors may become undesirable. When governments expect that such a "we are all one" attitude could emerge, they will tend to increase the rate at which they issue debt. Again, dynamic consistency gives rise to an argument for external restraints on the accumulation of national public debt.

5. How Asymmetric are European Shocks?

The arguments predicting more fiscal federalism in EMU and a possible bias toward excessive deficits in its anticipation rely on at least two important assumptions: (1) asymmetric disturbances are an important source of output fluctuations in the European context and (2) increasing market integration will lead to significant constraints on the tax-smoothing and income redistributive capabilities of the national fiscal authorities.

A number of articles have investigated the extent to which supply and demand shocks are asymmetric across members of the EC. With national currencies, exchange rate adjustment allows countries to pursue different monetary policies in the face of asymmetric macroeconomic shocks. As Mundell (1961) noted, if all shocks affect two regions symmetrically, then the benefits of using a common currency can be reaped without reducing the capacity of monetary policy for income stabilization. The greater the degree to which shocks are asymmetric across regions, the more important the loss of monetary autonomy becomes and the less likely that these regions form an optimum currency area. Bayoumi and Eichengreen (1993), Whitt (1993), and Cheung and Hutchison (1994) among others compare the cross-country correlations between shocks in Europe to their cross-country or cross-regional counterparts in other parts of the world.

Bayoumi and Eichengreen (1993) and Whitt (1993) use long-run identifying restrictions to distinguish temporary ("demand shocks") from permanent ("supply shocks") fluctuations in output and inflation rates and calculate the correlations between members of the EC separately for temporary and permanent shocks. Bayoumi and Eichengreen find that the correlation coefficients for both types of shocks are higher across seven regions of the United States than for the European countries. They find, however, positive correlations between fundamental disturbances in Germany and those in most other EC countries; the supply/demand correlations using annual data over the 1960-1988 period are particularly large for Belgium (.59/.33), Denmark (.59/.39), France (.54/.35), and the Netherlands (.59/.17), indicating that these countries may form a core of relatively good candidates for EMU with Germany.

They also compare the speed of adjustment to shocks for the EC and the United States, finding that adjustment is more sluggish in Europe than in the United States for both supply and demand disturbances.[10] This suggests that it may be more difficult to create a monetary union that includes all the EC countries than in the U.S. case, particularly since its formation could lead to greater industrial specialization (as with the United States), so that asymmetries of aggregate supply shocks could become even more pronounced than they are under the present exchange rate regime.

Whitt (1993) follows a similar approach using quarterly industrial production and wholesale price data (rather than annual GNP and deflator) for 1960-1992, arguing that these better reflect shocks to the tradable goods sector. Whitt finds less support for a core of EC members than do Eichengreen and Bayoumi, suggesting even greater difficulty in forming a monetary union. While supply shocks in the core group have similarly high correlations, demand shocks in Italy are almost uncorrelated with Germany, and demand shocks in France and the Netherlands are negatively correlated with German shocks. Whitt finds that only Canada and the United States are good candidates for monetary union among the countries considered (Canada, France, Germany, Great Britain, Italy, Japan, the Netherlands, and the United States).

These estimates may overstate the commonality of disturbances, however, as the correlation coefficients reflect both fundamental shocks and economic structure. For example, the disturbances identified in both these studies may be correlated with German shocks either because of symmetry in their fundamental disturbances or because German disturbances are being transmitted to these economies. The former is the appropriate indicator of fundamental domestic disturbances, and the latter captures the degree of economic linkage between countries, which in turn depends on the exchange rate regime.

Cheung and Hutchison (1994) attempt to control for structural linkages and exchange rate regimes when measuring the symmetry of disturbances between Germany and several European countries, focusing on Nordic members of the European Free Trade Association (Finland, Norway, and Sweden) in comparison with two small EC core members (Belgium and the Netherlands). The model includes real oil prices, German output (industrial production), German money, and the focus country output (industrial production). It is estimated with a vector error-correction methodology over the Bretton Woods and post-Bretton Woods exchange rate regimes using monthly data.

The correlations among the output disturbances for the two exchange rate regimes are shown in Table 1. A major question addressed is whether Belgium and the Netherlands have more symmetric output disturbances with Germany, and with each other, than the Nordic members of the European Free Trade Association considering EC membership at this writing. Cheung and Hutchison find that output disturbances across these small European nations generally are highly asymmetric, both with each other and with Germany. The two highest correlations are between Germany and the Netherlands during the Bretton Woods (.48) and post-Bretton Woods (.28) periods. Other correlations, particularly in the post-Bretton Woods period, are weak: Belgium, .15; Finland, .06; Norway, .05; and Sweden, .08.

The Netherlands has by far the strongest structural linkage with Germany, reflected in the estimated response of domestic output to a rise in German output,

Correlations Among Output Disturbances*
(Bretton Woods\Post-Bretton Woods)

Country	Germany	Nether-lands	Belgium	Sweden	Finland	Norway
Germany	1	.28	.15	.08	.06	.05
Netherlands	.47	1	.11	.11	.01	-.08
Belgium	.25	-.04	1	.06	.14	-.15
Sweden	.17	.02	.08	1	.17	.08
Finland	.02	.03	-.01	.12	1	-.01
Norway	.01	.08	-.07	-.14	.03	1

Adjustment Coefficient on Error Correction Term**

	Bretton Woods	Post-Bretton Woods
Netherlands	.012 (1.21)	-.504 (-7.04)
Belgium	.117 (3.70)	-.093 (-1.95)
Sweden	.000 (0.52)	NA
Finland	-.001 (-0.39)	NA
Norway	-.002 (-1.30)	NA

*Correlations of disturbances derived from vector error-correction model with real oil prices, German output, German money, and focus country output; monthly data. Upper panel represents post-Bretton Woods period (1974-1992) and lower panel represents Bretton Woods period (1960-1971).

**Adjustment coefficient is the estimated coefficient on the lagged error correction term in the vector error-correction model (focus country output equation); t-statistics in parentheses; NA denotes that no cointegrating vector (long-term equilibrium relation) was found for this country in the sample period given.

Table 1: Common Shocks and Output Linkages

the adjustment to disequilibrium, and the strength of the cointegrating relationship between the two countries.

In response to a 1% shock to German industrial production, Dutch production is estimated (over the post-Bretton Woods sample) to rise by almost .7% after one year. Adjustment to disequilibrium is also very rapid (lower panel, Table 1); roughly half of the deviation from the long-run equilibrium (cointegrating vector) is compensated for by changes in Dutch industrial production within one month.

Structural linkages between Germany and the other countries in the sample are much weaker. Only Belgium has a cointegrating relationship with Germany in the post-Bretton Woods period, and adjustment to disequilibrium is slow; only 9% of the deviation from long-run equilibrium is compensated for by changes in industrial production in Belgium within one month. The peak response of industrial production in Belgium to a 1% German output shock is about .25% at six months.

On balance, the evidence in these studies is consistent in finding fairly asymmetric shocks in Europe, indicating that the loss of the monetary and exchange rate instruments that comes with EMU could be costly. If the Single Market Program and EMU lead to greater industrial specialization (as in the United States), then the asymmetric nature of fundamental disturbances could be even greater. This indicates that pressures for national tax-smoothing policies or a fairly extensive form of fiscal federalism could be strong.

6. How Much Labor Mobility May be Expected in the Single Market?

The degree of factor mobility determines the potential for tax flight and acts as a constraint on the ability of governments to pursue tax-smoothing or redistributive policies. Redistributive policies are particularly problematic when asymmetric shocks are dominant, as with European countries, and only fiscal instruments are available (such as within EMU). This may provide an incentive to increase the extent of fiscal federalism.[11]

The degree of capital mobility in Europe is very high, and attempts to tax capital at high rates by international standards would most likely significantly slow the rate of new capital formation and erode the tax base. Indeed, attempts to further harmonize rates of capital taxation in Europe are commonplace. The degree of labor mobility in Europe is less clear, however. To what extent would a national fiscal program that results in lower after-tax real wages be likely to induce a substantial migration to other EC countries?

The act of changing job location is partly an investment decision, where the balance of costs and benefits takes into account pecuniary as well as nonpecuniary factors that are likely to change over time. Factors that tend to increase labor mobility, and potentially the extent of tax flight, are elements of the Single Market Program that reduce or eliminate barriers to the transference of the documentation of labor skills, such as the mutual recognition of educational degrees or skill accreditation and certification.

A number of studies have investigated the extent to which labor migration is sensitive to wage differentials, unemployment differentials, and other factors in Europe. Flanagan (1993) finds little evidence of real wage convergence in the EC since the Treaty of Rome increased the degree of labor mobility. However, European migration flows did rise, quadrupling between 1959 and 1965 and peaking in 1970 (Straubhaar, 1988). Nonetheless, the intra-European migration flows are small compared to the external flows from nonmember states to the EC. It does not appear that the EC did much to stimulate internal flows, and most flows that did occur do not appear highly correlated with wage dispersion.

Eichengreen (1992a) notes that although border controls and other statutory restrictions on European labor flows were eliminated by the 1992 Single Market Program, cultural and linguistic barriers remain. But these barriers are much less for migration between regions within any given EC country. Eichengreen (1992a, 1992b) estimates interregional migration equations for Britain, Italy, and the United States. The dependent variable is migration scaled by population, and the independent variables reflect various incentives to move: the change (or level) in log wages lagged and unemployment lagged. Lagged migration is also included to measure persistence. Eichengreen finds that U.S. migration is very sensitive to wage changes and to the level of regional unemployment and responds quickly (i.e., there is very little persistence). British and Italian migration sensitivity to wages and unemployment, by contrast, is an order of magnitude less than it is for the United States and demonstrates high persistence. Eichengreen argues that labor mobility within countries may be regarded as an upper bound on mobility between them and concludes that intra-EC migration will probably not play as important a role after monetary union in Europe as it does in the United States.

Why does not European labor respond to incentives to move as readily as U.S. residents? Flanagan (1993) argues that the existing economic incentives within Europe, with the exception of Italy in the 1960s, have been insufficient to overcome other nonlegal barriers associated with cultural differences, language differences, social ties, and so on. Nonetheless, he points out that Greece, Portugal, and Spain have more to gain within an integrated EC labor market in the 1990s than the Italians had in the 1960s. Wage differentials between these three countries and Northern Europe are several times that of the Italian wage differential at its peak.

Looking beyond regional data, another way of obtaining some indication of the potential upper bound on EC labor mobility over the next few decades is to consider the integrated Nordic labor market. The Scandinavian countries--Denmark, Finland, Iceland, Norway, and Sweden--have shared a common labor market for over 40 years. The labor market agreement, signed in Copenhagen in May 1954 and revised in March 1982, gives the right to Nordic citizens to settle anywhere in Scandinavia without either residency or work permits. The Nordic labor market may serve as a model of the single market for labor services strived for in the EC.

Information on employment opportunities is shared throughout the Nordic area, and Nordic immigrants are treated the same as native residents by the national authorities. Migrants can receive unemployment benefits for a job obtained at the destination. Although migrants generally have a higher probability of being unemployed, generous unemployment benefits throughout the Nordic area increase the expected gain from mobility.[12] These considerations, together with the similarity of culture and language[13] and geographic proximity, would seem to provide the Nordic area with all the ingredients of a well-functioning and integrated labor market.

In practice, however, the intra-Nordic immigration pattern has been dominated by Finnish migration to Sweden, especially in the 1960s and the beginning of the 1970s (Lundborg, 1988, 1991a, 1991b). There was also substantial net migration from Denmark to Sweden in the mid-1970s. Net migration between Denmark and Finland and between Finland and Norway, by contrast, was negligible, at least over the 1970-1990 period (Pedersen, 1993).

Nonetheless, economic incentives appear to play an important role in determining immigration patterns. In particular, large real wage differentials help to explain the Finnish-Swedish net labor flow.[14] Lundborg (1991b) investigates annual labor migration flows to Sweden from Denmark, Finland, and Norway in the period 1968-1985. He obtains elasticities of migration from a logistic human capital model, indicating that the behavior of Finnish workers, given similar incentives, is not systematically different than other Nordic residents. Finnish emigration to Sweden is explained rather well by real disposable wages and the unemployment rate in Sweden ("pull factors") and the real disposable wage in Finland ("push factor"). The closing of the wage gap seems to be the main explanation for the marked decline in Finnish emigration to Sweden since the mid-1970s.

Pedersen (1993) also investigates levels of unemployment, changes in employment, and changes in vacancies in the countries of origin and destination as causal factors in explaining intra-Nordic migration. He concludes that these labor market indicators are generally significant determinants of intra-Nordic labor flows, but the best indicator varies with each pair of countries. Net migration most sensitive to unemployment rate differentials is between Finland and Sweden. A rise in Finnish unemployment by one percentage point together with a fall in Swedish unemployment by one percentage point (widening the unemployment differential by two percentage points) is estimated to attract about 11,000 additional Finnish residents (about .22% of the population--workers as well as family members) to Sweden.

Lundborg (1991a) identifies generous unemployment schemes as an important hindrance to even more widespread labor migration within Scandinavia. The last year that Denmark had an unemployment rate on a level comparable with Norway and Sweden was 1973. But, with the exception of the jump in the mid-1970s, Danish emigration to Sweden remained at quite low levels despite a persistent and very high unemployment rate differential. Lundborg also notes that the rise in Danish unemployment was accompanied by substantial increases in real unemployment benefits (real "wages" of being unemployed) and argues that "adverse incentive" effects were created that inhibited migration.[15]

Schröder (forthcoming) regresses differentials, real wage differentials, unemployment differentials, education attainment, and other variables on the number of individuals moving between pairs of the Nordic countries (excepting Finland due to data limitations) during 1981-1989 as a share of home country population (ratio in natural logs). A one percentage point rise in home country unemployment relative to another Nordic country was estimated to increase migration (relative to population) by about .5% to .8% with a one-year lag. A 1% rise in the net real wage differential (against the home country) was estimated to increase migration by about .75%. Most interesting for our purposes is that only highly educated individuals (university education) were sensitive to wage differentials between Nordic countries. The individuals with relatively low educational attainment, by contrast, seemed to be most sensitive to unemployment rate differentials. This indicates that investment in human capital (highly educated individuals) may be very sensitive to real wage differentials between countries.

These studies find that intra-Nordic migration is generally responsive to real wage and unemployment differentials, but that this sensitivity appears to vary over time, on educational factors, and on the level of unemployment compensation. The response to real wage differentials appears strongest among the most highly educated, and the largest "barrier" to intra-Nordic migration in response to unemployment differentials appears to be the extensive safety net for unemployed workers. In particular, the reduction in Finnish migration appears related to the narrowing of real wage differentials with Sweden.[16] And the lack of a sustained and strong Danish response to high unemployment differentials appears related to adverse incentive effects of unemployment compensation.

If a single European labor market follows a similar path as the common Nordic labor market, then one can anticipate a significant rise in potential labor mobility, sensitivity to real wage differentials, and hence constraint on national tax-smoothing policies. The Nordic experience suggests, however, that the sensitivity of European countries to unemployment differentials will depend in large part on the nature of the unemployment compensation schemes in place.

Finally, the labor response to a permanent change in real wage differentials would presumably be larger than these estimates indicate. These estimates do not attempt to distinguish between temporary and permanent real wage differentials, presumably reflecting some average of the two. In this sense, the estimates may be taken as lower bounds on the responsiveness of labor movements to permanent changes in taxes. Indeed, we know little about how labor mobility responds to permanent differences in taxes in the long run, especially across generations. It seems reasonable to conclude, however, that international mobility of labor and other factors might impede efficient tax-smoothing in the presence of asymmetric shocks because optimal tax changes could possess permanent components.

7. Conclusion

The Maastricht treaty and its intellectual predecessors articulate concerns that member states of the EU will tend toward excessive public sector budget deficits and public debt accumulation in a monetary union. These fears find form in the fiscal convergence criteria of the treaty that are difficult to rationalize in terms of economic reasoning. Several authors have criticized the arbitrary choices of quantitative targets and of using particular measures of debt policies. The arguments that international spillovers or externalities necessarily give rise to a need for limiting public sector borrowing by national governments have also met criticism in the growing literature.

In this article, we have argued that there are important reasons, based on improving allocative efficiency, for an increasing role of the union-wide fiscal authority in Europe for stabilizing incomes and prices under monetary union. The empirical evidence suggests that asymmetric shocks across member states have both permanent and temporary components, leading to a need for asymmetric fiscal management when exchange rate adjustment and independent monetary policies are no longer available. Empirical evidence also indicates that asymmetric fiscal management on the national level will be increasingly constrained by rising capital and labor mobility in the EC.

We argue that expectations of eventual fiscal federalism in Europe might well lead to excessive deficits for national governments because they recognize that future tax burdens will not be entirely national tax burdens if an active role in regional stabilization is assumed by the union-wide level of government. Dynamic inconsistency of optimally coordinated national fiscal policies emerges with the potential for a high degree of tax flight in integrated European markets. In this light, some form of entry condition over deficit and debt levels seems to be justified in the period leading up to EMU.

Endnotes

1. This article was written for the Study Group on the Political Economy of European Integration sponsored by the Center for German and European Studies at the University of California, Berkeley. We thank Jeff Frieden for helpful comments.

2. See Fratianni, von Hagen, and Waller (1992) for a detailed description of the excess-deficit procedure.

3. Wihlborg (1994), however, argues that these three conditions impose unnecessary costs of adjustment on EC members in the period leading up to EMU. He argues that the currency reform--the introduction of the ecu--will automatically take care of inflation convergence, and national exchange rates will similarly disappear. Since exchange rate risk and capital controls would no longer be relevant, interest rate differentials would simply reflect default risk.

4. These include, for example, Bovenberg, Kremers, and Masson (1991), Buiter and Kletzer (1991a, 1991b, 1992), Buiter, Corsetti, and Roubini (1993), Eichengreen (1993), and Glick and Hutchison (1991, 1993).

5. Specifically, Buiter and Kletzer (1991a) use a Diamond overlapping-generations model with lump-sum taxes and transfers. Cooperation is unnecessary for achieving a Pareto optimum with respect to household welfare when national governments seek to maximize a generalized utilitarian social welfare function defined over residents' utilities in a (open-loop) Nash equilibrium. Dynamic efficiency of the equilibrium is assured in a noncooperative equilibrium because the social welfare function is Paretian with respect to residents' welfare. Cooperation is needed to achieve a Pareto optimum for the national social planners.

6. See Buiter and Kletzer (1991a and 1992).

7. Political instability and the weakness of governments help explain the inability of Italy to adjust its fiscal-financial policies. Partisan conflict and extensive political polarization can be associated with large fiscal deficits for Greece following the political economy models. As others have pointed out, elections that resulted in stable political majorities in Belgium, Denmark, and Ireland preceded significant reversals of fiscal policies away from large deficits, further confirming these ideas.

8. Buiter, Corsetti, and Roubini (1993) perform stationarity tests of the present value of outstanding public debt holding current deficit-financing policies constant.

9. See Eichengreen (1992a and 1993) for a literature review and analysis of the EC budget and budgets in countries with fiscal federalist structures. He focuses on

10. Bayoumi and Eichengreen (1993) also separate the United States into an industrial core (Northeast, Midwest, and Far West) and hinterland, showing that the correlations between regional shocks are much higher within the core subset than between the core and hinterland. They compare these results to a core and periphery for the EC, showing that the asymmetries of shocks are much lower among Belgium, Denmark, France, Germany, Luxembourg, and the Netherlands than within the entire EC. They suggest that this may lend support to proposals for a two-speed monetary union with the six core countries forming a currency union first to be joined later by the members of the periphery.

11. On the other hand, high labor mobility is one criterion often employed to judge the desirability of a monetary union. Labor mobility may partly substitute for price flexibility in offsetting region-specific demand shocks.

12. Lundborg (1991a) constructs measures of unemployment benefits in each Nordic country and enters them into migration equations.

13. Danish, Norwegian, and Swedish are very similar languages. Reading knowledge of one of these Scandinavian languages is sufficient to read in the other two. Verbal communication is more difficult, but easily overcome. Icelandic differs somewhat more from the other three as it remains closely related to Old Norse. Finnish, however, is a completely different language from the other Scandinavian languages. Nonetheless, Swedish is an important second language of Finland.

14. However, relatively high real wages in Denmark and Norway did not attract significant Finnish emigration.

15. This conclusion is consistent with Pedersen's (1993) observation that Danish entry into the EC in 1973 was also not accompanied by any significant "membership effect" on net migration flows.

16. Data available on Danish, Norwegian, and Swedish emigrants indicate that a substantial proportion return to their home countries after a few years. Pedersen (1993) finds, based on a sample of Scandinavian emigrants in 1981 between 15 and 65 years of age, that 50% of Danish and Norwegian nationals returned within three years and 50% of Swedes returned after seven years. It is not clear, however, whether this is motivated by narrowing real wage differentials or other factors

References

Alesina, Alberto, Cohen, G., and Roubini, Nouriel. "Macroeconomic Policy and Elections in OECD Economics." *Economics and Politics* 1992, 4: 1-30.

Alesina, Alberto, Cohen, G., and Roubini, Nouriel. "Political Business Cycles in Industrial Economies." *European Journal of Political Economy* 1993, 9: 1-23.

Barro, Robert J. "On the Determination of the Public Debt." *Journal of Political Economy* 1979, 87: 940-971.

Bayoumi, Tamim, and Eichengreen, Barry. "Shocking Aspects of European Monetary Unification." In Giavazzi, Francesco, and Torres, Francisco (eds.), *The Transition to Economic and Monetary Union in Europe*. Cambridge, England: Cambridge University Press, 1993.

Bovenberg, A. Lans, Kremers, Jerome J.M., and Masson, Paul. "Economic and Monetary Union in Europe and Constraints on National Budgetary Policies." *IMF Staff Papers* 1991, 38: 374-398.

Buiter, Willem H., and Kletzer, Kenneth M. "Reflections on the Fiscal Implications of a Common Currency." In Giovannini, A., and Mayer, C. (ed.), *European Financial Integration*. Cambridge, England: Cambridge University Press 1991a.

Buiter, Willem H., and Kletzer, Kenneth M. "The Welfare Economics of Cooperative and Noncooperative Fiscal Policy." *Journal of Economic Dynamics and Control*. 1991b, 15: 215-244.

Buiter, Willem H., and Kletzer, Kenneth M. "Fiscal Policy Coordination As Fiscal Federalism: Economic Integration, Public Goods and Efficiency in Growing Economies." *European Economic Review* 1992, 36: 647-653.

Buiter, Willem, Corsetti, Giancarlo, and Roubini, Nouriel. "Maastricht's Fiscal Rules." *Economic Policy* 1993, (April): 57-100.

Canzoneri, Matthew, and Diba, Behzad. "Fiscal Deficits, Financial Integration, and a Central Bank for Europe." *Journal of the Japanese and International Economies* 1991, 5: 381-403.

Cheung, Yin-Wong, and Hutchison, Michael. "Should Nordic EFTA Join a European Monetary Union? An Empirical Analysis." Group for International and Comparative Economic Studies Working Paper no. 285. University of California, Santa Cruz, March 1994.

Corsetti, Giancarlo, and Roubini, Nouriel. "The Design of Optimal Fiscal Rules for Europe After 1992." In Giavazzi, Francesco, and Torres, Francisco (eds.), *The Transition to Economic and Monetary Union in Europe*. Cambridge, England: Cambridge University Press, 1993.

Cukierman, Alex, Edwards, Sebastian, and Tabellini, Guido. "Seignorage and Political Instability." *American Economic Review* 1992, 82: 537-555.

Eichengreen, Barry. *Should the Maastricht Treaty Be Saved?* (Series: Princeton Studies in International Finance 74.) Princeton, NJ: Princeton University Press, 1992a.

Eichengreen, Barry. "Is Europe an Optimum Currency Area?" In Borner, Silvio, and Grubel, Herbert (eds.), *The European Community After 1992: The View from the Outside*. London: Macmillan, 1992b.

Eichengreen, Barry. "European Monetary Unification." *Journal of Economic Literature* 1993, 31: 1,321-1,357.

Flanagan, Robert J. "European Wage Equalization Since the Treaty of Rome." In Ulman, Lloyd, Eichengreen, Barry, and Dickens, William T. (eds.), *Labor and an Integrated Europe*. Washington, DC: Brookings Institution, 1993.

Fratianni, Michele, von Hagen, Jürgen, and Waller, Christopher. *The Maastricht Way to EMU*. (Series: Princeton Essays in International Finance 187). Princeton, NJ: Princeton University Press, 1992.

Glick, Reuven, and Hutchison, Michael. "Fiscal Constraints and Incentives with Monetary Coordination: Implications for Europe 1992." In Wihlborg, Clas,

Fratianni, Michele, and Willett, Thomas (eds.), *Financial Regulation and Monetary Arrangements After 1992*. Amsterdam: North-Holland, 1991.

Glick, Reuven, and Hutchison, Michael. "Fiscal Policy in Monetary Unions: Implications for Europe." *Open Economies Review* 1993, 4: 39-65.

Grilli, Vittorio, Masciandaro, Donato, and Tabellini, Guido. "Political and Monetary Institutions and Public Financial Policies in the Industrial Countries." *Economic Policy* 1991, 13: 341-392.

Ingram, James. "State and Regional Payments Mechanisms." *Quarterly Journal of Economics* 1959, 73: 619-632.

Lundborg, Per. "Den Gemensamma Nordiska Arbetsmarknaden. Migrations Bestämningsfaktorer och dess Ekonomiska Effekter." *Nordisk Tidskrift* 1988, 4: 349-357.

Lundborg, Per. "Determinants of Migration in the Nordic Labor Market." *Scandinavian Journal of Economics* 1991a, 93: 363-375.

Lundborg, Per. "An Interpretation of the Effects of Age on Migration: Nordic Migrants' Choice of Settlement in Sweden." *Southern Journal of Economics* 1991b, 58: 392-405.

Mundell, Robert. "A Theory of Optimum Currency Areas." *American Economic Review* 1961, 51: 657-665.

Musgrave, Richard A. *The Theory of Public Finance*. New York: McGraw-Hill, 1959.

Pedersen, Peder J. "Intra-Nordic and Nordic-EC Mobility." In Fagerberg, Jan, and Lundberg, Lars (eds.), *European Economic Integration: A Nordic Perspective*. Avebury, England: Aldershot, 1993.

Rogoff, Kenneth. "Reputation, Coordination and Monetary Policy." In Barro, Robert J. (ed.), *Modern Business Cycle Theory*. Cambridge, MA: Harvard University Press, 1989.

Roubini, Nouriel. "Economic and Political Determinants of Budget Deficits in Developing Countries." *Journal of International Money and Finance* 1991, 10: 549-572.

Roubini, Nouriel, and Sachs, Jeffrey. "Political and Economic Determinants of Budget Deficits in the Industrial Democracies." *European Economic Review* 1989a, 33: 903-933.

Roubini, Nouriel, and Sachs, Jeffrey. "Government Spending and Budget Deficits in the Industrial Countries." *Economic Policy* 1989b, 8: 99-132.

Schröder, Lena. "Skandinavisk Kompetensmigration i Perspektiv av EU:s Fria Arbetsmarknad." *Ekonomisk Debatt* (forthcoming).

Straubhaar, Thomas. "International Labour Migration Within a Common Market: Some Aspects of EC Experience." *Journal of Common Market Studies* 1988, 27: 45-62.

Whitt, Joseph. "European Monetary Union: Evidence from Structural VARs." Paper presented at the Federal Reserve System Committee on International Economic Analysis, October 1993.

Wihlborg, Clas. "Mikroekonomiska aspekter på en monetär union." Bilaga 4 Till EG-Konsekvensutredningen, Samhällsekonomi. 1993.

Wihlborg, Clas. "EMU--Economic Substance or Political Symbolism." *World Economy* 1994, 17(5): 651-661.

Wage Differentials: A Comparison of the European Union and the United States

Christopher L. Erickson[1]

This study compares wage differentials within manufacturing industries among the 50 U.S. states and the 12 European Union countries. The differentials are generally larger across EU countries than across U.S. states, but this gap is more pronounced at market exchange rates than at PPP exchange rates. This suggests, together with previous findings on the limited responsiveness of intra-European labor mobility to wage differentials, that the incentive for capital dislocation within Europe is large compared to the incentive for intra-U.S. capital mobility, while the incentive for labor mobility is much closer across the two continents. There are good reasons to believe, however, that even the response of capital to wage differentials might be sluggish.

1. Introduction

The implications of European unification for labor and capital mobility have been explored recently (see Flanagan, 1993, and Eichengreen, 1993, for the issue of labor mobility and Erickson and Kuruvilla, 1994, for the issue of capital mobility). The basic question is whether there will be massive movements of capital and labor in response to differentials in labor costs with the completion of the single market and the lowering of barriers to the movement of these factors. This study makes use of a natural analogy: the world's largest genuinely "free trade zone," the United States, to evaluate the magnitude of European Union (EU) wage differentials and thus to contribute to our understanding of the likely extent of capital and labor mobility in response to these differentials.

The underlying argument is that the proper analogy for understanding intra-EU capital and labor mobility from now on is to analyze intra-U.S. (or interstate) determinants of the movement of these factors. That is, while the literatures that might seem most relevant at first are the ones explaining cross-country differences in investment experience and labor mobility (see Agarwal, 1980, and Long, 1988, for summaries of these literatures), perhaps the better analogy in the emerging world of free trade zones is a large, single economy, separated to some extent by culture but basically barrier-free in movement of capital and labor: the United States. This analogy is even more salient for the question of what might happen once a single currency is adopted, when and if this occurs.

I will look at one of the key determinants (and perhaps the most obvious) of both capital and labor mobility, wage costs. While recent work, most notably Barro and Sala-i-Martin (1991) and Blanchard and Katz (1992), has examined convergence of incomes, wages, and unemployment rates and the migratory responses to these variables within the United States as an analogy for emerging free trade regions such as the EU, this study will attempt to draw additional lessons from the analogy by directly comparing wage differentials within manufacturing industries among the 50 U.S. states and the 12 EU countries. This comparison will shed further light on the question of the possible extent of both capital and labor mobility in the EU in response to wage differentials.

I will examine not only recent EU experience but also previous U.S. experience. For one thing, the evolution of EU wages since the Treaty of Rome has recently been documented elsewhere (Flanagan, 1993). Even more, the goal here is to get a sense of where the EU may be going, not where it has been. So, this article will summarize findings on cross-state convergence of wages, with an eye to the lessons we might draw for possible EU experience.

Yet, I want to be sure not to gloss over the concept of American exceptionalism, which goes back at least to de Tocqueville. That is, we need to keep in mind that Americans may have a more naturally mobile culture than Europeans. Even more, we need to balance the presumption that economic actors respond to explicit price signals (i.e. wages) with the recognition of the importance of other factors that help to determine the locational decisions of capital and labor (e.g., tax rates, infrastructure, and unionization may well be important determinants of capital mobility, while housing costs and cultural issues may be so for labor mobility).

Nevertheless, wages emerge as a key determinant in previous studies of the mobility of capital, surprisingly less so for labor mobility. Therefore, keeping in mind this caveat about the importance of noneconomic factors, the comparison of wage differentials in the EU and the United States seems relevant for the question of the possible comparative magnitude of intra-EU capital and (perhaps to a lesser extent) labor mobility.

I find that wage differentials are not dramatically larger in the EU compared to the United States at purchasing power parity (PPP) exchange rates, suggesting, along with previous findings on labor responsiveness to wages in Europe and the United States, that the implementation of the single market probably will not cause massively larger dislocations of labor compared to the U.S. experience. Note, however, that labor movements within Europe of the magnitude of intra-U.S. labor movements would be large by European standards and thus might present a major policy issue within Europe.

However, the differentials among regions in the EU at market exchange rates are about four times larger than the corresponding differentials in the United States, suggesting that there may be a significantly greater wage incentive for capital mobility within the EU compared to the United States, despite previous findings of minimal responsiveness of capital movements to labor cost differentials in the EU.

2. Determinants of Capital Mobility

The literature on capital mobility consistently finds that labor factors, including wages, importantly influence capital location decisions.

Crandall (1993) studied the regional distribution of U.S. employment and output. His review of the existing literature indicates that labor market variables (wages and unionization) have consistently been found to have an effect on capital movement:

> The literature on the determinants of business location has grown considerably in recent years. The focus of these studies varies substantially: business formations, new plant start-ups, direct foreign investment, employment growth in particular industries, manufacturing employment, nonfarm employment, personal income, and gross state product. The explanatory variables typically included in such studies are generally measures of taxes, tax incentives, public expenditures, wage rates, and the degree of unionization.
>
> Earlier studies often yielded inconclusive results on the effects of taxes and government expenditures on business activity, but recent studies tend to find that growth is inversely related to taxes.... The results for labor market variables in this literature are somewhat uneven. Most studies find that business growth is inversely related to wage rates or unionization, but the collinearity of wages with unionization makes the identification of these effects difficult (pp. 30-31).

In his own analysis of the determinants of manufacturing employment and gross state product across different states, Crandall found labor market effects to be the most consistently important:

> The results of the empirical analysis of state data thus point to labor market variables as the most persistent influences on differential growth rates, particularly in manufacturing. The degree of unionization and, to a somewhat lesser extent, wage rates are inversely related to employment and output growth in manufacturing. Government spending, infrastructure, and tax variables are less important at this level of aggregation (pp. 39-41).

Coughlin, Terza, and Arromdee (1991) examined the determinants of the location of manufacturing foreign direct investment (FDI) among U.S. states from 1981 to 1983. That is, once foreign interests have decided to locate in the United States, what are the characteristics of the states in which they are most likely to locate? Their conditional logit model of the spatial distribution of FDI among states indicates that higher wage rates deter FDI with an estimated elasticity of -4.4.[2] But, in addition, they find statistically significant effects from state per capita income (+), manufacturing employment per square mile (+), unemployment rates (+), taxes (-), measures of infrastructure (+), state expenditures to promote FDI (+), and unionization rate (+, surprisingly). If the EU will eventually resemble the United States in terms of the mobility of capital among countries (or the nature of the location choice for an outside investor), then their findings suggest that wages will indeed be an important determinant of location, but only one among many.

In addition, the cross-country FDI literature has indicated the importance of wages and other labor costs. There are several competing models in the FDI literature: those based on perfect markets suggest that differential rates of return and risk should be important determinants; those based on market imperfections suggest that differential firm advantages (such as financing or marketing skills) are important; those based on propensity to invest suggest that factors such as existing investment and exchange rates should be important; FDI inflow theories suggest that factors related to the host country, such as tax rates, political stability, and labor costs, should be important (Agarwal, 1980). What seems to be clear is that there is no existing general theory of FDI; among the possible explanatory variables, Erickson and Kuruvilla (1994), Cushman (1987), and Blair and Premus (1987), among others, have found labor costs to be important determinants of the capital location choice.

In their study of capital location within the 12 EU countries during the 1980s, Erickson and Kuruvilla (1994) found that higher unit labor costs are associated with less FDI with an elasticity ranging from -2.6 to -4.2, after controlling for gross domestic product and existing FDI stock. In addition, there is a strong raw correlation between net FDI (inflows minus outflows) to EU countries over the period 1980-1988 and 1980 unit labor costs, as indicated in Figure 1.

The Commission of the European Communities (1990: 98) identified five criteria to identify sectors with high risks of north/south relocation: "(i) share of labor costs

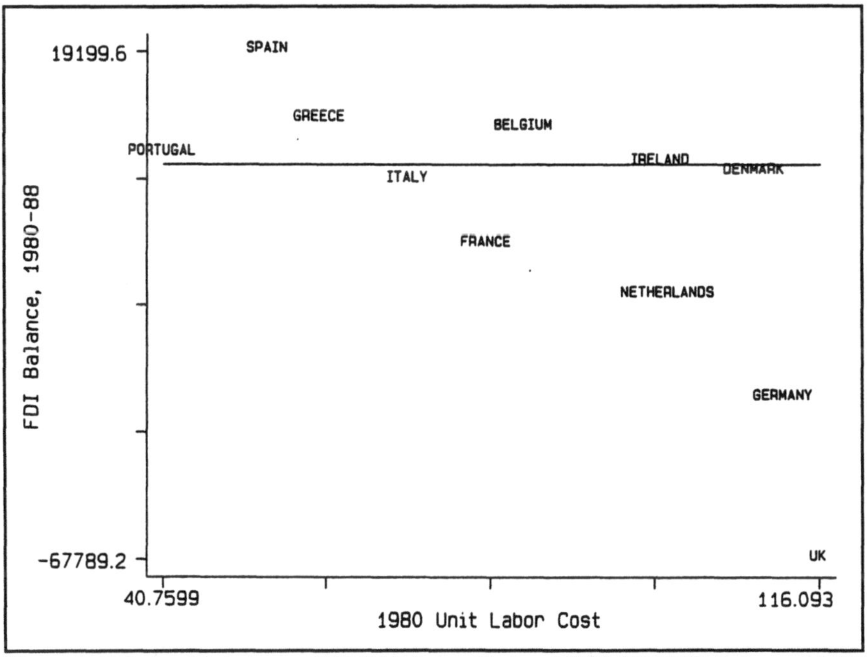

Figure 1: Relationship between 1980 Unit Labor Cost and 1980-1988 FDI Balance, 11 EU Countries. (Source: Erickson and Kuruvilla (1994)).

in the value of production above the industry average in the northern Member States; (ii) good competitive position in the southern Member States; (iii) differences in unit wage costs to the advantage of the southern Member States; (iv) major price differences for identical products between the Member States; and (v) low intensity in R&D expenses." On the basis of these criteria, the commission concluded that north/south relocation is most likely to occur in the fields of textiles/clothing/footwear, the ceramics industry, and toys.

These sets of findings certainly emphasize the lack of exclusive determinance of labor costs in the capital location choice. Nevertheless, they generally indicate that labor costs do importantly influence the capital location decision, within both the EU and the United States as well as across other countries. For the purposes of this article, these findings suggest that the comparison of wage differentials that will follow is, indeed, meaningful but is part of a much larger story that will not be fully told here.

3. Determinants of Labor Mobility

The literature on labor mobility has been less consistent in its findings on the importance of wages to location decisions. In fact, the determinants of within-country labor mobility, and labor mobility in general, remain somewhat of a mystery. Nevertheless, as in the capital location choice, wage differentials do appear to play an important role in explaining migration patterns.

Several recent studies have found significant effects of wages or per capita income on migration within countries. Eichengreen (1993), extending work by Pissarides and McMaster (1990), found that immigration among regions in Britain, Italy, and the United States responded positively and significantly to changes in local wages relative to national wage, as well as to the level of the unemployment rate. Similarly, Barro and Sala-i-Martin (1991) found that, all else equal, a higher level of state per capita income leads to a greater rate of immigration to that state.

Yet, the evidence on the importance of levels or changes in wage differentials to migration seems to be more mixed than the findings on capital location. Flanagan (1993), for example, found that intra-EC migration failed to respond to specific instances of reduction of legal barriers to migration since the 1957 Treaty of Rome as well as to large and growing wage differentials (he attributes the lack of responsiveness to nonlegal barriers such as language and culture). In his review of the literature on the determinants of migration, Greenwood (1975) found that migration does, indeed, occur from low- to high-income regions, but that "appreciable differences have been uncovered in the magnitudes in which income and other factors influence various population or labor force subgroups in their decisions regarding whether and where to migrate" (p. 411); he concluded that it was not possible to infer from the previous findings that wages are the chief determinant of migration.

More recently, Blanchard and Katz (1992) found that interstate migration in response to economic shocks appears to result more from changes in unemployment rates than from changes in wages.[3] And, both Pissarides and

McMaster (1990) and Barro and Sala-i-Martin (1991) emphasize that the response of migration to levels or changes in wage or income differentials is very slow; Barro and Sala-i-Martin, for example, found that a 10% rise in a U.S. state's per capita income leads to an increase in the state's population growth rate due to immigration of only .26% per year. Together, these econometric studies suggest that, both in the EU and in the United States, labor mobility is not remarkably responsive to wage (and income) differentials.

Survey-based research has reached similar conclusions regarding the importance (but lack of exclusive determinance) of employment-related factors to the migration decision. Long (1988) found that based on Annual Housing Surveys, "a rather parsimonious set of categories (job transfer, look for work, take new job, enter or leave armed forces, retirement, attend schools, be closer to relatives, or to seek a change of climate) usually account for 70 or 80 percent of the 'main' reasons for interstate or inter-regional moves" (p. 251).

Moreover, Long (1988) and Long and Boertlin (1974) found nontrivial differences in internal migration rates among a set of countries (including EU countries Belgium, France, Great Britain, and Ireland) from the 1960 and 1970 censuses, with Australia, Canada, and the United States having the most mobility. And, Eichengreen (1993) found that migration rates and the migratory response to wages within several European nations are much lower than the corresponding rates and responses within the United States.

Long and Boertlin (1974) nicely summarize a set of possible reasons for cross-country differences in intracountry mobility:

(1) The amount of geographic mobility is related to a country's level of industrialization and urban development.

(2) There is a long-run dynamic that is built into populations that are almost entirely descended from long-distance migrants.

(3) It is a firmly established principle that persons who have moved once are likely to move again.

(4) Successive waves of settlement established numerous urban centers in Australia, Canada, and the United States, geographically separated from one another, and today each country has an urban structure that is not clearly dominated by a single metropolis. None of the numerous metropolitan areas in these countries dominates life and commerce the way that London dominates English society or the way that other European capitals tend to be centers of trade, commerce, and industry in their respective countries.

(5) de Tocqueville attributed the high rate of geographic mobility in America to material abundance coupled with the lack of a hereditary class structure.

(6) Geographic size may be related to other factors that strongly influence the overall rate of moving.

(7) The broad conclusion seems to be that Australia, Canada, and the United States have high rates of short- and long-distance moving now because they have had high rates in the past.

Will integration lead the EU to look more like the United States along any of these dimensions? To the extent that geographic size has an independent influence, perhaps. Or to the extent that the EU now lacks a single dominant city (again assuming that this has an independent influence). But, most of the other determinants identified by Long and Boertlin (1974) seem more rooted in the culture of the two continents: the history of the frontier, the history of "nations of immigrants," and the lack of hereditary class structure all seem to be aspects of American (or American, Australian, and Canadian) exceptionalism. The question, then, is whether the legal barriers removed by the Single European Act were important at all, considering these factors mitigating against movement in Europe. Flanagan (1993) found that previous removal of legal barriers had little effect on migration; yet, we can still pose the question of whether the wage incentive for labor mobility is, in fact, present.

Recognizing, then, that a wide range of factors determine capital and labor locational choices, this study will now move to an analysis of wage differentials in the EU and the United States, with an understanding that wages are just one determinant albeit an important one. The questions addressed here are: how far apart are industry-level manufacturing wages across EU countries and the United States, are these gaps similar, and what might the evolution of wage differentials across U.S. states tell us about how the EU might evolve?

4. Comparing Wage Differentials

I now examine differentials in manufacturing production worker wages in the two free trade regions of the 50 U.S. states and the 12 EU countries. Table 1 presents max/min ratios and the standard deviation of log hourly earnings for U.S. states (in 1987) and EU countries (in 1988) for production workers in all of manufacturing and disaggregated manufacturing industries matched by Standard Industrial Classification and International Standard Industrial Classification codes.[4] That is, the two measures of wage differentials are the ratio of the wage in the highest wage U.S. state (or EU country) to the wage in the lowest wage state (or country) and the variance of log wages across all U.S. states (or EU countries).

There are no controls in the estimates presented in Table 1 for PPP; the European wages are converted at market exchange rates, and there are no controls for cost-of-living differentials across U.S. states. This is the more appropriate conversion factor for measuring the incentives facing holders of capital, assuming that holders of internationally mobile capital are concerned about the international market price at which they can purchase labor, not what the workers in particular countries can purchase with those wages.[5]

Table 1 indicates much larger inequality in the EU compared to the United States when no PPP controls are included; for manufacturing as a whole, for example, the measures of inequality are four times greater in the EU than the corresponding measures in the United States. This suggests a greater incentive for capital mobility in the EU than in the United States. Note, however, as Erickson and Kuruvilla (1994) point out, that unit labor costs may be an even better measure of incentives facing capital; if the productivity differences among the more-developed and less-developed EU countries are much greater than the productivity differences among

Table 1: Measures of Hourly Earnings Inequality Within Manufacturing Industries across U.S. States and EU Countries, not including PPP Adjustment

	U.S. States 1987		Europe 1988	
Industry	Max/Min	Std.Dev. of Logs	Max/Min	Std.Dev. of Logs
Manufacturing	1.70	.120	6.48	.535
Textile mill products	1.31	.075	6.71	.539
Apparel and other textile products	1.57	.121	6.66	.524
Leather and leather products	1.41	.103	6.05	.521
Lumber and wood products	1.93	.148	7.93	.638
Furniture and fixtures	1.76	.138	10.15	.669
Paper and allied products	2.11	.147	4.83	.478
Printing and publishing	1.43	.101	8.64	.598
Chemicals and allied products	1.62	.118	3.90	.450
Petroleum and coal products	1.27	.082	3.17	.496
Rubber and miscellaneous plastic prod.	1.95	.155	4.58	.484
Stone clay and glass products	1.66	.124	5.67	.510
Primary metal industries	2.23	.172	4.03	.504
Fabricated metal products	1.69	.129	6.01	.500
Machinery except electrical	1.64	.130	5.53	.521
Electrical and electronic equipment	1.73	.136	4.51	.493
Transportation equipment	1.98	.177	4.93	.468
Instruments and related products	1.63	.136	5.80	.483
Miscellaneous manufacturing industries	1.54	.138	8.38	.603

Sources: Hourly Earnings: U.S. Bureau of the Census, *Employment and Earnings*, ILO *Yearbook of Labor Statistics*.

the U.S. states, then this comparison of hourly earnings may overstate the difference in the incentives facing capital in the two regions. In particular, Erickson and Kuruvilla found average labor productivity rates up to five times higher in the more-developed EU countries than in the less-developed countries; it is unlikely that such wide productivity differentials are present in the United States.[6] An obvious extension of this work would be to explore meaningful ways to measure productivity differences (and thus unit labor costs) across U.S. states, as well as the relationship between changes in productivity and changes in wages.

Table 2 presents the same two measures of hourly earnings inequality, but now controlling for differences in cost of living among regions by converting the European wages at PPP exchange rates and by deflating the U.S. wages by state-level measures of PPP in 1992.[7] As noted above, these measures of wage inequality controlling for PPP are the most appropriate for the question of labor mobility, insofar as workers compare real wages among regions when making migration decisions (as opposed to owners of capital, who presumably compare market prices of labor instead).

Table 2: Measures of Hourly Earnings Inequality within Manufacturing Industries across US States and EU Countries, including PPP Adjustment

	U.S. States 1987		Europe 1988	
Industry	Max/Min	Std. Dev. of Logs	Max/Min	Std.Dev. of Logs
Manufacturing	1.87	.132	2.76	.320
Textile mill products	1.28	.074	3.32	.330
Apparel and other textile products	1.39	.070	2.83	.297
Leather and leather products	1.34	.082	2.57	.276
Lumber and wood products	1.79	.152	3.38	.389
Furniture and fixtures	1.64	.123	4.32	.437
Paper and allied products	2.44	.208	2.59	.272
Printing and publishing	1.46	.097	3.68	.378
Chemicals and allied products	1.91	.164	2.30	.254
Petroleum and coal products	1.29	.099	2.31	.291
Rubber and miscellaneous plastic prod.	2.14	.214	2.20	.263
Stone clay and glass products	1.67	.126	2.41	.281
Primary metal industries	2.49	.210	2.22	.278
Fabricated metal products	1.86	.143	2.56	.288
Machinery except electrical	1.60	.127	2.36	.297
Electrical and electronic equipment	2.18	.173	2.36	.268
Transportation equipment	1.79	.174	2.10	.245
Instruments and related products	1.66	.128	2.47	.261
Miscellaneous manufacturing	1.42	.111	3.57	.370

Sources: Hourly Earnings: U.S. Bureau of the Census, *Employment and Earnings*, ILO *Yearbook of Labor Statistics.* U.S. PP adjustment: Pear (1994)

Table 2 indicates a smaller difference between the EU and the United States in the magnitude of the PPP-adjusted wage differentials compared to the non-cost-of-living-adjusted estimates presented in Table 1; for example, the measures of inequality in manufacturing as a whole are more on the order of 2 to 2.5 times greater in the EU compared to the corresponding measures in the United States. Moreover, using this PPP correction, the ratios of highest wage to lowest wage and log wage variance in the EU and United States are very close for the industries of paper and allied products, chemicals and allied products, rubber and miscellaneous plastic products, primary metal, electrical and electronic equipment, and transportation equipment. To make it more concrete, the gap in wages for workers in paper and allied products in Oregon and Rhode Island (the highest and lowest wage states in this industry controlling for cost of living) was very close to the gap between wages for workers in this industry in Denmark and Greece, converted at PPP exchange rates; the same is true for the overall measure of dispersion of log wages in this industry among the regions within the two continents.

In short, while the ratio between the highest wage country (usually Belgium, Denmark, or Germany) and the lowest wage country (usually Greece or Portugal) in the EU (or the overall variance of log wages) calculated at market exchange rates is generally about four times higher than the corresponding measures among the U.S. states, the measures of inequality for the EU calculated at PPP exchange rates are generally closer to the U.S. ratios controlling for cost of living and are even equivalent in some industries. This suggests that cost-of-living differentials offset wage differentials to a much greater extent among EU countries than among U.S. states.

These results thus indicate that the wage incentives for labor mobility, at least, are not so much larger in the EU than in the United States. This suggests, along with the non employment-related reasons for greater labor mobility in the United States discussed above, that there is not much reason to expect massive labor movements within the EU with the completion of the single market, at least not that much more massive than present cross-U.S. state migration in response to wage differentials.[8]

On the other hand, to the extent that the market exchange rate is the proper metric for examining labor cost incentives for capital mobility, there does seem to be a significantly greater wage incentive for capital location in the lower-wage EU countries than for capital location in lower-wage U.S. states (compared to higher-wage countries and states, respectively). This conclusion is tempered, however, by the fact that labor productivity differentials are likely to be larger across EU countries than across U.S. states.

Yet, Erickson and Kuruvilla (1994) found that while capital movements within the EU did respond to the already existing labor cost (in this case, unit labor cost) differentials during the 1980s, the amount of capital flowing to the lower-cost countries was not very large. They argue that capital may have failed to respond massively to the large labor cost differentials thus far due to several possible factors, such as barriers to capital mobility that have only recently been removed, and due to uncertainty regarding the final terms of the Social Charter (and thus the environment for foreign investors). In addition, employers in the higher-cost countries may be choosing to pursue high-wage, high-skill, and high-value-added production systems or may be subject to agglomeration economies that make lower wages in more remote EU regions irrelevant to the investment decision. Finally, the availability of even lower-cost production sites outside the EU, as well as the low level of development in the less-developed EU countries, might diminish the attractiveness of the lower-wage EU countries as investment sites.

So, to the extent that recently removed barriers on the movement of capital and goods or uncertainty about the Social Charter have been the key barriers deterring capital movements to date, or to the extent that the low level of development in the lower-cost countries has deterred investment but will be significantly increased by the regional aid program, the EU may see large increases of FDI to the lower-cost countries in many industries in response to the large wage differentials at market exchange rates with the completion of unification (and the removal of these barriers). Alternatively, the lack of large capital flows to the less-developed EU countries during the 1980s may be an indication of future trends, due to the availability of even lower labor cost opportunities elsewhere in the world or due to agglomeration economies and the adoption of high-wage, high-skill production systems by the employers in the more-developed countries.

Yet, if wages adjust very rapidly to quantity (capital and labor) movements or to rapid increases in labor productivity, even the "capital will move massively post-1992" scenarios might not hold. In a direct analysis of wage dispersion in the EU, Flanagan (1993) found that the overall dispersion of hourly earnings among the original six EC and later nine EC countries fell in the late 1970s but rose again in the late 1980s, to a level near the dispersion in 1960; in contrast, using a different data set, Leamer (1993) concluded that a significant amount of wage equalization occurred in the EC between 1978 and 1989. So, while the question of past convergence of European wages is apparently open, we can also use the analogy with the United States to shed light on the question of the possible speed of future European wage convergence, with the caveat that the institutional structures of wage determination are quite different on the two continents.

Table 3 presents the same measures of wage inequality as the first two tables (max/min ratio and standard deviation of log wages across the available states) for production workers in all of manufacturing among U.S. states in 1951, 1961, 1971, 1981, and 1991.[9] These can be thought of as σ-convergence measures of the cross-sectional dispersion of wages (or, in the case of max/min ratios, measures of the extremes in a given cross-section) as opposed to the β-convergence measure of whether wages in poorer states are growing faster than wages in richer states, which is explored by Blanchard and Katz (1992).[10] The overall dispersion across states grew between 1951 and 1971 and was still above the 1951 level in 1981 before dropping between 1981 and 1991.[11] These results suggest that while wages have been growing faster in the states that had low wages in the early postwar period (Blanchard and Katz, 1992), the overall rate of dispersion has not fallen dramatically.

Table 3: Hourly Earnings Differentials in Manufacturing for U.S. states, 1951-1991

Variable	1951	1961	1971	1981	1991
Max/Min	1.88	2.11	2.17	1.97	1.68
Std. Dev. of logs	0.156	0.166	0.160	0.158	0.118

Source: U.S. Bureau of the Census, *Employment and Earnings.*

Thus, even in the United States, which is generally perceived to have more flexible labor markets than the EU,[12] overall wage inequality among states appears to persist. This suggests that the wage gaps documented here might provide more than short-run incentives for capital mobility in particular. Further, if rapid wage adjustment does not occur in response to capital flows, the comparison with the U.S. experience and previous findings on EU labor mobility suggest that we most likely will not see rapid convergence of EU wages due to labor mobility.

5. Conclusion

The literature on capital mobility, both within the United States and among countries, suggests the importance of wages as a determinant of the location decision. Erickson and Kuruvilla (1994) confirm this finding but do not find massive responsiveness of capital movements to wage differentials within the EU thus far. The literature on labor mobility within and across countries is less consistent in its findings on the importance of wages to the location decision. Flanagan (1993) finds that intra-EC migration has not responded to the removal of existing legal barriers since the Treaty of Rome, and the findings on the responsiveness of U.S. migration to wages are decidedly mixed.

This study indicates that the wage differentials between the highest-cost and lowest-cost EU countries in manufacturing industries (as well as the overall variance across countries) are about twice the size of the corresponding differentials among U.S. states at PPP exchange rates but are about four times larger at market exchange rates. This suggests that the incentive for capital mobility may be greater within the EU than within the United States (with the caveat that productivity differentials were not controlled for here), but that the incentive for labor mobility is comparable, especially given the exceptional proclivity of Americans to move. Wage convergence seems more likely to occur through capital mobility than through labor mobility, but the extent to which such convergence may occur remains an open question.

Endnotes

1. The author thanks Barry Eichengreen and Jeffry Frieden for helpful comments on earlier drafts. K. Thomas Chandy provided stellar research assistance.

2. That is, a 1% increase in the wage rate in a particular state is associated with a 4.4% lower probability of location in that state.

3. Miller (1973) also found that out-migration is much more responsive to the rate of growth of employment than to wages.

4. Observations for some states and countries are not reported in the sources for Table 1 for some of the industries; the table gives the max/min and standard deviation of logs among those states or countries that are reported (presumably those in which some activity did occur). Note in particular that industry-level observations are not available for Italy. Also, note that the table does not include Puerto Rico, the Virgin Islands, or Guam; including these would increase the measures of inequality for the United States for most industries.

5. On the other hand, the PPP-deflated wages can be interpreted as estimates of long-range labor costs for extended investment projects, accounting in some sense for the fluctuating nature of market exchange rates, rather than purchasing power.

6. On the other hand, these measures of average labor productivity differentials reflect differences in the existing capital stocks as well, which also likely vary much more across EU countries than across U.S. states.

7. Note that cost-of-living estimates are not available directly from the U.S. government at the state level; the source of these data is the Research Department of the American Federation of Teachers, as reported in Pear (1994). I also used separate estimates of housing prices in major Metropolitan Statistical Areas as reported in "Cost of Living Index: Selected Metropolitan Areas" (1993), following the approach of Blanchard and Katz (1992), who used city house prices for 39 cities from the National Association of Realtors to deflate their historical series of state-level wages. I do not report these results, however, as they are qualitatively similar to the results using the Pear (1994) data.

8. Note, however, that labor movements within the United States are large by European standards; if the nonwage factors keeping European labor mobility low relative to intra-U.S. mobility turn out to be unimportant relative to the wage incentive (which would be contrary to the recent findings of Eichengreen, 1993, and Flanagan, 1993), then intra-European labor mobility on the order of intra-U.S. labor mobility could pose a genuine crisis in the EU. For example, the share of U.S. population in the Northeast census region in 1950, 26.1%, was almost double the share in the West region, 13.3%; by 1990, the West had a larger share, 21.2%,

than the Northeast, 20.4% (source: U.S. Bureau of the Census). While these data do not separate within-U.S. migration from natural increase and immigration and do not measure the extent to which the migration portion was due to wage differentials, they are nevertheless suggestive of the extent of population shifts in the United States. One might think of the U.S. experience as being somewhere between present European experience and worst-case-scenario European experience.

9. Note that the wage measures used to calculate these two indicators of wage differentials are the same as those used by Coughlin, Terza, and Arromdee (1991) in their study of cross-state FDI location.

10. This σ-convergence versus β-convergence distinction comes from Barro and Sala-i-Martin (1991). Blanchard and Katz (1992) compare the average rate of growth of hourly manufacturing wages in the 50 states from 1950 to 1990 to their value in 1950, finding that the growth rate of wages is strongly negatively related to the starting value.

11. Note that these measures are based on non-PPP- adjusted data.

12. See, for example, Organization for Economic Cooperation and Development (1986).

References

Agarwal, J.P. "Determinants of Foreign Direct Investment: A Survey." *Weltwirtschaftliches Archiv* 1980, 116:739-773.

Barro, Robert, and Sala-i-Martin, Xavier. "Convergence Across States and Regions." *Brookings Papers on Economic Activity* 1991, 1:107-158.

Blair, John P., and Premus, Robert. "Major Factors in Industrial Location: A Review." *Economic Development Quarterly* 1987, 1:72-85.

Blanchard, Olivier J., and Katz, Lawrence F. "Regional Evolutions." *Brookings Papers on Economic Activity* 1992, 1:1-75.

Commission of the European Communities. "Social Europe." *European Economy* 1990, special issue.

"Cost of Living Index: Selected Metropolitan Areas." *Statistical Abstract of the United States*. Washington, DC: Government Printing Office, Series No. 763, 1993.

Coughlin, Cletus C., Terza, Joseph V., and Arromdee, Vachira. "State Characteristics and the Location of FDI within the United States." *Review of Economics and Statistics* 1991, 675-683.

Crandall, Robert W. *Manufacturing on the Move.* Washington, DC: Brookings Institution, 1993.

Cushman, David O. "The Effects of Real Wages and Labor Productivity on FDI." *Southern Economic Journal* 1987, 54: 174-185.

Eichengreen, Barry. "Labor Markets and European Monetary Unification." In Masson, Paul R., and Taylor, Mark P. (eds.), *Policy Issues in the Operation of Currency Unions*. Cambridge, England: Cambridge University Press, 1993.

Erickson, Christopher L., and Kuruvilla, Sarosh. "Labor Costs and the Social Dumping Debate in the European Union." *Industrial and Labor Relations Review* 1994, 48:28-47.

Flanagan, Robert J. "European Wage Equalization since the Treaty of Rome." In Ullman, Lloyd, Eichengreen, Barry, and Dickens, William T. (eds.), *Labor and an Integrated Europe*. Washington, DC: Brookings Institution, 1993.

Greenwood, Michael J. "Research on Internal Migration in the United States: A Survey." *Journal of Economic Literature* 1975, 8:397-433.

Leamer, Edward E. "Wage Effects of a US-Mexican Free Trade Agreement." In Garber, Peter (ed.), *The US-Mexico Free Trade Agreement.* Cambridge, MA: MIT Press, 1993.

Long, Larry E. *Migration and Residential Mobility in the United States.* New York: Russell Sage Foundation, 1988.

Long, Larry E., and Boertlin, Celia G. *The Geographical Mobility of Americans: An International Comparison*. Washington, DC: Bureau of the Census, Current Population Reports, Special Studies, Series P-23, No. 64, 1974.

Miller, Edward. "Is Out-Migration Affected by Economic Conditions?" *Southern Economic Journal* 1973, 39:396-405.

Organization for Economic Cooperation and Development. *Flexibility in the Labour Market: The Current Debate*. Geneva: International Labor Organization, 1986.

Pear, Robert. "Auditors Say Poverty Line Should Vary Across Nation." *New York Times* August 5, 1994, A10.

Pissarides, Christopher, and McMaster, Ian. "Regional Migration, Wages and Unemployment: Empirical Evidence and Implications for Policy." *Oxford Economic Papers* 1990, 42:812-831.

Economic Integration and Unemployment in the EFTA Countries

Karl Ove Moene and Michael Wallerstein[1]

The rate of unemployment differed dramatically between the EU and the EFTA countries in the 1970s and 1980s, but not in the 1990s. In this article, we present a model that can explain the persistence of both high and low levels of unemployment as a consequence of employers' choice of employment policy. We contrast two employment policies: (1) a policy of cutting costs through layoffs when production is currently unprofitable and (2) a no-layoff policy that maintains a larger than necessary workforce during downturns in order to be assured of an adequate supply of labor during upturns. We show that either policy may be more profitable, provided enough other firms follow the same policy. We conclude with a discussion of the impact of economic integration on the sustainability of full employment in the EFTA countries.

1. Introduction

The Scandinavian countries of Denmark, Norway, and Sweden are alike in many ways. The three are all relatively small and homogeneous societies with open economies. In all three, the Social Democrats have been the largest party in parliament since the 1920s. The three countries share a reputation for high taxes, generous welfare policies, and a relatively egalitarian distribution of income. Unions are exceptionally strong, at least if strength is measured by union membership, and employers are among the most highly organized in the world. All three countries had highly centralized systems of wage-setting at the national level throughout the 1970s (Lange, Wallerstein, and Golden, 1995).

There is at least one way, however, that Denmark has differed from the other Scandinavian countries since the mid-1970s. While all three countries enjoyed extremely low levels of unemployment during the 1960s and early 1970s, Danish unemployment jumped dramatically after 1973, and then again after 1979, eventually peaking above 10% in the early 1980s[2]. Thereafter, the unemployment rate in Denmark never fell much below 8%, even during the height of the economic expansion in 1986-1987. In contrast, unemployment rates in Norway and Sweden increased only slightly, from 2% in the 1970s to an average of 2.5% in the early and mid-1980s.

There is another difference between Denmark, on the one hand, and Norway and Sweden, on the other. Denmark joined the European Community (EC) in 1973, while Norway and Sweden remained outside. A comparison of unemployment rates in the eight major members of the EC since 1973 and in the five continental members of the European Free Trade Association (EFTA) that remained outside the EC — Austria, Finland, Norway, Sweden, and Switzerland — reveals analogous differences, as shown in Table 1[3]. The average unemployment rate in the EC countries was over three times the average in the EFTA countries during the late 1970s and 1980s. Moreover, in the 1982-1988 period, every EC country had an unemployment rate above the highest level of unemployment found in any EFTA country.

Table 1: Average Rate of Unemployment in EC and EFTA Countries, 1975-1992

Country	1975-1981	1982-1988	1989-1992
EC Countries			
Belgium	7.8	11.4	7.5
Denmark	6.7	9.1	10.1
France	5.4	9.6	9.5
Germany	3.5	6.7	4.9
Ireland	8.2	15.4	14.8
Italy	7.1	9.8	10.4
Netherlands	5.9	10.6	7.4
United Kingdom	6.1	11.0	8.1
EC average	6.3	10.4	9.1
EFTA Countries			
Austria	1.7	3.5	3.4
Finland	4.9	5.1	6.8
Norway	1.8	2.7	5.4
Sweden	2.0	2.7	2.6
Switzerland	0.3	0.7	1.3
EFTA average	2.1	2.9	3.9

Notes: The unemployment rates are the standardized rates except in Austria, Denmark, Ireland, and Switzerland where standardized rates are unavailable. German unemployment figures exclude East Germany. Source: Organization for Economic Cooperation and Development (1992: 218-219).

More recently, as the Nordic countries moved closer to joining the EU, unemployment rates increased dramatically. In preparation for possible membership in the EU and the European Monetary System, Finland, Norway, and Sweden adopted new monetary policies in the late 1980s and early 1990s that gave priority to the maintenance of a fixed exchange rate over the maintenance of full employment (Notermans, 1993; Moses, 1994). All three currencies were pegged to the ecu between the fall of 1990 and the spring of 1991. Shortly thereafter, the three countries experienced their worst recession since the 1930s.

In Norway, unemployment rose from below 2% in 1987 to over 6% by 1993. In Sweden, the rise in unemployment came later but faster. In 1990, unemployment in Sweden was still below 2%. By 1992, Swedish unemployment had risen above 5%. In 1993, the Swedish unemployment rate reached 8.5%. Moreover, standard unemployment figures do not include the participants in active labor market policies. Including workers enrolled in active labor market programs would increase the Swedish unemployment rate by 50% (Organization for Economic Cooperation and Development, 1994). In Finland, unemployment jumped from 3.5% in 1990 to 19% in four years, a decline in employment that far exceeds the worst years of the Great Depression. Although the rise in unemployment has been more moderate in non-Nordic EFTA members, the gap between unemployment in the EC and in the EFTA countries is much reduced today.

Economists have adopted the term *hysteresis* to describe the observation that the level of unemployment that is compatible with a stable rate of inflation depends on past levels of unemployment. The higher the level of unemployment in the present, the higher the level of unemployment corresponding to a given macroeconomic policy stance in the future. Put another way, there seem to be multiple equilibriums in the labor market, depending on the current level of unemployment.

Several explanations have been offered for such hysteresis. The insider-outsider hypothesis, developed by Lindbeck and Snower (1988) and Blanchard and Summers (1990), is premised on the claim that unions try to protect the employment of only their current membership. According to this argument, once workers lose their jobs, they lose their insider status in the union and are ignored in the wage-setting process. When demand improves, the insiders push wages up rather than allow employment to be extended to outsiders. Other authors have emphasized the effect of sudden demand shocks on the stock of capital in the economy. Soskice and Carlin (1989) focus on the decline in physical capital as firms reduce investment when demand falls. Layard, Nickell, and Jackman (1991) emphasize the loss of human capital as skills deteriorate among the unemployed.

None of these explanations seems to capture the recent changes in the labor market in the Nordic countries. Local union leaders may primarily represent the interests of employed union members, as suggested in the insider-outside model, but wage bargaining in the Nordic countries is dominated on the labor side by either the national unions or the central union confederations. There is little evidence that the national union leaders show less concern for unemployed union members than those who remain employed. Neither do the approaches that emphasize the decline in physical and human capital appear to capture the entire story. Evidence of hysteresis remains even after controlling for the stock of physical capital, as we discuss below. The decline in human capital may have an impact, but all of the Nordic countries employ an extensive set of active labor market policies designed to *upgrade* the skills of those without work.

In this article, we present an alternative approach to understanding the stability of both high unemployment and full employment. Our explanation of hysteresis in the labor market is based on the contrast between firms that hire for the long run and do not lay off workers during temporary declines in demand and firms that hire and fire on a short-term basis. The interaction between the choice of employment policies and the tightness of the labor market can induce herdlike behavior among employers. The more employers converge on a common employment policy, the more profitable it is for all employers to follow the herd. Firms are more likely to lay off workers when neighboring firms have laid off workers. Firms are more likely to hoard labor when other employers are also hoarding labor.

Consider, for example, the case where most firms offer implicit long-term employment guarantees. As a consequence, the flow into the pool of idle workers is small. If the number of jobs is sufficiently large to employ the workforce, unemployment will also be low. With low unemployment, employers perceive potential labor shortages in the future. Consequently, employers are reluctant to release their workers and lose them to other firms, even when demand for their particular product is low, provided demand is expected to increase again in the future. The more firms hoard labor, the lower the level of unemployment, which, in turn, increases firms' fears of labor shortages and the incentive to hoard labor. If, instead, unemployment is high, firms can more safely cut costs with layoffs whenever demand falls. Since labor shortages are unlikely in the near future, workers are laid off whenever current production is unprofitable. As labor hoarding declines, aggregate unemployment increases, which increases the relative profitability of following a short-term employment policy. In both cases, it is most profitable to follow the policy followed by others. Those who deviate from the employment policy chosen by others do worse.

In the next two sections, we show that both a labor market with long-term implicit employment contracts and a labor market that operates as a spot market may constitute equilibriums in the sense that both can be sustained on the basis of profit-maximizing behavior. In the following section, we consider the implications of our analysis for the question of whether or not different national equilibriums can coexist within a single integrated economic area.

2. Variable- and Fixed-Employment Policies

To define different employment policies and study the choice between them, we need a simple model of the economic environment. Consider a labor market in which the capital-labor ratio in production is technologically determined and the capital stock is given. Each worker, when employed, produces output that can be sold by the firm for $p(t)$, where the price (or workers' productivity) is a stochastic function of time. We assume, initially, that the wage is fixed. One might interpret the model as one of an industry covered by an industry-wide labor agreement that fixes the wage independently of individual firms' employment policy[4]. With an exogenous wage of w, employers earn $p(t)-w$ per period per employee. We will assume that the wage is high enough so that workers prefer to be employed and actively search for employment when they are laid off.

If employers can always obtain a sufficient supply of labor, their profit-maximizing strategy would be obvious: hire workers whenever $p(t)-w \geq 0$ and lay off workers whenever $p(t)-w < 0$. If employers are sometimes unable to find appropriate workers, however, employers may prefer to keep current workers on the payroll in periods when the price is low and current profits are negative in order to be assured of an adequate supply of labor in the future when the price rises again. We will use the term *variable-employment policy* to denote the first policy of laying off when the price falls below the wage and hiring when the price rises above the wage. We will use the term *fixed-employment policy* to denote the second strategy in which workers are hired with an implicit long-term labor contract that excludes layoffs when the price is temporarily low.

To investigate the equilibriums of this market, we need to specify the stochastic behavior of $p(t)$. One of the simplest formulations is to assume that the price follows a continuous time Markov process with two states — a high price, p_H, and a low price, p_L — and stationary transition parameters — λ_D and λ_I — as illustrated in Figure 1. When the price is high, there is a probability of $\lambda_D dt$ that the price will fall within the small time period dt. Similarly, $\lambda_I dt$ is the probability that the price will increase within dt when it is low. Another way to understand the meaning of parameters λ_D and λ_I is in terms of the expected length of time before the price changes. The average length of time a high price will remain high

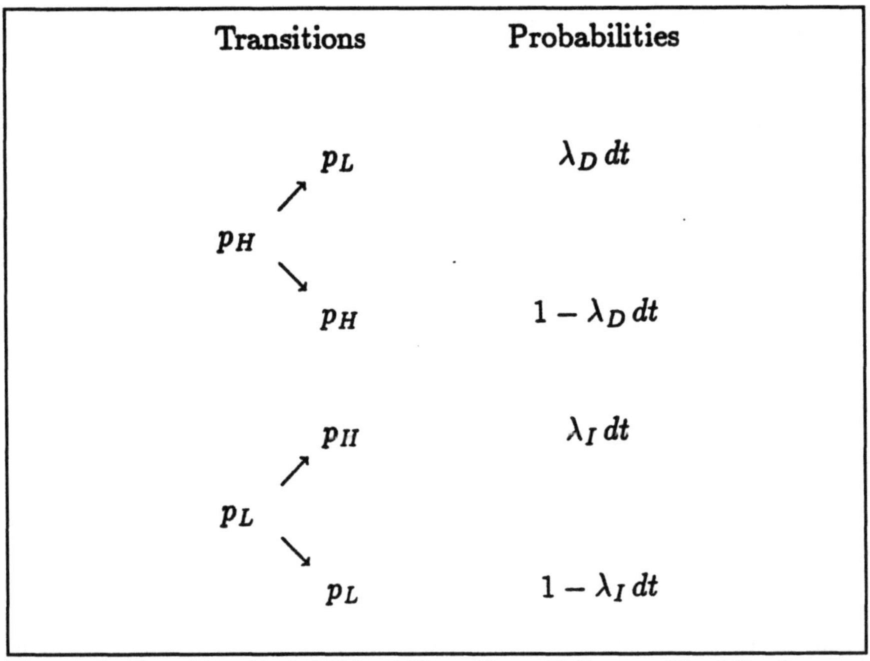

Figure 1: Transition Probabilities When Firms Follow a Fixed-Employment Policy.

is $1/\lambda_D$, while $1/\lambda_I$ is the average length of time a low price will remain low.

We want to compare the variable-employment and fixed-employment policies in terms of the present value of the profit stream per worker. If $w>p_H$, production would not be profitable with either strategy. If $w\leq p_L$, employers would always want to hire as much labor as the existing stock of capital allows. The interesting case, therefore, is when $p_L<w<p_H$. We will also assume that the unemployed workers receive an unemployment benefit, b, such that $p_L<b<w$. The assumption that $p_L<b$ implies that employers cannot cut wages sufficiently to operate profitably when the price is low and still attract labor.

Consider first a policy of no layoffs. The value of each job when a firm follows the fixed-employment policy of hiring in both good times and bad, denoted V^f, can be most easily derived from the asset equation that states that the current return on an asset, rV^f (where r is the rate of interest), is equal to income received (p-w where $p=p_H$ or p_L) plus the expected change in the value of the asset due to the possibility of a price shift. When the price is high, the asset equation is

$$rV^f(p_H) = (p_H - w) - \lambda_D[V^f(p_H) - V^f(p_L)]. \tag{1}$$

When the price is low, the asset equation becomes

$$rV^f(p_L) = (p_L - w) + \lambda_I[V^f(p_H) - V^f(p_L)]. \tag{2}$$

Combining Equations 1 and 2, we can solve for $V^f(p_H)$ and $V^f(p_L)$. The one we need is

$$V^f(p_L) = \frac{\lambda_I p_H + (r+\lambda_D)p_L - (r+\lambda_D+\lambda_I)w}{r(r+\lambda_D+\lambda_I)}. \tag{3}$$

Equation 3 indicates that the value of a job with an employee is simply the weighted average of the present value of the earnings streams that would be generated by each of the two possible prices: $(p$-$w)/r$ for $p=p_H$ or $p=p_L$. If $r=0$, the weights would be determined by the share of time that the price spends, on average, in each state. With $r>0$, the initial state with $p=p_L$ is weighted more heavily. If there is no chance the price will increase, that is, if $\lambda_I=0$, then $V^f(p_L)=(p_L-w)/r<0$ since $p_L<w$. In contrast, if the price rises as soon as it falls with certainty, or if $\lambda_I\rightarrow\infty$, then $V^f(p_L)\rightarrow(p_H-w)/r$. Note that $V^f(p_L)$ may be either positive or negative, depending on the relationship between w and the weighted average of the two prices. If $V^f(p_L)<0$, it is never profitable for a firm to adopt the fixed-employment policy, as we show below.

The alternative policy is to lay off workers when the price is low and hire when the price is high. Clearly, if employers could hire workers instantaneously and costlessly when the price rises, they earn higher profits by not hoarding labor when the price is low. To be able to hire workers costlessly is not realistic, however. In practice, firms spend a significant amount of money to find and hire appropriate workers. Here, the only hiring cost we include in the model is the cost of the time it takes to fill a vacancy. Let the time it takes a firm to hire a worker once a firm starts searching be exponentially distributed with the parameter μ. This implies that the average time it takes a firm to fill a position is $1/\mu$.

Now we must keep track of whether the price is high or low and whether the job is filled or vacant. We will write $(p_H,0)$ to indicate an empty slot when the price is high and $(p_H,1)$ to indicate a filled position when the price is high. Since employers following a variable-employment policy lay off their workers when the price is low, these three combinations exhaust the possible states. The transition scheme is illustrated in Figure 2. If the firm is seeking to fill a vacancy, that is, if the current state is $(p_H,0)$, there is a probability of μt that a worker will be found within dt, a probability of $\lambda_D t$ that the price will fall within dt and the firm will stop searching, and a probability of $(1-\mu dt-\lambda_D dt)$ that at the end of dt the vacancy will remain unfilled and the price will remain high[5].

Transitions		Probabilities
$(p_H,0)$	→ $(p_H,1)$	$\mu\, dt$
	→ $(p_L,0)$	$\lambda_D\, dt$
	→ $(p_H,0)$	$1-\mu\, dt-\lambda_D\, dt$
$(p_H,1)$	→ $(p_L,0)$	$\lambda_D\, dt$
	→ $(p_H,1)$	$1-\lambda_D\, dt$
$(p_L,0)$	→ $(p_H,0)$	$\lambda_I\, dt$
	→ $(p_L,0)$	$1-\lambda_I\, dt$

Figure 2: Transition Probabilities When Firms Follow a Variable-Employment Policy.

Let V^v denote the present value of a job when the firm follows a variable-employment policy. Now we have three asset conditions:

$$rV^v(p_H,0) = \mu[V^v(p_H,1)-V^v(p_H,0)]-\lambda_D[V^v(p_H,0)-V^v(p_L,0)], \tag{4}$$

$$rV^v(p_H,1) = (p_H-w)-\lambda_D[V^v(p_H,1)-V^v(p_H,0)], \quad \textit{and} \tag{5}$$

$$rV^v(p_L,0) = \lambda_I[V^v(p_H,0)-V^v(p_L,0)]. \tag{6}$$

We have three equations to determine $V^v(p_H,0)$, $V^v(p_H,1)$, and $V^v(p_L,0)$. The one we will need is

$$V^v(p_L,0) = \left(\frac{\mu}{r+\mu+\lambda_D}\right)\left(\frac{\lambda_I}{r+\lambda_D+\lambda_I}\right)\left(\frac{p_H-w}{r}\right). \tag{7}$$

On the one hand, employers who lay off workers during downturns avoid the loss of p_L-w when the price is low. On the other hand, employers following a variable-employment policy lose potential revenues of p_H-w while they are searching for a worker when the price is high. Which employment policy is more profitable for employers? The answer is given by comparing equations for the value of the two policies when the price is low (Equations 3 and 7), since that is when employers face the choice of whether to lay off or to hoard currently unprofitable labor.

In Figure 3, the two strategies are compared as a function of the wage rate. In both cases, the value of a job is a declining linear function of the wage rate, but the value per job when following the variable-employment policy has a lower slope. Which strategy is best for the firm depends on the wage. When $w=w^*$, where

$$w^* = \left(\frac{\lambda_I}{r+\mu+\lambda_D+\lambda_I}\right)p_H + \left(\frac{r+\mu+\lambda_D}{r+\mu+\lambda_D+\lambda_I}\right)p_L,$$

firms are indifferent between the two strategies. If $w>w^*$, the cost of carrying workers during low-price periods exceeds the present value of forgone profits during high-price periods and the variable-employment policy is more profitable. If $w<w^*$, however, employers earn higher profits by hoarding labor during downturns.

For our purposes, however, the most useful way to compare the two strategies is in terms of the ease of filling vacancies, as represented by the transition rate μ. If μ=0, then V^v=0, since vacancies remain unfilled forever. In this case, the fixed-employment strategy is superior provided the wage is low enough relative to the prices and transition parameters such that V^f is positive. If μ sufficiently large, however, the spot-market strategy is superior since, as $\mu\rightarrow\infty$, the variable-

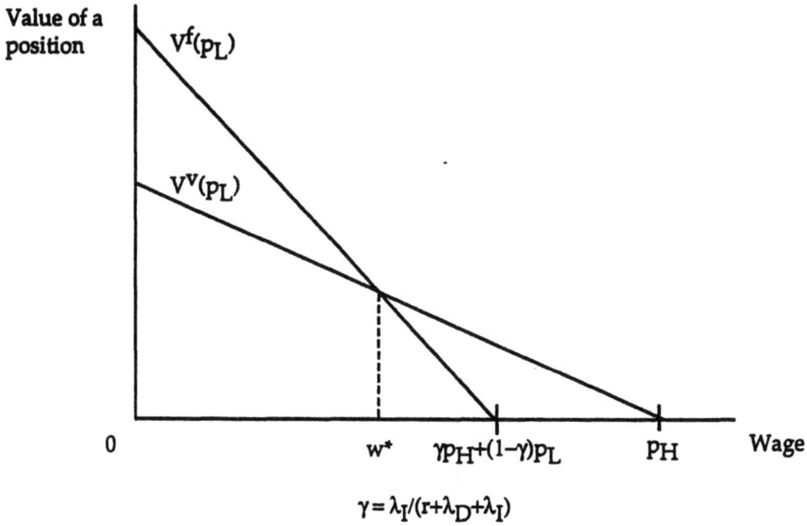

Figure 3: The Value of a Position When the Price is Low as a Function of the Wage.

employment policy approaches the best of all possible worlds for employers, where they can lay off workers whenever the price is low and immediately fill vacancies when the price rises again. In general, the fixed-employment strategy is superior from employers' point of view whenever μ is less than a critical value μ^*, where μ^* is given by

$$\mu^* = \frac{\lambda_I p_H + (r+\lambda_D) p_L - (r+\lambda_D+\lambda_I) w}{w - p_L} \tag{8}$$

If $\mu>\mu^*$, the variable-employment policy is superior. If $\mu<\mu^*$, employers earn higher profits by retaining workers even when the current price makes production unprofitable. Note that $\mu^*>0$ if and only if $V^f>0$. The values of the two policies as functions of μ (for the case in which $V^f>0$) are illustrated in Figure 4.

The comparative statics of the tipping point μ^* can be easily derived from Equation 8. An increase in the wage or the interest rate lowers μ^*. A higher wage increases the loss from maintaining workers when the price is low and reduces the gain from having employees when the price is high. An increase in the interest rate increases the weight given to current losses relative to future gains. Both lower the threshold at which the variable employment-policy is superior. A decline in business conditions as represented by a lower λ_I or a higher λ_D also reduces μ^*. The longer the expected period when the price is low, or the shorter the expected period when the price is high, the more likely a variable-employment policy will be better from the employers' point of view.

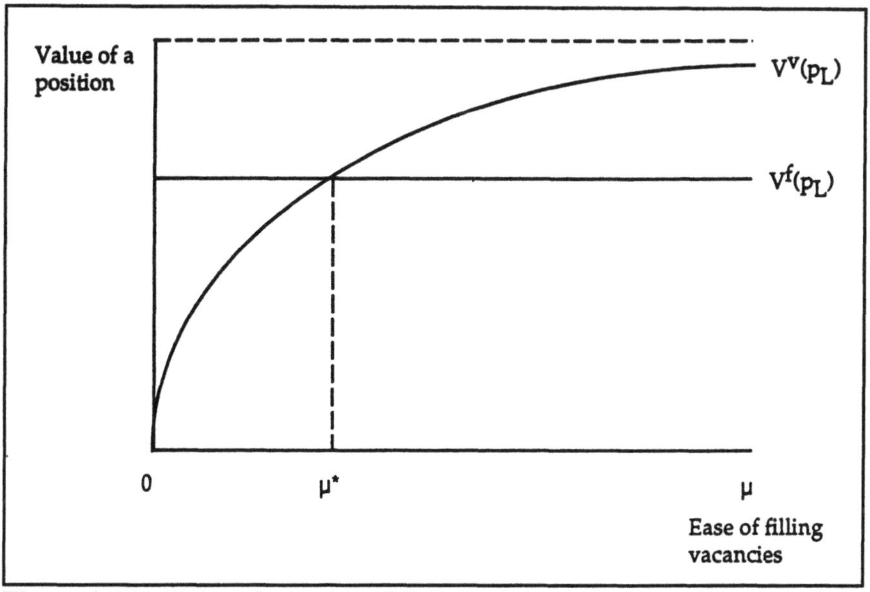

Figure 4: The Value of a Position When the Price is Low as a Function of the Ease of Filling Future Vacancies.

So far we have assumed that the wage is unaffected by firms' choice of employment policy. This might be a reasonable approximation for centralized systems of wage determination where the wage is independent of the layoff strategies chosen by any particular firm or industry. Even in the Nordic countries, however, a significant part of the wage increase is negotiated at the local level. If workers are not indifferent between different strategies, and if workers' preferences have some impact on the wage, either through the operation of a competitive labor market or through local bargaining, the assumption of an exogenous wage is restrictive.

One alternative is to assume that competition in the labor market equalizes workers' utility (assuming that workers are equally skilled). In this case, workers in firms without a long-term employment commitment must receive a compensating wage differential such that they are indifferent between accepting a job with permanent employment or a job that will last only as long as the price remains high. This imposes an additional cost on firms that adopt a variable-employment policy, since they must pay a higher wage to compensate their workers for the threat of unemployment. The need to pay a compensating wage differential reduces the slope of the V^v curve in Figure 4 and increases the threshold μ^*, possibly to infinity.

Another alternative is to assume that firms pay workers a premium over workers' outside option to induce workers to provide sufficient effort on the job. The idea is that workers who are paid so little that they are indifferent between keeping their job or being laid off have little incentive to work diligently[6]. This, again, implies that firms following a variable-employment policy have to pay a higher wage than firms following a fixed-employment policy. The wage premium that firms have to pay to assure a supply of high-quality labor is greater when workers know that they will be laid off no matter how hard they work when the price falls. Again, the slope of the V^v curve in Figure 4 is lowered and μ^* is increased.

Compensating wage differentials and efficiency wages provide additional reasons why long-term employment relations might benefit firms, but these modifications add little to the basic story. In the case with a fixed wage, if $V^f(p_L) \leq 0$, then $V^v(p_L) > V^f(p_L)$ for any $\mu > 0$, since $V^v(p_L)$ is always positive. With other models of wage determination, there are combinations of parameters that imply that a fixed-employment policy is always superior. In all cases, however, there is a range of prices and transition probabilities such that $V^v(p_L) < V^f(p_L)$ for low values of μ and $V^v(p_L) > V^f(p_L)$ for high values of μ as illustrated in Figure 4.

3. The Cost of Filling Vacancies

We have implicitly assumed in our analysis that firms are small enough relative to the labor market such that μ is exogenous for any individual employer. In aggregate, however, the likelihood of finding an appropriate worker depends on the total number of vacancies and unemployed workers looking for work, which, in turn, depends on the employment policies followed by employers. In the previous section we examined the effect of the likelihood of filling a vacancy on employers' choice of employment policy. In this section, we study the effect of employers' choices on the likelihood of filling vacancies and characterize the resulting equilibriums.

The core of the labor market is the process by which unemployed workers are matched to vacant jobs. It has become standard practice to conceptualize the matching of unemployed workers with vacant jobs as an outcome that requires searching efforts by both workers and employers (Mortensen, 1986; Pissarides, 1990). Formally, it is assumed that the number of matches each period, M, is an increasing function of the number of unemployed workers who are searching for jobs, u, and of the number of vacancies that employers are seeking to fill, v, or $M=M(u,v)$. An increase in the number of job seekers or job vacancies will lead to an increase in the number of successful matches. Assuming that all vacancies are equally likely to be filled, we can write the probability of filling an empty position as

$$\mu dt = \frac{M(u,v)}{v}. \tag{9}$$

It is common to assume that the matching function exhibits constant returns to scale (Pissarides, 1990). This implies that a doubling of the number of unemployed workers and the number of vacancies would double the number of matches. It is not obvious, however, that the assumption of constant returns to scale in the matching function is realistic. Models of the search process by Howitt and McAfee (1987) and Moene and Wallerstein (1995), for example, imply that matches are more difficult in "thin" labor markets where the number of unemployed and job vacancies are both low. If matching is easier in "thick" labor markets, then the matching process is characterized by increasing returns to scale. In this article, therefore, we assume that $M(u,v)$ is a homogeneous function with either constant or increasing returns to scale. Mathematically, we assume that $M(u,v)$ can be written as

$$M(u,v) = v^k M(u/v,1) = v^k m(u/v), \tag{10}$$

where $k \geq 1$ and $m'(\cdot) > 0$. If $k=1$, the matching function has constant returns to scale and the proportion of vacancies that are filled each period depends only on the ratio of unemployed workers to job vacancies, or $\mu dt = v^{k-1} m(u/v) = m(u/v)$. If $k>1$, the matching function has increasing returns to scale and the probability of finding a worker depends positively on both the number of unemployment workers per vacancy, (u/v), and the scale of the labor market.

According to Equations 9 and 10, the probability of filling a vacancy depends on the number of unemployed workers, u, and the number of job vacancies, v, which depend, in turn, on the distribution of high and low prices and the employment policies of employers. We assume, for simplicity, that all firms face the same price distribution, p_H and p_L with transition parameters λ_D and λ_I, but that price changes are job-specific. In every period, the price for some jobs' output is high while the price for other jobs' output is low. With constant transition parameters, the economy will evolve to a stationary equilibrium where the shares of job positions with a high price and a low price are constant as individual positions jump from one state to the other[7].

Consider first the case where all firms follow a variable-employment policy. Then any position may be in one of three states. Let $\theta^v(p_L,0)$, $\theta^v(p_H,0)$, and $\theta^v(p_H,1)$ be the shares of positions with a low price, a high price with a job vacancy, and a high price with an employed worker, respectively. In stationary equilibrium, the expected number of positions leaving the low-price state each period must equal the expected number of positions entering the low-price state, or

$$\lambda_I \theta^v(p_L,0) = \lambda_D[\theta^v(p_H,0) + \theta^v(p_H,1)].$$

Similarly, the expected number of positions leaving the state with a high price and a job vacancy, either because the position is filled or because the price drops, must equal the expected number of new vacancies:

$$(\mu + \lambda_D)\theta^v(p_H,0) = \lambda_I \theta^v(p_L,0).$$

To complete the set of equilibrium conditions, we can use either the equality between expected exit and entry into the state with a high price and an employed worker

$$\lambda_D \theta^v(p_H,1) = \mu \theta^v(p_H,0)$$

or the condition that the three states exhaust all possibilities $\theta^v(p_L,0)+\theta^v(p_H,0)+\theta^v(p_H,1)=1$.

Solving for the equilibrium shares $\theta^v(p_L,0)$, $\theta^v(p_H,0)$, and $\theta^v(p_H,1)$, we have

$$\theta^v(p_L,0) = \left(\frac{\lambda_D}{\lambda_D+\lambda_I}\right), \tag{11}$$

$$\theta^v(p_H,0) = \left(\frac{\lambda_D}{\mu+\lambda_D}\right)\left(\frac{\lambda_I}{\lambda_D+\lambda_I}\right), \quad and \tag{12}$$

$$\theta^v(p_H,1) = \left(\frac{\mu}{\mu+\lambda_D}\right)\left(\frac{\lambda_I}{\lambda_D+\lambda_I}\right). \tag{13}$$

Letting N denote the total number of positions, the average number of vacancies when all employers follow a variable-employment policy is given by

$$v^v = \theta^v(p_H,0)N = \left(\frac{\lambda_D}{\mu+\lambda_D}\right)\left(\frac{\lambda_I}{\lambda_D+\lambda_I}\right)N. \tag{14}$$

Letting L denote the total number of workers, the expected number of unemployed workers when employers follow a variable-employment policy is given by

$$u^v = L-\theta^v(p_H,1)N = L-\left(\frac{\mu}{\mu+\lambda_D}\right)\left(\frac{\lambda_I}{\lambda_D+\lambda_I}\right)N.$$

Finally, if the number of available workers equals the number of positions, or $L=N$, the expected number of unemployed workers is

$$u^v = \left(\frac{\mu+\lambda_D+\lambda_I}{\mu+\lambda_D}\right)\left(\frac{\lambda_D}{\lambda_D+\lambda_I}\right)N$$

and the ratio of unemployed per vacancy is given by

$$\left(\frac{u}{v}\right)^v = \frac{\mu+\lambda_D+\lambda_I}{\lambda_I}. \tag{15}$$

Note that the number of unemployed workers exceeds the number of vacancies, even though the total number of workers and positions is equal since some firms with an empty position are not interested in hiring at the current price.

Parallel calculations when all firms follow a fixed-employment policy, however, run into difficulty. With no layoffs and $L=N$, $u^f=v^f=0$ and $(u/v)^f$ is undefined. This problem can be overcome by incorporating exogenous turnover into the model. In reality, some separations occur through quits and retirements, regardless of a firm's employment policy. Thus even firms that offer implicit, long-term employment guarantees do have vacancies to fill periodically. Until now, we have ignored such turnover since it plays no role in our analysis. But now we have to introduce exogenous turnover to determine $(u/v)^f$. We can then take the limit as such turnover goes to zero to keep our analysis consistent.

We introduce, therefore, a new parameter, δ, such that δdt represents the likelihood of a worker quitting within the period dt. Let $\theta^f(1)$ be the share of positions that are filled when firms follow a fixed-employment policy. Then the stationary distribution of filled and empty positions can be found from the condition that the expected number of matches must equal the expected number of separations

$$\mu[1-\theta^f(1)] = \delta\theta^f(1) ,$$

which can be solved to yield

$$\theta^f(1) = \frac{\mu}{\mu+\delta}. \tag{16}$$

When all firms follow a fixed-employment policy, the expected number of vacancies is

$$v^f = [1-\theta^f(1)]N = \left(\frac{\delta}{\mu+\delta}\right)N. \tag{17}$$

while the expected number of unemployed workers is

$$u^f = L-\theta^f(1)N = L-\left(\frac{\mu}{\mu+\delta}\right)N.$$

If $L=N$, then $v^f=u^f$ and $(u/v)^f=1$. Taking the limit as δ approaches zero, we have

$$v^f = 0 \text{ and } (u/v)^f = 1. \tag{18}$$

Now we can compare the likelihood of filling a vacancy depending on the employment policies of firms. Equations 14 and 18 imply that $v^v>v^f$, while Equations 15 and 18 imply that $(u/v)^v>(u/v)^f$. When employers follow a variable-employment policy, there are both more vacancies and more unemployed workers per vacancy. For both reasons (according to Equations 9 and 10), the likelihood of filling a vacancy is higher when other firms follow a variable-employment policy than when other firms follow a fixed-employment policy, or $\mu^v>\mu^f$. The more firms follow a variable-employment policy, the higher the likelihood of filling a position, and, as illustrated in Figure 4, the greater the likelihood of filling a position, the more profitable a variable-employment policy.

There are three possible cases to consider. If $\mu^*<\mu^f$, where μ^* is the tipping value of μ where employers are indifferent between the two employment policies (as given in Equation 8), then the only equilibrium is one in which all firms choose the variable-employment policy. In this case, the likelihood of filling vacancies is sufficiently high to make the variable-employment policy employers' dominant strategy. If $\mu^*>\mu^v$, then the only equilibrium is one where all firms follow a fixed-employment policy. In this case, the cost of filling vacancies is sufficiently high that the fixed-employment policy is always more profitable.

If $\mu^f<\mu^*<\mu^v$, however, there are two locally stable equilibriums. If, on the one hand, all firms follow a variable-employment policy, the cost of filling vacancies is sufficiently low such that a variable-employment policy is the most profitable. If, on the other hand, all firms follow a fixed-employment policy, the cost of filling a vacancy is high enough to induce profit-maximizing firms to hoard labor during periods of a low price in order to be assured of being able to produce when the price increases. Conditions of labor scarcity induce firms to hoard labor, which has the effect of reinforcing labor scarcity. Conditions of high unemployment induce firms to cease hoarding labor, which increases unemployment.

4. Unemployment and Economic Integration

If our argument is right, the small EFTA countries maintained conditions of full employment, in part, because past conditions of labor scarcity encouraged firms to hoard labor during times of slack demand. Does economic integration necessarily destroy the possibility of sustaining full employment equilibriums under conditions of high unemployment elsewhere in Europe?

The answer depends on what sort of integration occurs. In any conceivable model of unemployment, the movement of labor into the countries with low unemployment could cause unemployment rates to converge. Yet labor mobility within the EC has remained limited in spite of large differences in real wages. The elimination of barriers to labor mobility within the EC is recent, and labor mobility may increase dramatically in the long run. The four Nordic countries, however, eliminated all barriers to labor mobility within the Nordic region in the mid-1970s. In addition, the Danish, Norwegian, and Swedish languages are similar enough so that the language barrier is low. Yet Danish unemployment rates of over 10% coexisted with labor shortages in Norway and Sweden for most of the 1970s and 1980s.

Another, perhaps more important, channel by which economic integration may alter the equilibrium is via capital outflows. Suppose, to be concrete, that all countries have the same labor productivity and the same price distribution. If markets are not integrated, different equilibriums may exist in different locations. In some, jobs may last for a short duration and unemployment may be high, while in others jobs may be permanent and unemployment low. In general, the rate of profit will differ, depending on differences in wages and on the prevailing layoff policies.

Capital mobility implies the disappearance of differences in profit rates between countries. Assume, temporarily, that the wage is either the same in all markets or is higher in markets with lower unemployment, as implied by the literature on the real-wage curve (Carlin and Soskice, 1990). In this case, all countries will end up with the same type of equilibrium in the labor market after integration. If the high unemployment equilibrium prevailed in at least one country prior to integration, and if this labor market is sufficiently large, then the high unemployment equilibrium will prevail in all labor markets after integration. The reason why is illustrated in Figure 4. Profits are higher in the equilibrium with short-term employment relationships for a given wage and price distribution if both equilibriums exist. If firms have the choice of investing in either equilibrium, they will locate in the market in which variable-employment policies prevail. As firms move production out of the market with long-term employment, unemployment rises. With rising unemployment, the difficulty of filling vacancies eases and the equilibrium may shift toward short-term employment relationships. If the wage is lower in the equilibrium with higher unemployment, the incentive for firms to leave markets with a low unemployment equilibrium is even greater.

The assumptions that underlie this analysis of the impact of capital mobility are restrictive. Labor productivity is not the same in different countries. Firms compare labor costs, not wages. It is not clear that labor costs are the same or higher in countries with lower unemployment. In addition, some theories of wage formation imply that wages would be lower in the low-unemployment equilibrium than in the high-unemployment equilibrium, even if productivity were the same. For example, employers who offer an implicit long-term employment contract may be able to attract workers with a lower wage than employers who offer employment only until the next downturn. Alternatively, firms may have to pay a higher wage to deter shirking if employees know that they may lose their job at any time for reasons unrelated to job performance (Moene and Wallerstein, 1995).

The strongest effect of economic integration on the sustainability of full-employment equilibriums may be via the constraints imposed on macroeconomic policy. A sudden decline in demand, a decline in λ_I or an increase in λ_D in our model, may reduce the expected delay in filling a vacancy at which firms are indifferent between labor-hoarding and labor-releasing policies to such an extent that firms find it profitable to lay off when their price is low irrespective of other firms' behavior. In this case, employment would rise rapidly if the initial equilibrium was one of full employment. Moreover, unemployment would remain high, even if the demand parameters, λ_I and λ_D, subsequently returned to their prior levels. A temporary fall in demand can cause a long-lasting increase in unemployment.

Avoiding the high-unemployment trap requires keeping both the wage sufficiently low and demand sufficiently high. Apart from Switzerland, the EFTA countries relied on centralized systems of wage bargaining to moderate wage growth and both devaluations and increased government spending to make up for declines in foreign or private domestic demand[8]. In this context, economic integration has two counteracting effects. On the one hand, greater economic integration may make the attainment of wage moderation easier, as employment becomes more sensitive to increases in labor costs. On the other hand, increased economic integration has made the management of aggregate demand more difficult. The lack of a clear picture of the constraints on macroeconomic policy that membership in the EC will entail, however, makes it impossible to make predictions regarding the impact of economic integration with any confidence.

5. Conclusion

In an environment of labor scarcity, firms that offer workers long-term employment contracts may earn higher profits than firms that use layoffs to reduce costs when the price falls. Thus, labor scarcity can encourage the growth of firms that follow a no-layoff policy. In contrast, in an environment with a large pool of unemployed workers, companies that act quickly to reduce costs through layoffs may earn higher profits than firms that offer long-term employment guarantees. In this way, the pool of unemployed may promote the relative growth of firms that respond to low prices with layoffs. In both high- and low-unemployment equilibriums, firms do worse if they deviate from the employment policies followed by other firms.

In a study of Norwegian employment in manufacturing, mining, and construction from 1966 to 1989, Moene and Nymoen (1991) found the demand for labor to be a negative function of the level of unemployment after controlling for the usual explanatory variables such as aggregate demand, real product wages, the rate of interest, and the stock of capital. According to their estimates, a 1,000-person increase in the pool of unemployed workers induces firms to hire 350 fewer workers at a fixed level of demand and input prices. Thus, negative demand shocks increase the level of unemployment corresponding to a given macroeconomic policy stance, while positive demand shocks have the reverse effect.

In sum, the EFTA countries were able to maintain lower levels of unemployment than other European countries for most of the 1970s and 1980s for three reasons: (1) wage-setting institutions that kept wage growth moderate, (2) a policy commitment to full employment, and (3) the presence of low levels of unemployment in the recent past. Today, the centralized wage-setting institutions are weakened, the commitment to full employment has been eroded, and unemployment is high. It is unlikely that future EFTA unemployment rates will diverge as much from levels of unemployment in other European countries as they did in the past 20 years.

Endnotes

1. An earlier version of this article was presented at the meeting of the Study Group on the Political Economy of European Integration sponsored by the Center for German and European Studies at the University of California, Berkeley, November 12, 1993. We thank Steinar Holden, Karl Pedersen, Asbjørn Rødseth, Torben Andersen and the participants of the conference for their comments. Financial support from the Center for German and European Studies and the Research Council of Norway is gratefully acknowledged.

2. The source for all unemployment figures through 1992 is the Organization for Economic Cooperation and Development (1992, 1993).

3. Table 1 omits Luxembourg (a member of the EC) and Iceland (a member of EFTA).

4. Alternative formulations in which the wage is endogenous in different ways are discussed at the end of this section.

5. Note that the probability that both the price will fall and the position will be filled within *dt* goes to zero as *dt* goes to zero.

6. See Weiss (1990) for an overview of models in which firms pay a premium to obtain higher quality workers or to induce greater effort on the job.

7. In this framework, a recession is represented by an increase in λ_D or a decline in λ_I, which leads to an increase in the fraction of firms facing the low price.

8. Switzerland is the exception among the EFTA countries, both in its decentralized system of wage setting and in the little use made of countercyclical policies. More than other countries in Europe, Switzerland has kept unemployment low when employment declines by expelling guest workers.

References

Blanchard, Olivier J., and Summers, Lawrence H. Hysteresis and the European Unemployment Problem. In Summers, Lawrence H.(ed.), *Understanding Unemployment*. Cambridge, MA: MIT Press, 1990).

Carlin, Wendy, and Soskice, David. *Macroeconomics and the Wage Bargain: A Modern Approach to Employment, Inflation and the Exchange Rate*. Oxford, England: Oxford University Press, 1990.

Howitt, Peter, and McAfee, R. Preston. Costly Search and Recruiting. *International Economic Review* 1987, 28: 89--107.

Lange, Peter, Wallerstein, Michael, and Golden, Miriam. The End of Corporatism? Wage Setting in the Nordic and Germanic Countries. In Jacoby, Sanford (ed.), *Workers of Nations: Industrial Relations in a Global Economy.* Oxford, England: Oxford University Press, 1995.

Layard, Richard, Nickell, Stephen, and Jackman, Richard. *Unemployment, Macroeconomic Performance and the Labour Market.* Oxford, England: Oxford University Press, 1991.

Lindbeck, Assar, and Snower, Dennis J. *The Insider-Outsider Theory of Employment and Unemployment.* Cambridge, MA: MIT Press, 1988.

Moene, Karl Ove, and Nymoen, Ragnar. The Dependency of Labour Demand on Unemployment: Norwegian Industry 1966(1)--1986(4). Oslo: Bank of Norway, Working Paper 91/3, 1991.

Moene, Karl Ove and Wallerstein, Michael. Full Employment as a Worker Discipline Device. In Roemer, John (ed.), *Property Rights, Incentives and Welfare.* London: Macmillan Press, 1995.

Mortensen, Dale T. 1986. Job Search and Labor Market Analysis. In Ashenfelter, Orley C., and Layard, Richard (eds.), *Handbook of Labor Economics* Volume 2. Amsterdam: North-Holland, 1986.

Moses, Jonathan W. Abdication from National Political Autonomy: What's Left to Leave. *Politics and Society* 1994, 22: 125--148.

Notermans, Ton. The Abdication from National Policy Autonomy: Why the Macroeconomic Policy Regime Has Become so Unfavorable to Labor. *Politics and Society* 1993, 21: 133--167.

Organization for Economic Cooperation and Development. *OECD Economic Outlook,* 52 (December). Paris: Organization for Economic Cooperation and Development, 1992.

Organization for Economic Cooperation and Development. *OECD Economic Outlook,* 53 (June). Paris: Organization for Economic Cooperation and Development, 1993.

Organization for Economic Cooperation and Development. *OECD Economic Surveys--Sweden.* Paris: Organization for Economic Cooperation and Development, 1994.

Pissarides, C. A. *Equilibrium Unemployment Theory.* Oxford, England: Basil Blackwell, 1990.

Soskice, David, and Carlin, Wendy. Medium-Run Keynesianism: Hysteresis and Capital Scrapping. In Davidson, Paul and Kregel, Jan (eds.), *Macroeconomic Problems and Policies of Income Distribution.* London: Edward Elgar Press, 1989.

Weiss, Andrew. *Efficiency Wages.* Princeton, NJ: Princeton University Press, 1990.

European Integration and the Regionalization of World Trade and Currencies: The Economics and the Politics

Jeffrey A. Frankel and Shang-Jin Wei[1]

1. Introduction

In the 1990s the possible breakup of the world economy into economic blocs has become a special focus of interest -- largely in response to such projects as the European Monetary System, Europe 1992, the enlargement of the European Union, the North American Free Trade Agreement that went into effect in 1994, and suspicions of a Japanese sphere of influence in Asia. The possible regionalization of the world economy raises important issues for policy. Given that worldwide free trade is difficult to attain politically, should it be pursued first within regional Free Trade Areas or in Preferential Trading Arrangements? What gets higher priority: expanding the number of countries participating in regional Preferential Trading Arrangements, reducing intraregional barriers to zero, or reducing the average level of trade barriers worldwide? Within given geographic groupings, what should be the sequencing among steps such as financial integration, currency integration, trade integration, and labor market integration? The list of important research topics is quite long. These questions are perhaps more salient in Europe than anywhere else. Regional arrangements have seen a steady expansion in scope since World War II. The succession of labels tells the story of extension in purview, from production and trade matters in a few economic sectors to a contemplation of all-encompassing economic and political integration: The European Coal and Steel Community, the Common Market, the European Economic Community, the European Community, and finally the European Union. At the same time, the European grouping has expanded along the geographic dimension as well: from the original six countries to nine, then to 12, and now to 15. Four members of the European Free Trade Association negotiated accession to the European Union in 1994 (Austria, Finland, Sweden, and Norway, with Norwegian voters blocking it). The trade-off between expansion in scope and expansion in membership has been a very live issue for Europeans.

This article considers the statistical record on the extent of European integration along two dimensions, trade links and currency links, and the interaction between the two. That these two dimensions of integration may be closely intertwined is evident in that a major motivation behind attempts to strengthen currency links within Europe is to reduce the extent to which exchange-rate risk discourages imports and exports and thereby to promote stronger trade links. Other important aspects, such as financial links within regions or the extent to which countries within a region share common economic disturbances, are not considered here.[2]

Specifically, the article looks econometrically at three questions: (1) Is trade biased toward intraregional partners within each of the three potential major blocs? (2) Are exchange rates more stable within each of the three potential blocs than across them? (3) To the extent exchange rates are stabilized within a bloc, does that contribute to intrabloc trade?

A central motivating question is the extent to which stabilization of exchange rates within Europe has been a contributing factor to the increase in intraregional trade there. Despite still-official plans for European Monetary Union by 1999, the setbacks that the Exchange Rate Mechanism has suffered in the crises of September 1992 and August 1993 mean that a return to the higher levels of exchange-rate variability that held in the past is a real possibility. To what extent would that reduce intra-European trade?

Using the gravity model to examine bilateral trade patterns throughout the world, we find clear evidence of trading blocs in Europe, the Western Hemisphere (WH), and East Asia and the Pacific. In Europe, it is the European Community (EC) that operates as a bloc, not including the European Free Trade Association (EFTA). Two EC members are estimated to trade an extra 48% more with each other beyond what can be explained by proximity, size, and per capita gross national product (GNP). Even though the blocs fall along natural geographic lines, they may actually be "super-natural," by which we mean intraregional trade bias in excess of what can be justified by natural geography. On the other hand, at the same time we find grounds for encouragement in an apparent tendency for the formation of customs unions to build political momentum to liberalize trade with respect to nonmembers. The best example is the EC, where a term to capture the openness of members to global trade is positive and statistically significant in our equation. Ever since the formation of the European Economic Community, there have been fears among nonmembers of a "Fortress Europe." These fears were exacerbated in the late 1980s when Jacques Delors launched the EC 1992 initiative (Arndt and Willett, 1991; Dickens, 1992; Greenaway, 1991; Kreinen, 1981; Schott, 1989). But there is no evidence in our results that the EC has diverted trade away from nonmembers. The only grouping that shows clear evidence of a negative coefficient, indicating trade diversion, is EFTA.

Turning to the possibility of currency blocs, we find a degree of intraregional stabilization of exchange rates, especially in Europe. Not surprisingly, the European currencies link to the deutsche mark (DM), and WH countries peg to the dollar. East Asian countries, however, link to the dollar, not the yen. We also find some tentative cross-section evidence that bilateral exchange-rate stability may have a (small) effect on trade.

We conclude with a discussion of the political economy of regional integration. Is economic regionalism compatible with progress toward a liberal multilateral trading system?

2. Is Europe a Trade Bloc?

There is more talk of regionalization--of whether the world is breaking up into three great trading blocs or currency blocs (Europe, WH, and East Asia; or ecu, dollar, and yen blocs)--than there are attempts at hard quantitative analysis. Often studies simply report measures of the relative size of the blocs, such as shares of world trade.

Many observers base their belief that world trade is becoming more regionalized on a simple statistic: the share of trade that is intraregional. This share has always been higher for Europe than for other continents: .36 in the EC (or .50 in Western Europe as a whole) in 1965, as opposed to .20 in East Asia and .31 in the WH. It also has increased over time: to .42 in 1980 and .47 in 1990 for the EC (or .54 and .60, respectively, in Western Europe as a whole). That the share of intraregional trade is high, or increasing, within a given grouping, however, does not necessarily mean that the members of this grouping are undertaking explicit discriminatory trade policy measures to bring this about. A high level of intraregional trade, or a rapid increase in the share, could be the result of natural factors, such as proximity or rapid economic growth, as we shall see.

A natural way to adjust for the determinants of bilateral trade is by means of the gravity model. The gravity model says that trade between two countries is proportionate to the product of their GNPs and inversely related to the distance between them, by analogy to the formula for gravitational attraction between two masses. It has a fairly long history and fits the data remarkably well empirically.[3]

In addition to the variables for size and distance, we also add the product of their per capita GNPs and an "Adjacent" dummy variable to indicate when two countries share a common land border. A dummy variable can then be added to represent when both countries in a given pair belong to the same regional grouping. The goal is to see how much of the high level of trade within each region can be explained by simple economic factors common to bilateral trade throughout the world and how much is left over to be attributed to a special regional effect. The great advantage of the Ordinary Least Squares (OLS) regression technique is that it can separate out the effects of the various different factors (provided the linear equation is correctly specified). In this way we can avoid attributing what is really the effect of, say, proximity or a common border to the apparent effect of common membership in a preferential trading arrangement.

Table 1 reports results of the gravity model estimation for the years 1980, 1985, and 1990. The variable we seek to explain is trade (exports plus imports), in log form, between pairs of countries. We have 63 countries in our data set, so there are 1,953 data points (63 x 62/2) for a given year. The results differ from those reported in earlier articles, particularly by the presence of three terms to capture bilateral differences in factor endowments across countries. The inclusion of differences in capital/labor ratios (K/L), education levels (Edu), and land/labor ratios (Land/L) is meant to capture classic Heckscher-Ohlin-type influences on trade, which one expects to play a role alongside more-modern considerations of product differentiation and increasing returns to scale. These variables are sometimes significantly greater than zero, though the pattern is not consistent enough to make one question the modern models. In any case there is little effect on the questions of interest here.

We find all four standard gravity variables to be highly statistically significant (.01 level), though some of the coefficient estimates fluctuate a bit. The estimated coefficient for the log of the product of the two countries' GNPs is about .7, indicating that, though trade increases with size, it increases less than proportionately (by .7% for every 1% increase in size, holding constant the per capita GNP). This reflects the familiar pattern that small economies tend to be more dependent on international trade than larger, more diversified economies. The estimated coefficient on the product of per capita GNPs is about .3, indicating that richer countries trade more. The coefficient on the log of distance is about -.5. This means that when the distance between two nonadjacent countries is higher by 1%, the trade between them falls by about .5%. The coefficient on the dummy variable representing Adjacency is about .7, indicating that two countries that share a common border trade roughly twice as much [exp(.7) = 2.0] as would two otherwise-similar countries.

If there were nothing to the notion of trading blocs, then these four or five basic variables might soak up most of the explanatory power. There would be little left to attribute to a dummy variable representing whether two trading partners are both located in the same regional grouping. (These dummy variables are the ones in Table 1 represented by a "2" suffix.) In this case the level and trend in intraregional trade would be due solely to the proximity of the countries and to their rates of overall economic growth.

To a surprising extent, this is in fact the case. The gravity model results suggest that up through 1980, the high level and increase in intra-European trade can be partly explained by the size, per capita GNP, proximity, and common borders of European countries. A bit of the intraregional trade remains to be attributed to the EC. The point estimate of the effect on trade among EC members is 36% [exp(.31) = 1.36]. But the estimated coefficient on the EC is only of borderline significance. (Furthermore, the 1980 estimate diminishes, as we shall see, when a dummy variable is added to capture the overall openness of European countries. This dummy variable is defined to equal one when *either one* of the two countries in a given pair is located in Europe, as opposed to both.)

By 1985 the EC dummy had become statistically significant. The coefficient implies that two EC members trade an extra 60% with each other [exp(.47) = 1.60]. It is clear that it is the EC in particular that is having an influence, as terms for EFTA and for Europe overall are not significant statistically.[4]

The EC coefficient in 1990 is again significant, though no higher than in 1985. The effect is 48% [exp(.39) = 1.477]. The EFTA and Europe effects are again nonsignificant.

Table 1: Factor Endowments in a Gravity Model of Bilateral Trade

Year	GNP	GNP/ capita	Dist	Adjac	WH2	EAsia2	APEC2	EC2	EFTA2	K/L	Edu	Land/L	Adj.R^2/ SEE	n
1980	.71***	.38***	-.49***	.54**	1.07***	.95***	1.70***	.30*	.03	.08**			.78/.98	656
	.02	.02	.06	.21	.27	.26	.19	.17	.34	.03				
	.65***	.44***	-.48***	.51**	1.00***	.95***	1.67***	.28*	.06		.10***		.79/.98	656
	.03	.03	.06	.21	.27	.26	.19	.17	.19		.03			
	.72***	.41***	-.45***	.55***	1.06***	.80***	1.79***	.29*	-.01			-.08**	.78/.99	656
	.02	.03	.06	.21	.28	.27	.19	.17	.34			.03		
	.65***	.42***	-.46***	.56***	1.06***	.86***	1.72***	.31*	.10	.08**	.10***	-.06**	.79/.98	656
	.03	.03	.06	.21	.27	.27	.19	.17	.33	.03	.03	.03		
1985	.73***	.40***	-.60***	.52**	.79***	.73***	1.34***	.46***	-.27	.03			.80/.95	652
	.02	.03	.05	.21	.28	.25	.18	.16	.33	.03				
	.74***	.40***	-.60***	.51**	.78***	.72**	1.34***	.46***	-.29		-.004		.80/.96	652
	.02	.03	.05	.21	.28	.25	.18	.16	.33		.03			

	.74***	.41***	-.57***	.53***	.79***	.62**	1.40***	.47***	-.29			-.06*	.81/.95	652
	.02	.03	.05	.21	.28	.25	.18	.16	.32			.03		
	.74***	.40***	-.58***	.54**	.81***	.63***	1.40***	.47***	-.27	.03	-.01	-.06	.81/.95	652
	.02	.03	.05	.21	.28	.26	.18	.16	.32	.03	.03	.03		
1990	.65***	.15***	-.48***	.75***	1.36***	.51**	1.34***	.40***	-.31	.01			.82/.87	655
	.02	.02	.05	.21	.24	.23	.17	.15	.30	.03				
	.62***	.17***	-.48***	.74***	1.33***	.52***	1.33***	.40***	-.29		.04		.82/.87	655
	.03	.03	.05	.19	.24	.23	.17	.15	.30		.03			
	.64***	.15***	-.50***	.72***	1.33***	.63***	1.28***	.39***	-.32			.06**	.82/.87	655
	.02	.02	.05	.19	.24	.24	.17	.15	.30			.03		
	.62***	.17***	-.51***	.72***	1.32***	.67***	1.26***	.39***	-.28	.02	.04	.07**	.82/.87	655
	.02	.02	.05	.19	.24	.24	.17	.15	.30	.03	.03	.03		

Notes: All regressions have an intercept, which is not reported here. All variables except the dummies are in logs. The endowment variables are for 1980 only, but used in regressions for 1985 and 1990 as well. Standard errors of coefficients are reported in parentheses.
APEC = Asian Pacific Economic Cooperation.
***, **, and * denote significant at the .01, .05, and .10 levels, respectively.

Table 2: Linguistic Links in a Gravity Model of Bilateral Trade: All Merchandise

Variable	1965	1970	1975	1980	1985	1990
GNP	0.64**	0.63**	0.70**	0.72**	0.50**	0.74**
	(0.02)	(0.02)	(0.02)	(0.02)	(0.02)	(0.02)
GNP/	0.39**	0.46**	0.37**	0.35**	0.07**	0.17*
capita	(0.03)	(0.03)	(0.03)	(0.02)	(0.03)	(0.02)
Distance	-0.40**	-0.51**	-0.66**	-0.58**	-0.43**	-0.64**
	(0.06)	(0.06)	(0.07)	(0.06)	(0.06)	(0.05)
Adjacency	0.58**	0.69**	0.54**	0.64**	0.75**	0.66**
	(0.17)	(0.17)	(0.18)	(0.17)	(0.19)	(0.16)
English	0.77**	0.44**	0.53**	0.90**	0.46**	0.60**
	(0.11)	(0.11)	(0.12)	(0.11)	(0.12)	(0.10)
Spanish	-0.22	0.15	0.06	-0.17	0.03	-0.13
	(0.20)	(0.20)	(0.21)	(0.20)	(0.25)	(0.18)
Chinese	1.05*	2.15**	0.79	0.98	1.08	1.32
	(0.54)	(0.77)	(0.83)	(0.55)	(0.57)	(0.48)
Arabic	0.09	-0.42*	-0.28	-0.19	-0.19	-0.16
	(0.27)	(0.29)	(0.26)	(0.26)	(0.37)	(0.25)
French	0.19	0.12	0.07	0.23	0.09	0.45*
	(0.22)	(0.22)	(0.23)	(0.23)	(0.26)	(0.21)
WH2	0.32*	0.08	0.49*	1.07**	0.21	1.21**
	(0.19)	(0.19)	(0.20)	(0.19)	(0.22)	(0.17)
EAEC2	1.77**	1.78**	1.00**	0.93**	-0.27	0.69**
	(0.29)	(0.30)	(0.31)	(0.27)	(0.29)	(0.24)
APEC2	-0.02	0.42	0.58*	0.96**	1.66**	0.74**
	(0.22)	(0.22)	(0.23)	(0.19)	(0.21)	(0.17)
EEC2	-0.09	-0.23	-0.41*	-0.006	1.15**	0.21
	(0.17)	(0.17)	(0.19)	(0.18)	(0.19)	(0.16)
EFTA2	0.23	0.20	0.16	0.34	0.67*	0.14
	(0.29)	(0.29)	(0.31)	(0.31)	(0.34)	(0.28)
WH1	-0.29**	-0.21*	-0.25*	-0.04	0.31**	0.20**
	(0.10)	(0.10)	(0.09)	(0.08)	(0.10)	(0.08)
EAEC1	0.78**	0.55**	0.60**	0.85**	-0.51**	1.05**
	(0.14)	(0.14)	(0.14)	(0.12)	(0.13)	(0.10)
APEC1	-0.55**	0.38**	-0.35*	-0.37	0.26	0.62**
	(0.13)	(0.13)	(0.14)	(0.12)	(0.14)	(0.11)
EEC1	0.12	0.10	0.12	0.38**	0.44**	0.13*
	(0.09)	(0.09)	(0.09)	(0.08)	(0.09)	(0.08)
EFTA1	-0.48**	0.48**	0.55**	-0.19*	-0.59**	0.43**
	(0.10)	(0.10)	(0.10)	(0.09)	(0.11)	(0.09)
n	1,194	1,274	1,453	1,708	1,343	1,573
SEE	1.01	1.05	1.14	1.14	1.20	1.01
Adj.R^2	0.71	0.73	0.73	0.74	0.57	0.79

Note: ***, **, and * denote significant at the .01, .05, and .10 levels, respectively. (Standard errors of coefficients are reported in parentheses)

Why did the EC strengthen in the early 1980s? One possibility is the accession of Greece, Portugal, and Spain (which are included in the definition of EC countries throughout the sample). Another possible contributing factor, considered below, is the stabilization of exchange rates under the European Monetary System (EMS).

In Table 2 we extend the results in two directions. We report the results of a test for trade diversion. At the same time, we include terms to capture when two countries share a common language or past colonial links. Table 3 does the same in a test for trade in manufactured goods alone, excluding agriculture and other raw materials.

In both sets of results, English and Chinese are the two languages that show statistically significant effects; Arabic, French, and Spanish show less clear effects. A pair of English-speaking countries in 1990 trades 82% more than two otherwise-similar countries [exp(.6) = 1.82]. When all languages are constrained to have the same coefficient (including Dutch, German, Japanese, and Portuguese as well as the five major languages reported individually here), the effect is a highly significant 36% [exp(.3) = 1.36; not reported here].

The variables that appear in Table 3 with a "1" suffix are dummy variables that capture when *one country or the other* out of the pair in question is a member of the particular grouping. If a regional trading arrangement works to divert trade away from nonmembers, then the coefficient of this dummy variable should be negative.

The results show no evidence of trade diversion by the EC. Indeed, the coefficient on EC1 is positive. A positive coefficient like this indicates that EC countries are more open to trade worldwide, not just to trade with each other, compared to typical countries in the sample. One might wonder how the formation of a common market could lead to "less than zero" trade diversion. In theory, the reduction of trade barriers within the region should not encourage trade with other countries; if anything, it should discourage it, because the outsiders' goods are now more expensive than those of fellow members of the club. The answer is that countries in a given region may somewhat reduce barriers with respect to nonmembers at the same time that they reduce or eliminate barriers internally. Indeed, the two policy changes may be related in a political economy sense. Some have argued that the constellation of political forces that allows liberalization with respect to trade with regional neighbors may be similar to what is required to allow liberalization more generally. We consider these issues in the last section of this article.

3. Currency Blocs

The attempt to link the currencies of the EC member countries has been a centerpiece of plans for European integration. The hope is that stable bilateral exchange rates will promote trade and that trade links and currency links will in turn help promote other kinds of integration.

Table 3: Linguistic Links in a Gravity Model of Bilateral Trade: Manufactures

Variable	1965	1970	1975	1980	1985
GNP	0.65**	0.68**	0.77**	0.76**	0.74**
	(0.02)	(0.02)	(0.02)	(0.02)	(0.02)
GNP/capita	0.39**	0.34**	0.33**	0.33**	0.30**
	(0.03)	(0.03)	(0.03)	(0.02)	(0.02)
Distance	-0.40**	-0.52**	-0.60**	-0.52**	-0.68**
	(0.06)	(0.07)	(0.17)	(0.06)	(0.06)
Adjacency	0.58**	0.81**	0.60**	0.54**	0.76**
	(0.17)	(0.18)	(0.17)	(0.17)	(0.18)
English	0.77**	0.52**	0.82**	1.13**	0.45**
	(0.11)	(0.13)	(0.11)	(0.11)	(0.10)
Spanish	-0.22	-0.02	-0.07	-0.26	0.20
	(0.20)	(0.21)	(0.20)	(0.20)	(0.21)
Chinese	1.05*	3.04**	1.51*	1.44**	1.07*
	(0.54)	(0.77)	(0.76)	(0.53)	(0.54)
Arabic	0.09	0.48	0.19	-0.21	-0.02
	(0.27)	(0.37)	(0.28)	(0.28)	(0.27)
French	0.19	-0.16	0.12	0.38*	0.30
	(0.22)	(0.23)	(0.22)	(0.23)	(0.23)
WH2	0.32*	0.11	0.83**	1.48**	0.61**
	(0.19)	(0.20)	(0.19)	(0.19)	(0.19)
EAEC2	1.77**	1.24**	1.01**	0.98**	0.61*
	(0.29)	(0.30)	(0.29)	(0.26)	(0.26)
APEC2	-0.02	0.25	0.32*	0.83**	0.98**
	(0.22)	(0.22)	(0.21)	(0.18)	(0.19)
EEC2	-0.09	0.15	0.03	0.43*	0.16
	(0.17)	(0.18)	(0.17)	(0.17)	(0.18)
EFTA2	0.23	0.72*	0.72*	0.80*	0.35
	(0.29)	(0.29)	(0.29)	(0.31)	(0.31)
WH1	-0.29**	-0.08	-0.06	-0.04	-0.01
	(0.10)	(0.11)	(0.09)	(0.08)	(0.08)
EAEC1	0.78**	0.64**	1.00**	1.21**	0.67**
	(0.14)	(0.16)	(0.14)	(0.21)	(0.11)
APEC1	-0.55**	-0.30*	-0.52**	-0.53**	-0.38**
	(0.13)	(0.14)	(0.13)	(0.12)	(0.12)
EEC1	0.12	0.22*	0.36**	0.53**	0.45**
	(0.09)	(0.10)	(0.08)	(0.08)	(0.08)
EFTA1	-0.48**	-0.15	-0.03	0.25**	-0.36**
	(0.10)	(0.11)	(0.10)	(0.09)	(0.09)
n	1,194	1,118	1,287	1,614	1,647
SEE	1.01	1.05	1.04	1.12	1.12
Adj. R^2	0.71	0.72	0.77	0.75	0.76

Note: ** and * denote significant at the .01 and .05 levels. (Standard errors of coefficients are reported in parentheses.

Table 4: Weights Assigned to Foreign Currencies in Determining Changes in Value of EC Currencies

Time Period	Const	USD (b1)	Yen (b2)	DM (b3)	Adj.R^2 /DW	Chow/ White	S.E.R T-test b1+b2+b3=1
France							
1974-	-.001	-.273	.148	.370***	.31/	2.29/	.018
1978	.002	.357	.103	.127	1.79	7.86	-2.12
1979-	-.005***	-.170	.078**	.812***	.70/	1.02/	.013
1983	.002	.119	.039	.071	2.25	3.59	-1.39
1984-	-.001	-.046	-.031	.841***	.86/	1.83/	.009
1987	.001	.137	.074	.077	2.08	11.54	-1.05
1988-	.000	-.185***	-.024	.806***	.94/	.94/	.005
1992	.001	.069	.032	.052	2.21	4.68	-2.64
Italy							
1974-	-.005**	-.246	.076	.054	-.01/	.40/	.023
1978	.003	.451	.092	.169	1.85	9.57	-2.42
1979-	-.006***	.023	.052	.742***	.74/	1.01/	.010
1983	.001	.088	.037	.053	2.17	5.46	-1.16
1984-	-.003***	.426***	-.082**	.933***	.89/	2.54/	.007
1987	.001	.136	.037	.052	2.11	20.30	2.32
1988-	-.003	-.174*	-.063**	.713***	.93/	.22/	.005
1992	.001	.089	.029	.062	1.78	9.35	-3.51
Belgium							
1974-	.000	-.169**	-.056	.933***	.92/	3.33/	.007
1978	.001	.083	.035	.045	1.93	6.44	-2.19
1979-	-.004***	-.154	.044	.859***	.77/	1.02/	.012
1983	.001	.119	.030	.041	1.76	2.37	-1.42
1984-	-.000	-.090	-.029	.938***	.98/	.31/	.004
1987	.001	.070	.018	.040	2.38	12.83	-1.95
1988-	.000	-.133***	-.042**	.909***	.97/	.45/	.004
1992	.000	.048	.021	.034	2.72	3.71	-2.40
Britain							
1974-	.001	-1.74***	-.036	-.428**	.97/	4.52**/	.003
1978	.000	.05	.020	.020	1.92	21.94	-59.04
1979-	-.000	-1.71***	-.002	-.461**	.97/	23.52***/	.003
1983	.000	.052	.010	.023	1.94	19.71	-65.78
1984-	-.001	-2.50***	-.062*	-.513**	.96/	16.83***/	.005
1987	.001	.161	.031	.047	1.60	37.1***	-30.97
1988-	-.000	-1.98***	.011	-.63**	.99/	9.67***/	.002
1992	.000	.032	.013	.020	2.46	20.99	-57.38
Denmark							
1974-	-.002	-.031	-.010	.849***	.77/	1.82/	.011
1978	.002	.121	.048	.065	1.98	5.36	-.87
1979-	-.005***	.073	.116**	.884***	.86/	.32/	.009
1983	.001	.129	.051	.041	2.10	33.80	.56

continued

Time Period	Const	USD (b1)	Yen (b2)	DM (b3)	Adj.R^2 /DW	Chow/ White	S.E.R. T-test b1+b2+b3=1
1984-	-.001	-.145**	-.011	.877***	-.94/	1.43/	.006
1987	.001	.112	.038	.078	2.46	7.93	-1.79
1988-	-.000	-.007	-.035	.902***	.92/	.52/	.006
1992	.001	.011	.041	.073	2.02	8.21	-.77
Netherlands							
1974-	-.001	-.177*	-.047	.875***	.82/	1.52/	.010
1978	.001	.098	.043	.065	2.53	3.09	-1.71
1979-	-.001	-.163**	-.002	.853***	-.93/	1.15/	.006
1983	.001	.066	.022	.035	1.77	5.69	-3.52
1984-	-.000	-.122**-	.002	.942***	.97/	1.56/	.004
1987	.001	.064	.023	.036	2.81	4.16	-1.71
1988-	-.000	-.118*	-.019	.934***	.94/	.37/	.005
1992	.001	.066	.039	.041	2.82	3.52	-1.21
Greece							
1974-	-.005***	.203*	-.043	.294**	.17/	2.48/	.011
1978	.002	.111	.076	.142	1.52	48.31	-2.47
1979-	-.013***	-.061	.055	.309***	.04/	.89/	.027
1983	.003	.311	.077	.119	2.10	2.58	-1.70
1984-	-.014***	.481	.065	.835***	.27/	1.55/	.027
1987	.004	.375	.092	.186	1.88	3.01	.55
1988-	-.008***	-.249***	.541	.599***	.88/	1.11/	.006
1992	.001	.090	.053	.060	1.63	10.37	-3.49
Ireland							
1974-	.001**	-1.74***	-.036*	-.428***	.97/	4.51**/	.003
1978	.000	.051	.020	.020	1.92	21.93	-58.99
1979-	-.004***	-.13	.028	.765***	.80/	.78/	.009
1983	.001	.089	.029	.054	2.13	1.90	-2.41
1984-	-.002	.53***	.066	.592***	.79/	.73/	.011
1987	.002	.197	.090	.151	2.05	6.54	-2.97
1988-	.000	-.18***	-.022	.808***	.97/	1.42/	.003
1992	.000	.04	.024	.036	2.49	9.65	-3.69
Portugal							
1974-	-.012***	-.016	-.135	.499***	.10/	.88/	.028
1978	.003	.208	.106	.107	2.04	2.71	-1.15
1979-	-.012***	-.41	.051	.315***	.12/	3.13/	.025
1983	.003	.282	.064	.114	1.89	3.53	-2.75
1984-	-.009***	-.24***	.068***	.535**	.96/	4.29/	.004
1987	.001	.06	.024	.038	1.16	9.02	-6.81
1988-	-.001	-.38***	.075	.461***	.77/	1.93/	.009
1992	.001	.133	.048	.091	1.98	6.40	-3.16
Spain							
1974-	.005	.30*	.142	.162*	-.03/	.37/	.033
1978	.084	.171	.089	.091	1.94	1.37	-.60

Time Period	Const	USD (b1)	Yen (b2)	DM (b3)	Adj.R^2 /DW	Chow/ White	S.E.R. T-est b1+b2+b3=1
1979-	-.010***	-.128	-.076	.204**	.06/	1.01/	.016
1983	.002	.161	.088	.092	2.04	13.83	-3.99
1984-	-.001	.009	-.821	.708***	.73/	1.14/	.011
1987	.002	.148	.087	.107	1.92	17.70	-1.04
1988-	-.001	-.576***	.020	.418***	.73/	1.83/	.011
1992	.001	.176	.066	.121	2.14	8.13	-3.45

Notes : All currencies are measured in terms of SDR (USD 0.42, DM 0.19, Yen 0.15, French Franc 0.12, Pound 0.12). Heteroscedasticity-consistent standard errors are reported below coefficient estimates. Standard errors are reported below coefficients.
***, **, and *denote significant at the .01, .05, and .10 levels, respectively.

3.1 Stabilization of Exchange Rates Within the Blocs

It is instructive to look at statistics on the variability of exchange rates among various groupings of countries. Worldwide, monthly exchange-rate variability rose in the 1980s, from a standard deviation of .33% in 1980 to .38% in 1990. The latter figure suggests that for a typical pair of countries, approximately 95% of monthly exchange-rate changes are smaller than .76% (two standard deviations, under the simplifying assumption of a log-normal distribution).

There is a tendency for exchange-rate variability to be lower within each of the groups than across groups, supporting the idea of currency blocs (see Frankel and Wei, forthcoming, Table 5). The lowest variability occurs within Europe. The 1980 statistic is a monthly standard deviation of .04%, and it falls by half during the course of the decade. Even though the members of the EC correspond roughly to the members of the EMS,[5] non-EC members in Europe show as much stability in exchange rates (both vis-à-vis themselves and vis-à-vis other European countries) as EC members. These results no doubt in part reflect that England and the Mediterranean countries have not been consistent members of the Exchange Rate Mechanism, especially not with the narrow margins that the others observed until 1993. But we shall see it also reflects that such EFTA countries as Austria are loyal members of the currency club de facto, even though they are not at all in that club de jure.

3.2 Links from Smaller European Currencies to the DM, Versus Other Major Currencies

Next we examine the influences that the most important international currencies have on the determination of the values of currencies of smaller countries. One way that countries in a given area could achieve the observed lower levels of intraregional bilateral exchange-rate variability is to link their currencies to the single most important currency in the region. In a simple version of the currency-bloc hypothesis, one would expect that the dollar has dominant influence in the WH, the yen in East Asia, and the mark (or ecu) in Europe.

The equation to be estimated is

$$\Delta(\textit{value of currency } i) = \alpha + \beta_1 \Delta(\textit{value of } \$) + \beta_2 \Delta(\textit{value of yen}) + \beta_3 \Delta(\textit{value of DM}) + \epsilon \,. \quad [1]$$

where the change in the value of each currency is computed logarithmically. The goal is to see whether countries try to stabilize their currencies in terms of a particular major currency. Such an equation is exceptionally well-specified under a particular null hypothesis, namely, that the value of the local currency is determined as a basket peg (perhaps a crawling peg, since we allow for a constant term). By "exceptionally well-specified," we mean that the coefficients should be highly significant and the R^2 should be close to 1.

In 1988, for example, there were 31 countries that were officially classified by the International Monetary Fund as following a basket peg of their own design (plus another eight pegged to the Special Drawing Right, SDR). They included Austria, Finland, Iceland, Norway, and Sweden. Most basket-peggers keep the weights in the basket secret, so that one can only infer the weight statistically from observed exchange-rate movements. Previous tests have suggested that countries that are officially classified as basket-peggers in practice often exhibit a sufficiently wide range of variation around the basket index (or else alter the parity or weights sufficiently often) that they are difficult to distinguish from countries classified as managed floaters.

In applying Equation 1 to a wide variety of countries, we realize that most do not follow a basket peg. If policymakers monitor an index that is a weighted average of their trading partners, even though they allow deviations from the index depending on current macroeconomic considerations or speculative sentiments, we can meaningfully estimate the coefficients in the equation under the (restrictive) assumption that these local deviations -- the error term -- are uncorrelated with the values of the major currencies.

There is a methodological question of what numeraire should be used to measure the value of the currencies. Here we use the SDR as the numeraire. The earlier tests on Asian currencies tried other numeraires (Frankel, 1993). Under the basket-peg null hypothesis, the choice of numeraire makes no difference in the estimation of the weights (though more generally it does make some difference).

Table 4 reports estimates of the implicit basket weights for nine EC currencies. The sample period is 1974-1992, broken into four subsamples. Here we do not impose the constraint that the coefficients on the DM, dollar, and yen sum to one, though we would expect this to emerge from the estimates. If a country follows a relatively tight peg, whether to a single currency or a basket, we would expect a high R^2 and highly significant coefficients. If the peg is to a single major currency, we would expect the weight on that currency to be close to one.

The EC countries, as expected, give heavy weight to the DM. The DM weight is highly significant and in the range .8 to .9 throughout 1974-1992 for the

Belgian franc, Danish krone, and Dutch guilder. It is also quite high during the EMS period 1979-1992 for the French franc, Italian lira, Irish punt, and fairly high for the Spanish peseta, Portuguese escudo, and Greek drachma. Rarely are there significant positive weights on the dollar or yen.

We have also allowed for the possibility of some effect of a fourth major currency, pound sterling, in memory of the role it once played as the world's international currency (Frankel and Wei, forthcoming, Tables 6 and 7). We impose the constraint that the weights on the four currencies sum to one (by subtracting the change in the value of the pound from each of the other variables). The results are similar to those reported here, but sharper as a result of the constraint. There is little role for the pound.[6] For such currencies as the Belgian franc, krone, and guilder, the weight on the DM is insignificantly less than 1.0. For the lira, escudo, and drachma, however, there is also a significant weight on the dollar, averaging about .1.

The DM also has the dominate influence on the six EFTA countries, shown in Table 5. Austria exhibits an extremely tight peg to the DM, as expected. Switzerland also gives heavy weight to the DM. The Swiss franc gives significant weight to the yen as well at times. Finland, Norway, and Sweden give most of their weight to the DM, though the dollar is also significant statistically when the coefficients are constrained to sum to 1.

In the WH, most of the countries tested give dominant weight to the dollar (Frankel and Wei, forthcoming). The pattern of linking to the major currency of the region is broken in East Asia, however. The weight on the dollar is very high in most East Asian countries, with no special role for the yen. The Japanese currency is statistically significant in Singapore and occasionally in some of the other countries in the region, but the coefficient is low. The same is true of the DM and pound (they are significant, for example, in Singapore). Each of the Asian countries is more properly classed in a dollar bloc than in a yen bloc.

3.3 Estimating the Effect of Exchange-Rate Variability on Trade

One rationale for a country to assign weight to a particular currency in determining its exchange rate is the assumption that a more stable bilateral exchange rate will help promote bilateral trade with the partner in question. This is a major motivation for exchange-rate stabilization in Europe.[7] There have been quite a few time-series studies of the effect of exchange-rate uncertainty on trade overall,[8] but fewer cross-section studies of bilateral trade.

Two exceptions are De Grauwe (1988), which looks at only 10 industrialized countries, and Brada and Mendez (1988). We will reexamine the question here using a data set that is more recent as well as broader, covering 63 countries. We return to the gravity model of bilateral trade represented by Equation 1, but add an additional variable to capture the effect of exchange-rate variability alongside the other variables. A problem of simultaneous causality should be noted at the outset: if exchange-rate variability shows up with an apparent negative effect on the volume of bilateral trade, the correlation could be due to the government's

Table 5: Weights Assigned to Foreign Currencies in Determining Changes in Value of EFTA Currencies

Time Period	Const	USD (b1)	Yen (b2)	DM (b3)	Adj.R^2/ DW	Chow/ White	SER	T-test (b1+b2+b3=1)
Austria								
1974-	.001	.017	.009	.910***	.93/	.76/	.006	-.54
1978	.001	.041	.025	.040	2.03	2.81		
1979-	-.001	-.003	-.011	1.035***	.98/	3.27/	.024	.48
1983	.000	.026	.014	.028	1.79	20.41		
1984-	-.000	.022	-.020	1.001***	.99/	.76/	.003	.04
1987	.000	.039	.019	.021	2.02	8.07		
1988-	.000	.039	.025	1.003***	.96/	1.20/	.004	.48
1992	.001	.077	.024	.055	2.71	1.64		
Finland								
1974-	-.003*	-.029	.022	.446***	.31/	1.78/	.015	-1.82
1978	.002	.134	.050	.097	2.00	3.95		
1979-	-.002	.018	.115**	.401***	.28/	.87/	.016	-1.88
1983	.002	.068	.050	.052	1.80	1.06		
1984-	-.001	-.370***	.047	.487***	.90/	1.86/	.006	-5.81
1987	.001	.080	.029	.048	2.13	9.17		
1988-	-.001	1.199**	.016	.285**	.44/	1.07/	.015	-2.56
1992	.002	.132	.050	.127	2.00	1.79		
Norway								
1974-	-.003	.114	-.048	.811***	.65/	1.23/	.013	-.47
1978	.002	.147	.052	.113	1.80	6.04		
1979-	-.003**	.025	.100**	.397***	.43/	2.13/	.012	-2.71
1983	.001	.134	.050	.066	1.53	4.23		
1984-	.005***	-.281	.045	.563***	.64/	.91/	.014	-1.83
1987	.002	.201	.075	.140	1.94	10.05		
1988-	-.000	-.396***	-.017	.398***	.75/	3.23/	.008	-4.00
1992	.001	.151	.046	.092	1.88	6.82		
Sweden								
1974-	-.004	.272*	-.015	.816***	.51/	1.69/	.017	.22
1978	.003	.151	.062	.110	1.91	3.06		
1979-	-.006**	.149	.147*	.246	.09/	2.55/	.024	-2.09
1983	.003	.123	.078	.153	1.81	2.19		
1984-	-.001**	-.129*	.061**	.447***	.90/	1.19/	.005	-5.42
1987	.001	.071	.025	.040	1.76	7.66		
1988-	.001	-.310**	-.030	.371***	.71/	1.78/	.008	-3.96
1992	.001	.127	.046	.082	1.90	17.29		
Switzerland								
1974-	-.005	-.143	.103	.843***	.47/	.64/	.023	-.43
1978	.003	.348	.143	.149	1.89	25.58		
1979-	-.002	-.103	.136**	.960***	.66/	.92/	.017	-.03
1983	.002	.192	.059	.110	1.78	6.15		

Time Period	Const	USD (b1)	Yen (b2)	DM (b3)	Adj.R^2/ DW	Chow/ White	SER	T-test (b1+b2+b3=1)
1984-	-.002	-.515***	.307***	.653***	.88/	.78/	.010	-2.15
1987	.001	.155	.077	.101	1.67	20.31		
1988-	-.002	-.255	.038	.727***	.69/	.50/	.013	-1.21
1992	.002	.208	.093	.144	1.90	12.21		
Iceland								
1974-	-.022***	1.23***	-.034	.088	.03/	2.28/	.047	.30
1978	.006	.462	.168	.237	2.17	3.90		
1979-	-.035***	.829**	-.048	.404	.02/	2.38/	.042	.29
1983	.005	.401	.105	.265	2.11	6.30		
1984-	.010**	.142	-.064	.367*	.02/	1.45/	.026	-.84
1987	.004	.184	.088	.192	2.00	2.32		
1988-	-.008***	-.390*	.027	.277	.25/	4.21/5	.019	-1.81
1992	.003	.232	.083	.202	1.93	.56		

Note: Standard errors are reported below coefficients. ***, **, and * denote significant at the .01, .05, and .10 levels, respectively.

deliberate efforts to stabilize the currency vis-à-vis a valued trading partner, as easily as to the effects of stabilization on trade.

Volatility is defined to be the standard deviation of the first difference of the logarithmic exchange rate. We start with the volatility of nominal exchange rates and embed this term in our gravity equation. The results are reported in Table 6. Table 7 does the same for the volatility of real exchange rates. Most coefficients are similar to those reported in the earlier results without exchange-rate variability (Tables 1-3): the WH, East Asia, Asian Pacific Economic Cooperation grouping (APEC), and the EC all show statistically significant bloc effects.

The OLS results show a negative effect of exchange-rate volatility (whether nominal or real) on bilateral trade that is highly significant in 1965, 1970, and 1975, as well as 1980, though the estimated effect is small in magnitude. Only in 1985 and 1990 does the negative effect disappear (indeed, turn positive).

Interpretations of the estimates in Tables 6 and 7, small as they may be, are complicated by the likelihood of simultaneity bias in the above regressions. Governments may choose deliberately to stabilize bilateral exchange rates with their major trading partners. This has certainly been the case in Europe. Hence, there could be a strong observed correlation between trade patterns and currency linkages even if exchange-rate volatility does not depress trade.

To address this problem, we use the method of instrumental variable estimation, with the standard deviation of relative money supply as our instrument for the volatility of exchange rates. The argument in favor of this choice of instrument is that relative money supplies and bilateral exchange rates are highly correlated in theory (they are directly linked under the monetary theory of exchange-rate determination) and in our data as well, but monetary policies are less likely than exchange-rate policies to be set in response to bilateral trade patterns. The Instrumental Variables results show the same sign pattern across the years as the

Table 6: Nominal Exchange-Rate Volatility in a Gravity Model of Bilateral Trade

Variable	1965	1970	1975	1980	1985	1990
GNP	0.63***	0.64***	0.72***	0.76***	0.76***	0.76***
	(0.02)	(0.02)	(0.02)	(0.02)	(0.02)	(0.02)
GNP per	0.27***	0.36***	0.27***	0.27***	0.25***	0.12***
capita	(0.02)	(0.02)	(0.02)	(0.02)	(0.02)	(0.02)
Distance	-0.40***	-0.51***	-0.68***	-0.62***	-0.71***	-0.60***
	(0.04)	(0.04)	(0.05)	(0.04)	(0.04)	(0.04)
Adjacency	0.78***	0.69***	0.53***	0.64***	0.73***	0.68***
	(0.17)	(0.17)	(0.18)	(0.18)	(0.18)	(0.16)
Nominal	-3.81***	-2.47***	-1.49**	-7.65***	0.13	2.24***
Variability	(0.60)	(0.09)	(0.74)	(0.08)	(0.34)	(0.27)
WH2	0.05	0.01	0.26*	0.44***	0.34**	0.71***
	(0.16)	(0.14)	(0.15)	(0.15)	(0.16)	(0.14)
EAEC2	1.59***	1.60***	0.87***	0.81***	0.60**	0.67***
	(0.31)	(0.29)	(0.33)	(0.26)	(0.28)	(0.25)
APEC2	0.60***	0.70***	0.87***	1.35***	1.21***	1.39***
	(0.22)	(0.17)	(0.23)	(0.18)	(0.19)	(0.17)
EC2	0.20	0.08	-0.10	0.01	0.45**	0.51***
	(0.16)	(0.21)	(0.18)	(0.18)	(0.18)	(0.16)
n	1,115	1,231	1,401	1,653	1,589	1,519
Adj. R^2	0.70	0.72	0.72	0.72	0.74	0.78
SEE	1.04	1.06	1.18	1.18	1.17	1.05

Notes: Standard errors are in parentheses. All variables except the dummies are in logarithms.
*** denotes significant at .01 level (t=>2.576); ** denotes significant at .05 level (t=>1.96);
* denotes significant at .10 level (t=>1.645)

OLS estimates, but the negative effect is statistically significant only in 1965 (Frankel and Wei, forthcoming, Table 13).

These results, while less robust than most of the other gravity equation findings, are generally consistent with the hypothesis that real exchange-rate volatility has depressed bilateral trade a bit in the past. More specifically, these results would appear to confirm that the stabilization of exchange rates within Europe helped a bit to promote intra-European trade from 1965 to 1980. But the evidence for a negative trade effect, which starts out relatively strongly in 1965, diminishes steadily in the 1970s and 1980s. The proliferation of currency options, forward contracts, and other hedging instruments over this period may explain why even the small effect that appears once to have been there has more recently disappeared.

4. Conclusions Regarding European Economic Integration

Trade within Europe was at a high level even before the 1980s and increased rapidly during that decade. Much of the tendency to trade intraregionally can be

Table 7: Real Exchange-Rate Volatility in a Gravity Model of Bilateral Trade

Variable	1965	1970	1975	1980	1985	1990
GNP	0.72***	0.65***	0.72***	0.74***	0.76***	0.76***
	(0.02)	(0.02)	(0.02)	(0.02)	(0.02)	(0.02)
GNP per capita	0.24***	0.36***	0.27***	0.26***	0.25***	0.12***
	(0.03)	(0.02)	(0.02)	(0.02)	(0.02)	(0.02)
Distance	-0.53***	-0.50***	-0.67***	-0.62***	-0.71***	-0.57***
	(0.05)	(0.04)	(0.05)	(0.04)	(0.04)	(0.04)
Adjacency	0.59***	0.77***	0.58***	0.73***	0.73***	0.80***
	(0.18)	(0.16)	(0.18)	(0.18)	(0.18)	(0.16)
WH2	0.02	0.02	0.27*	0.42***	0.30*	0.74***
	(0.15)	(0.13)	(0.15)	(0.15)	(0.15)	(0.14)
EAEC2	0.99**	1.80***	0.85***	0.76***	0.60**	0.71***
	(0.50)	(0.32)	(0.32)	(0.26)	(0.27)	(0.25)
APEC2	0.44*	0.67***	0.90***	1.35***	1.16***	1.38***
	(0.26)	(0.21)	(0.22)	(0.18)	(0.18)	(0.17)
EC2	0.04	0.08	-0.06	0.02	0.40**	0.57***
	(0.17)	(0.16)	(0.18)	(0.18)	(0.17)	(0.16)
Real exchange-	-3.02***	-2.72***	-1.57**	-6.97***	0.12	3.19***
rate volatility	(0.67)	(0.83)	(0.82)	(0.08)	(0.37)	(0.27)
n	773	1,053	1,316	1,503	1,500	1,494
Adj. R^2	0.76	0.76	0.74	0.75	0.75	0.78
SEE	0.94	0.99	2.21	1.13	1.14	1.04

Notes: Standard errors are in parentheses. All variables except the dummies are in logarithms.
***, **, and * denote significant at .01, .05, and .10 levels, respectively.

explained by natural economic factors: the size of the GNPs, the levels of per capita GNP, the proximity of the countries, the sharing of common borders and common languages, and the openness of the economies. Some of the increase in intraregional trade in the 1970s and 1980s can be explained by an increase in per capita GNP (though to a lesser extent than in Pacific Asia).

There was also a highly significant increase in the degree of intraregional trade bias in the course of the 1980s, most readily explained by deliberate policy initiatives of the EC. Our estimates in Table 1 suggest that a country joining the EC would have experienced an increase in trade with other members of about 50% by 1990. No such effect is observed for EFTA.

We have considered the possibility that the stabilization of exchange rates was a significant contributor to the increase in intraregional trade. The standard deviation of exchange rates fell among EFTA countries by about half in the 1980s and among EC countries by slightly more. Among both groups, the currencies in effect linked themselves to the DM, much as WH (and East Asia) currencies in effect link themselves to the dollar.

We have found some possible cross-section evidence that real exchange-rate variability has had an effect on trade volume. There is much more evidence that this factor is statistically significant in the period 1965-1980 than in 1985 or 1990. A possible explanation is the spread of hedging instruments. In any case, even when the estimated effect is at its peak, it explains only a very small fraction of the intraregional trade bias. It does not appear that the stabilization of European exchange rates in the 1980s played a large role in the increase in intraregional trade.

5. Political Implications of Economic Regionalism

Many observers fear a repeat of the malign form of regionalism practiced in the 1930s. We have seen in econometric tests that there is indeed evidence of a trend toward regionalization of trade and financial relationships over the last 25 years. What are the implications for economic welfare and for politics? In this section we review many arguments commonly made regarding economic regionalization, to the effect that it is good or that it is bad. Although some of the arguments on both sides are fully valid, others merit skepticism. We shall attempt an overall verdict on regionalization.

Economists and political scientists both try to take hard-headed views of how countries behave, and even of how their own country should behave. For economists, the usual presumption is that the national goal is to maximize national economic welfare (most conveniently measured by GNP, but more properly adjusted for such nonmarket factors as pollution). For some political scientists, particularly those called realists, the usual presumption is that the goal is to maximize the *relative* standing of the country vis-à-vis competitors. GNP is important as one of the determinants of power (along with other determinants such as the size of one's military, the possession of colonies or a sphere of influence, and the state of one's technology). But it is relative GNP that is usually thought to matter, not absolute GNP.

The economists' perspective still leaves a lot of room for interesting political-economic interactions. We divide our review of the issues in three parts. First, we consider the implications of regionalization from the standpoint of economic welfare, taking the level of worldwide liberalization as politically given. Second, we consider how regional initiatives might interact with trade policy more generally; thus we introduce political economy considerations but continue to assume that the objective should be to maximize economic welfare. Finally, we consider briefly broader political objectives, including the possibility that relative GNP is important for reasons of power and rivalry.

5.1 Implications of Free Trade for Economic Welfare

The formation of blocs in the 1930s was associated with a sharp fall in worldwide trade and with the Great Depression. The postwar multilateral trading system founded on the General Agreement on Tariffs and Trade (GATT) was associated with a dramatic increase in the volume of world trade and with worldwide economic growth. It is thus natural to worry that the reemergence of regional blocs might lead to a resumption of less satisfactory growth performance like that of the 1930s and be harmful for economic welfare.

A point to note right away is that economists continue to believe that worldwide free trade is the first-best strategy. New arguments, whether political or economic, ultimately do little to change the bottom line. Political arguments are made that, with the end of the Cold War, the United States can no longer afford economic sacrifices for the sake of the liberal international system. But these arguments become irrelevant if it is recognized that *each* country's economic welfare is in general maximized under worldwide free trade. No sacrifice is required. Economic arguments are made that in the presence of imperfect competition, increasing returns to scale, and endogenous technology, an individual country can theoretically raise economic welfare by imposing just the right tariffs or subsidies. But the introduction of imperfect competition does at least as much to strengthen the arguments for free trade as to weaken them. In most of these models, intervention works only if the foreign country fails to retaliate. In reality, countries do retaliate and emulate. An equilibrium in which all countries are effectively prevented from intervening, for example, by means of the GATT or the World Trade Organization, is better for all than the noncooperative equilibrium in which everyone intervenes.

Although the multilateral system has made large strides toward freer trade, most recently in the form of the successful conclusion of the Uruguay Round negotiations in December 1993, political constraints inevitably prevent the immediate attainment of the economists' nirvana. Since influential producer interest groups in each country typically stand to lose from free trade, unilateral liberalization rarely occurs, and the world must instead await the outcome of step-by-step multilateral negotiations, in which countries trade concessions with each other in such a way that at each step the percentage of the population that stands to gain is sufficiently high to overcome the political opposition.

In this light, the case in favor of regional trading arrangements is a second-best argument that takes as given the impossibility of further most-favored nation (MFN) liberalization. The uninitiated might assume that free-trade economists would under these circumstances necessarily support Free Trade Areas (FTAs). But from the standpoint of static economic welfare, trade economists are in fact ambivalent about the desirability of FTAs. So long as tariffs and other barriers against third countries remain in place, the elimination of barriers between two FTA members can as easily intensify distortions as eliminate them. The classical distinction is between the harmful trade-diverting effects of FTAs and their beneficial trade-creating effects. Although modern theories of trade have gone far beyond the diversion/creation distinction, it is still a useful intuitive guide to likely welfare effects.[9] Grossman and Helpman (1993) find in a median-voter model that an FTA is most likely to be adopted when trade diversion outweighs trade creation, which unfortunately is also when it is most likely to reduce aggregate welfare.

5.2 Negative Political Implication for Multilateral Trade Liberalization

There are a variety of arguments as to how the adoption of a regional trading area might undermine movement toward unilateral or multilateral liberalization for political reasons: these fall under the headings "incentive to protect," scarce negotiator resources, median-voter dead end, and manipulation of the process by special interests. We consider these antiregionalization arguments first, before considering some arguments that go the other way.

The standard experiment presumes that the level of trade barriers against outsiders remains unchanged when an FTA is established. However, Krugman (1991) shows how, in a world consisting of a few large blocs, each unit will have more monopoly power and thus will be more tempted to seek to shift the terms of trade in its favor by raising tariffs against the other blocs. This temptation will be strengthened in a world of many small trading blocs (or of MFNs, i.e., each country is its own bloc). A world of a few large blocs is thus one in which the noncooperative equilibrium features a higher level of interbloc tariffs and a lower level of economic welfare.

Bagwell and Staiger (1993a) examine the condition under which multilateral tariff liberalization is self-enforcing (through anticipation of future retaliation). They find that this condition holds only during the early stages of customs union formation, but not when the customs union is complete and able to exercise its full monopoly power. (The sequence is reversed in Bagwell and Staiger, 1993b, where FTAs are considered: members do not set external tariffs jointly and thus cannot exercise collective monopoly power as in a customs union.)

In reality, in one sense, governments are less capable of national economic optimization than the Krugman and Bagwell-Staiger models presuppose, and in another sense they are more capable. They are less capable in that maximum exploitation of the terms of trade (through imposition of the "optimum tariff") is in practice one of the *less* prevalent determinants of trade policy. More commonly seen are arguments regarding infant industries, protecting the scarce factor of production, increasing employment, and adjustment costs. Governments are *more* capable in that they have already instituted the cooperative international regime of the GATT, as Bergsten (1991) pointed out in his comment on Krugman (1991a): Article XXIV explicitly rules out Krugman's concern. (This provision allows deviations from the MFN principle only for FTAs that do not raise the average level of their tariffs against nonmembers. Bagwell and Staiger, 1993a, fn. 25, point out, however, that exacerbation of the incentive to protect in customs unions can take the form of "gray-area" measures when explicit tariff increases are ruled out.) In both respects, large trading blocs are less vulnerable to the incentive to raise tariffs against each other than under Krugman's assumptions.

Even when tariff increases are ruled out, the distortions created by a few large FTAs can reduce world welfare. But preferential trading areas drawn along continental boundaries can *raise* welfare, if the degree of preferences does not exceed a natural level justified by intercontinental transport costs (Krugman, 1991b; Frankel, Stein, and Wei, forthcoming; and Stein, 1994: 84-93).

The scarce-negotiator-resources argument points out that negotiations are not costless. If they were, then the world would have achieved free trade by now. If the U.S. Special Trade Representative is spending all his or her time -- and spending all the White House's political capital with Congress -- on a regional agreement (e.g., the North American Free Trade Agreement, NAFTA), there is presumably less time or capital left over to spend on multilateral negotiations (e.g., the Uruguay Round). As with the incentive-to-protect argument, regional trading arrangements may set back the process of negotiating worldwide trade liberalization under the GATT.

Some authors have suggested political models in which the forces in favor of liberalization might win out over protectionists if the only choice is between the status quo and multilateral liberalization, but that when offered the option of a regional FTA, the political process might then take the regional route to the exclusion of the multilateral route. Bhagwati (1993: 28-29) worries that businessmen and bureaucrats, after having achieved regional integration, might then find the effort involved in multilateral negotiation too difficult.

Levy (1993) offers what might be called a median-voter dead-end model, in which a bilateral free trade agreement can undermine political support for multilateral liberalization because it is a dead end. As in Grossman and Helpman (1993), it is assumed that trade policy is determined by the median voter. Trade itself is determined in some sectors by differences in factor endowments (which the extra terms in our Table 1 attempt to capture) and in others by considerations of imperfect substitutes (which is the rationale behind the gravity model's basic proportionality between trade and country size). As others have argued, the intra-industry sort of trade that is generated in imperfect substitutes is easier to accept politically than the other kind of trade. The reason is that adjustment to import competition requires workers only to move from the assembly line for one product variety to the assembly line for another variety of the same product. Trade based on differences in factor endowments is much more difficult to accept politically, because it requires workers in previously protected industries to move to different industries (and at lower wages, in the case of capital-intensive industrialized countries).

Levy argues that policy toward trade is thus always a trade-off between the gains afforded by increased varieties and the losses inflicted by a fall in the relative price of the product that is intensive in the scarce factor (e.g., labor, in the case of industrialized countries). If liberalization is not attainable, it is because the losses from factor-endowment trade dominate. If a vote is held first on whether to join a bilateral FTA, it is more likely to pass when the potential partner has similar factor endowments (it is easier politically to achieve a European Community than a NAFTA). The reason is that the gains from increased trade in imperfect substitutes will be large, while the losses from a fall in the relative price of labor-intensive products will be small. But if a vote is then held on multilateral liberalization, it will fail: those key sectors that stand to profit from trade in imperfect substitutes will already have reaped those gains, and there will be no political force to countervail the sectors that lose from the additional factor-endowment trade. In this way regional free trade agreements undermine political support for multilateral liberalization in this model.

The special-interests argument points out that the process of instituting a regional trading arrangement features abundant opportunities for trade-sensitive industries, particularly those that might be adversely affected, to manipulate the process. Examples abound. First, Wonnacott and Lutz (1989: 65-66) emphasize that negotiators frequently seek to exclude from regional FTAs precisely those of their sectors that would be most threatened by welfare-enhancing trade creation. Grossman and Helpman (1993: 34-43) have used their median-voter model to understand how the possibility of such industry exclusions increases the chances of FTAs being adopted. This was the primary reason for another restriction that the GATT Article XXIV places on FTAs, that "substantially all" barriers within the region be removed. In practice, FTAs have tended to comply less than completely with this provision. Examples include the European Economic Community's exclusion of agriculture and, in practice, steel and many other goods.[10]

Second, Anne Krueger (1993) emphasizes the exploitation of rules of origin. An FTA, unlike a customs union, does not involve the setting of common external tariffs. Rules of origin are a mechanism with which a country can prevent imports coming in from nonmembers, transshipped via the FTA partner, in those sectors where the partner has lower tariffs. Krueger shows how individual industries in the FTA negotiation can enhance the extent of protection they receive when their governments use rules of origin to enable them to capture their FTA partner's market in addition to their own.

Bhagwati (1993: 30-31) points out that large countries like the United States may use their overwhelming bargaining power within regional groupings to obtain from small countries distorting concessions that they might not obtain in more balanced multilateral negotiations. Perroni and Whalley (1994) point out that small countries have been the enthusiasts in recent regional agreements and show why large countries have all the bargaining power on their side.

5.3 Positive Political Implications for Multilateral Trade Liberalization

Other arguments go the other way. They offer the hope that the adoption of a regional trading area might undermine protectionism and reinforce movement toward liberalization more generally. The arguments concern locking in unilateral liberalization, mobilizing regional solidarity, building export constituencies, and creating political momentum.

In the late 1980s, Mexican President Salinas reversed a half-century of Mexican protectionism and imposed sweeping unilateral liberalization measures. Future presidents of Mexico might not be so enlightened. Thus, a good argument for NAFTA from the American and Canadian viewpoint was that it locked in the Salinas reforms in a manner that would be difficult to reverse in the future. Elsewhere, leaders have used popular support for regional solidarity to achieve liberalization that would be politically impossible if pursued unilaterally. De Melo,

Panagariya, and Rodrik (1993, section 3) model the process whereby governments can adopt rules or institutions in a regional grouping to insulate themselves from pressure by private sector lobbies for intervention on their behalf.

Wei and Frankel (1994) have made a primitive start at modeling an argument regarding political constituencies. We consider the problem of building export constituencies in a system where a country chooses its trade policies by majority vote. Our hypothesis is that, under certain conditions, leaders might not be able to obtain a majority vote in favor of multilateral liberalization, much less unilateral liberalization, and yet might be able to obtain a majority vote in favor of regional liberalization, which, when completed, then shifts the economic incentives so as to produce a majority in favor of wider liberalization.

This model is inspired by Fernandez and Rodrik (1991), who consider a situation where the majority would vote against unilateral liberalization, even though a majority would ex post gain from it economically. Essentially they divide the population into three groups: those who know they would gain from liberalization because they are confident of their ability to compete on world markets, those who will eventually gain from liberalization because they will turn out to be competitive on world markets but do not know this ex ante, and those who lose from liberalization because of new import competition but do not know this ex ante. If all those who are uncertain have as little as a 49% chance of gaining, all those who are uncertain--and thus a majority of the entire population--will oppose liberalization ex ante, even though a majority of the population gains ex post (say .49 x 2/3 plus the 1/3 who are sure gainers). The interesting aspect of the model is that if the leaders are somehow able to push liberalization through anyway and a new vote is taken after the uncertainty is resolved, a majority will then vote in favor of maintaining the new liberalized status quo. In essence, the act of liberalization itself builds a constituency for liberalization, as those who are good at exporting discover their previously unknown talents. Similar conclusions could be reached in a model where capital and labor moved from previously protected sectors to new trade-oriented sectors, though the status quo bias in this case would hold for reforms that did not benefit a majority in addition to those that did.

In the Wei and Frankel (1994) version, political leaders may be able to obtain a majority vote in favor of regional liberalization because fewer sectors are adversely affected. More firms then discover their export potential, making it possible to obtain a majority support for previously unattainable MFN liberalization. The story is thus a counter-example to the (perhaps overly strong) claim of Levy (1993) that "bilateral free trade agreements can never increase political support for multilateral free trade."

A possible illustration is bankers in Italy and Spain who had become lazy and inefficient when protected from competition but who responded to the threat of competition in 1992 from northern European banks by merging. The hope is that, thinned out, they are now less likely to seek protection from international competition in multilateral negotiations.

A final illustration of building political momentum is President Clinton's "Triple Play" of late 1993. By upgrading the Seattle meeting of APEC ministers that had been scheduled for November 1993 into a high-profile Leaders' Meeting, he signaled to the Europeans that if they continued to allow French farmers to hold up the Uruguay Round, other countries might proceed without them. This message carried credibility because of its fortunate timing, coming as it did on the heels of the hard-fought approval of NAFTA in the U.S. Congress. Thus, the NAFTA outcome demonstrated the political will necessary for meaningful agreements, while the APEC meeting demonstrated the possibility that agreements would cover a fraction of the world economy that was sufficiently large and dynamic to give the Europeans cause for worry at the prospect of being left out. German policymakers have reportedly confirmed that this was part of their motive for concluding the Uruguay Round in December. In this episode at least, it appears that regional initiatives helped bring about multilateral agreement.

In short, there are a variety of possible channels of political causation running from regionalism to multilateralism, some positive and some negative. How can one get an idea as to which effects dominate in practice?

The gravity equation results of Tables 2 and 3 can shed some light on the net effect of political interactions like the ones we have described, as they have actually played themselves out over the last 25 years. If tariffs on imports from nonmembers remain unchanged when a given regional grouping is formed, then the coefficient on the variable with a "1" suffix (the dummy variable indicating when at least one country of the pair is a member of the grouping in question) should be negative, indicating trade diversion. Trade creation is indicated by a positive coefficient on the variable with a "2" suffix (the dummy variable indicating when both countries in the pair are members of the grouping in question). If trade diversion is large enough relative to trade creation, then the FTA may reduce economic welfare. If trade diversion is small, the FTA is likely to improve welfare. A third possibility is that adoption of a regional FTA is associated with political momentum in favor of more widespread liberalization (for any of the reasons enumerated in this section). In this case, the best outcome from the standpoint of economic welfare, the coefficient on the variable with a "1" suffix would be positive.

The results in Tables 2 and 3 suggest that the third possibility is the relevant one in the cases of East Asia, the WH, and the EC. These countries have tended to open up with respect to all trading partners at the same time that they have opened up with respect to other members of their own grouping. Only for the EFTA grouping, which is not a significant bloc, is there evidence of trade diversion.

Thus, the verdict seems to be that the net political effect of the removal of regional barriers has tended to support liberalization with respect to nonmembers as well and that the effect of further liberalization has been more than enough to offset any trade diversion resulting directly from the original regional arrangements themselves. From the economists' viewpoint, this verdict is an encouraging one.

5.4 Implications for International Political Relations

There remains the question of power relationships and noneconomic goals. Smaller countries often fear that close economic integration with a large neighbor will bring political domination. Albert Hirschman (1945) argued that a small country that comes to depend on trade with a large neighbor for a high share of its GNP is unlikely to side against that neighbor in times of political or military conflict.

Of course, what may be politically disadvantageous from the standpoint of the small country is by construction politically advantageous for its large neighbor. In the grand tradition of realist international relations, a major power that sits at the center of a large and cohesive trading bloc and whose currency is widely used will be at a political advantage vis-à-vis rival powers.

We incline toward a more benign interpretation of the political causes and effects of economic regionalism in the postwar period (as opposed to the 1930s). Promoting democracy, peace, and stability can be a political goal of regional economic arrangements. This describes the EC's motive in the late 1970s for admitting the previous right-wing dictatorships of Greece, Portugal, and Spain. The original (and still-paramount) motive underlying the EC and its predecessors was to bind together France and Germany and thereby ensure that there would not be a repeat of the three wars the two neighbors had fought over the preceding century. To the extent that the European Union sees fit to continue to extend its membership eastward in the 1990s, a primary motive will be to promote democracy, peace, and stability among previous members of the Warsaw Pact.

Endnotes

1. This article was written for the Study Group on the Political Economy of European Integration at the University of California, organized by Barry Eichengreen and Jeffry Frieden. The authors would like to thank Jeffry Frieden for valuable suggestions.

2. Among recent studies on the regional patterns of economic disturbances are Bayoumi and Eichengreen (1992). Chinn and Frankel (1994) study whether interest rates in small countries are more responsive to the region's major financial center than to the world's other major financial centers. (The finding is generally no for Asia, even though it is yes for Europe.) Stabilization of exchange rates within regions can help promote financial integration, as measured by interest rate differentials, in addition to helping promote trade as examined in this article.

3. Antecedents include Linneman (1966) and stretch back at least as far as the 1940s and ultimately to Sir Isaac Newton. Two recent applications to Europe are Hamilton and Winters (1992) and Havrylyshyn and Pritchett (1991). Eichengreen and Irwin (forthcoming) adopt the gravity model approach to the trading bloc question and apply it to the interwar period. Further recent references are given in Frankel, Stein, and Wei (forthcoming).

4. This is the same result found by Hamilton and Winters (1992), a significant coefficient of .7 on the EC and zero on EFTA. But it is the opposite of the conclusion one might draw from simple statistics on the magnitudes of intraregional trade in the EC and in Western Europe as a whole, if one did not hold constant for proximity (Grant, Papadakis, and Richardson, 1993).

5. Of the EC, only Greece had not joined the Exchange Rate Mechanism by early 1992 (though Italy and England dropped out soon thereafter).

6. For Ireland, the implicit coefficient on the pound ranges between .1 and .2.

7. Recent analyses of European currency integration include Eichengreen (1990) and Eichengreen and Wyplosz (1993).

8. See, for example, Akhtar and Hilton (1984). The literature is reviewed in Edison and Melvin (1990).

9. Stein and Frankel (1994) show in a model of imperfect competition that a simulation comparison of the magnitudes of trade creation and trade diversion provides the right answer to the question whether FTAs raise the welfare of the representative consumer under many plausible parameter values though not all.

10. Such "new issue areas" as trade in services and government procurement have been widely excluded from regional FTAs in the past. Only recently has the European Union begun to address these issues seriously, although these regional groupings have progressed more rapidly in services and procurement than proved possible multilaterally in the Uruguay Round.

References

Akhtar, M. Akbar, and Hilton, Spence. "Effects of Exchange Rate Uncertainty on German and U.S. Trade." *Federal Reserve Bank of New York Quarterly Review* 1984, 9/1: 7-16.

Arndt, Sven, and Willett, Thomas. "EC 1992 from a North American Perspective." *The Economic Journal* 1991, 101(409): 1,567-1,579.

Bagwell, Kyle, and Staiger, Robert. "Multilateral Cooperation During the Formation of Free Trade Areas." *National Bureau of Economic Research Working Paper* no. 4543, 1993a.

Bagwell, Kyle, and Staiger, Robert. "Multilateral Cooperation During the Formation of Free Trade Areas." *National Bureau of Economic Research Working Paper* no. 4364, 1993b.

Bayoumi, Tamim, and Eichengreen, Barry. "One Money or Many? On Analyzing the Prospects for Monetary Unification in Europe and Other Parts of the World." International Monetary Fund and University of California at Berkeley, August 1992.

Bergsten, C. Fred. "Commentary: The Move Toward Free Trade Zones." In *Policy Implications of Trade and Currency Zones*. A Symposium Sponsored by the Federal Reserve Bank of Kansas City, Jackson Hole, Wyoming, August 1991.

Bhagwati, Jagdish. "Regionalism and Multilateralism: An Overview." In de Melo, J., and Panagariya, A. (eds.), *New Dimensions in Regional Integration*. New York: Cambridge University Press, 1993.

Brada, Josef, and Mendez, Jose. "Exchange Rate Risk, Exchange Rate Regimes and the Level of International Trade." *Kyklos* 1988, 41(2): 198.

Chinn, Menzie, and Frankel, Jeffrey. "Financial Links Around the Pacific Rim: 1982-1992." In Glick, R., and Hutchison, M. (eds.), *Exchange Rate Policy and Interdependence: Perspectives from the Pacific Basin*. Cambridge, England: Cambridge University Press, 1994.

De Grauwe, Paul. "Exchange Rate Variability and the Slowdown in Growth of International Trade." *IMF Staff Papers* 1988, 35: 63-84.

de Melo, Jaime, Panagariya, Arvind, and Rodrik, Dani. "The New Regionalism: A Country Perspective." In de Melo, J., and Panagariya, A. (eds.), *New Dimensions in Regional Integration*. New York: Cambridge University Press, 1993.

Dickens, William. *The U.S. Labor Market Effects of European Economic Integration: Policy Considerations*. Washington, DC: National Commission for Employment Policy, November 1992.

Edison, Hali, and Melvin, Michael. "The Determinants and Implications of the Choice of an Exchange Rate System." In Haraf, William, and Willett, Thomas (eds.), *Monetary Policy for a Volatile Global Economy*. Washington, DC: AEI Press, 1990.

Eichengreen, Barry. "One Money for Europe? Lessons from the US Currency Union." *Economic Policy* 1990, 10: 117-189.

Eichengreen, Barry, and Irwin, Douglas. "Trade Blocs, Currency Blocs and the Disintegration of World Trade in the 1930s." *Journal of International Economics*, forthcoming.

Eichengreen, Barry, and Wyplosz, Charles. "The Unstable EMS." *Brookings Papers on Economic Activity* 1993, 1: 51-143.

Fernandez, Raquel, and Rodrik, Dani. "Resistance to Reform: Status Quo Bias in the Presence of Individual-Specific Uncertainty." *American Economic Review* 1991, 81: 1,146-1,155.

Frankel, Jeffrey. "Is Japan Creating a Yen Bloc in East Asia and the Pacific?" In Frankel, Jeffrey, and Kahler, Miles (eds.), *Regionalism and Rivalry: Japan and the U.S. in Pacific Asia.* Chicago: University of Chicago Press, 1993.

Frankel, Jeffrey, Stein, Ernesto, and Wei, Shang-Jin. "Trading Blocs and the Americas: The Natural, the Unnatural, and the Super-Natural." *Journal of Development Economics*, forthcoming.

Frankel, Jeffrey, and Wei, Shang-Jin. "Emerging Currency Blocs." In Genberg, Hans (ed.), *The Future of the International Monetary System and Its Institutions*. Geneva: International Center for Monetary and Banking Studies, forthcoming.

Grant, Richard, Papadakis, Maria, and Richardson, J. David. "Global Trade Flows: Old Structures, New Issues, Empirical Evidence." In Bergsten, C.F., and Noland, M. (eds.), *Twentieth Pacific Trade and Development Conference*. Washington, DC: Institute for International Economics, 1993.

Greenaway, David. *Implications of the EC 1992 Programme for Outside Countries*. New York: United Nations, 1991.

Grossman, Gene, and Helpman, Ehlanan. "The Politics of Free Trade Agreements." *National Bureau of Economic Research Working Paper* no. 4597, 1993.

Hamilton, Carl, and Winters, L. Alan. "Opening Up International Trade in Eastern Europe." *Economic Policy* 1992, 14: 77-116.

Havrylyshyn, Oleg, and Pritchett, Lant. "European Trade Patterns After the Transition." *Policy, Research and External Affairs Working Paper Series* no. 748. Washington, DC: World Bank, 1991.

Hirschman, Albert O. *National Power and the Structure of Foreign Trade* (expanded 1980 edition). Berkeley: University of California Press, 1945.

Kreinen, Mordecai. "Static Effect of EC Enlargement on Trade Flows in Manufactured Products." *Kyklos* 1981, 34: 60-71.

Krueger, Anne. "Free Trade Agreements as Protectionist Devices: Rules of Origin." *National Bureau of Economic Research Working Paper* no. 4352, 1993.

Krugman, Paul. "Is Bilateralism Bad?" In Helpman, E., and Razin, A. (eds.), *International Trade and Trade Policy*. Cambridge, MA: MIT Press, 1991a.

Krugman, Paul. "The Move Toward Free Trade Zones." In *Policy Implications of Trade and Currency Zones*. A Symposium Sponsored by the Federal Reserve Bank of Kansas City, Jackson Hole, Wyoming, August 1991b.

Levy, Philip. "A Political Economic Analysis of Free Trade Agreements." *Center for Economic Policy Research Publication* no. 347. Stanford University, 1993.

Linneman, Hans. *An Econometric Study of International Trade Flows.* Amsterdam: North-Holland, 1966.

Perroni, Carlo, and Whalley, John. "The New Regionalism: Trade Liberalization or Insurance?" *National Bureau of Economic Research Working Paper* no. 4626, 1994.

Schott, Jeffrey. *Free Trade Areas and U.S. Trade Policy* Washington, DC: Institute for International Economics, 1989.

Stein, Ernesto. "The Welfare Implications of Asymmetric Trading Blocs." *Essays on the Welfare Implications of Trading Blocs with Transport Costs and on Political Cycles of Inflation* (Chapter 2). Ph.D. dissertation, University of California, Berkeley, 1994.

Stein, Ernesto, and Frankel, Jeffrey. "The Welfare Implications of Continental Trading Blocs in a Model with Transport Costs." Pacific Basin Working Paper Series no. PB94-03, Federal Reserve Bank of San Francisco, May 1994.

Wei, Shang-Jin, and Frankel, Jeffrey. *Can Regional Blocs be Stepping Stones to Global Free Trade?* Washington, DC: Institute for International Economics, 1994.

Wonnacott, Paul, and Lutz, Mark. "Is There a Case for Free Trade Areas?" In Schott, Jeffrey (ed.), *Free Trade Areas and U.S. Trade Policy*. Washington, DC: Institute for International Economics, 1989.

Contributors and Editors

Giancarlo Corsetti: Researcher, Terza Università di Roma.

Barry Eichengreen: John L. Simpson Professor of Economics and Professor of Political Science, University of California, Berkeley.

Chris Erickson: Assistant Professor, Anderson Graduate School of Management, UCLA.

Jeffrey A. Frankel: Professor of Economics, University of California, Berkeley, and Senior Fellow, Institute for International Economics, Washington, D. C.

Jeffry Frieden: Professor of Political Science, UCLA.

Geoffrey Garrett: Assistant Professor of Political Science, Stanford University.

Michael M. Hutchison: Professor of Economics, University of California, Santa Cruz.

Kenneth M. Kletzer: Professor of Economics, University of California, Santa Cruz.

Karl Ove Moene: Professor of Economics, University of Oslo.

Maurice Obstfeld: Professor of Economics, University of California, Berkeley.

Andrew Rose: Associate Professor and Chair of Economic Analysis and Policy, Haas School of Business, University of California Berkeley.

Nouriel Roubini: Professor of Economics, Yale University.

Lars E.O. Svensson: Professor of International Economics, Institute for International Economic Studies, Stockholm University.

Jürgen von Hagen: Professor of Economics, University of Mannheim, Germany.

Michael Wallerstein: Professor of Political Science, Northwestern University.

Carl Walsh: Professor of Economics, University of California, Santa Cruz.

Christopher Way: PhD candidate, Department of Political Science, Stanford University.

Shang-Jin Wei: Assistant Professor of Public Policy, Kennedy School of Government, Harvard University, Cambridge.

Index

Springer-Verlag and the Environment

We at Springer-Verlag firmly believe that an international science publisher has a special obligation to the environment, and our corporate policies consistently reflect this conviction.

We also expect our business partners – paper mills, printers, packaging manufacturers, etc. – to commit themselves to using environmentally friendly materials and production processes.

The paper in this book is made from low- or no-chlorine pulp and is acid free, in conformance with international standards for paper permanency.

FSC
www.fsc.org
MIX
Papier aus verantwortungsvollen Quellen
Paper from responsible sources
FSC® C105338

If you have any concerns about our products,
you can contact us on
ProductSafety@springernature.com

In case Publisher is established outside the EU,
the EU authorized representative is:
Springer Nature Customer Service Center GmbH
Europaplatz 3, 69115 Heidelberg, Germany

Printed by Libri Plureos GmbH
in Hamburg, Germany